1987

GEN
Rossi, Alfred.
Astonish us in the morning :

3 0301 00084363 7

Astonish Us in the Morning

ASTONISH US IN THE MORNING

TYRONE GUTHRIE REMEMBERED

Alfred Rossi

Wayne State University Press   Detroit, 1980

LIBRARY
College of St. Francis
JOLIET, ILLINOIS

Originally published by Hutchinson & Co., Ltd., London, 1977.
Copyright © 1977 by Alfred Rossi. All rights are reserved.
No part of this book may be reproduced without formal
permission from the publisher.

Library of Congress Cataloging in Publication Data
Rossi, Alfred.
  Astonish us in the morning.

  Reprint of the 1977 ed. published by Hutchinson, London.
  Includes index.
    1. Guthrie, Tyrone, Sir, 1900–1971.   2. Theatrical producers
and directors—Great Britain—Biography.
I. Title.
[PN2598.G85R67 1980]   792'.023'0924 [B] 80–11855
ISBN 0–8143–1669–7
ISBN 0–8143–1670–0 (pbk.)

*This edition is published in the
United States and Canada by
Wayne State University Press
Detroit, Michigan 48202.
Manufactured in the United States of America.*

792.023
R830

*For Paul, Damien, and Tonio
who never knew Tony Guthrie,
and, especially, for Helen
who did.*

123,448

Contents

Acknowledgements 11

Introduction 13

Conversations
  Anthony Quayle 19
  J. C. Trewin 31
  Annette Prevost 39
  Tanya Moiseiwitsch 50
  Alec Guinness 58
  John Gielgud 65
  Robert Morley 77
  Sybil Thorndike 87
  Laurence Olivier 93
  Coral Browne 104
  Stella Adler 111
  Harry Andrews 114
  Andrew Cruickshank 118
  Stanley Baxter 122
  John Mills 134
  Robert Hardy 137
  John Gibson 144
  Constance Tomkinson 153
  Kenneth Griffith 161
  Paul Rogers 169
  Leo McKern 177
  William Hutt 181
  Arthur Hill 186
  Alec McCowen 192
  Kurt Kasznar 198
  Norman Ginsbury 202
  Walter Slezak 205
  Peter Donat 210
  George Grizzard 214

Ellen Geer   218

Hume Cronyn and Jessica Tandy   227

Ken Ruta   238

Barrie Stavis   250

Len Cariou   267

Michael Langham   276

An Impression of the Memorial Service held on Wednesday, 16 June 1971 at St Paul's, Covent Garden, for Sir Tyrone Guthrie, by Constance Tomkinson   289

Address Delivered by Alec Guinness at Sir Tyrone Guthrie's Memorial Service   291

Appendix: A Representative Listing of Stage Productions Directed by Tyrone Guthrie   297

Index   303

Illustrations

Between pages 112 and 113

Tyrone Guthrie at a rehearsal of *Tamburlaine the Great*, New York City, 1956. (*Reproduced by kind permission of Anthony Quayle*)

A Sadler's Wells party in 1933, showing Flora Robson, Judith Guthrie, Charles Laughton, Lilian Baylis, James Mason, Elsa Lanchester and Tyrone Guthrie. (*Reproduced by permission of Peter Roberts and the Sadler's Wells Foundation*)

Vivien Leigh, Tyrone Guthrie, Laurence Olivier and an unidentified person at Elsinore in 1937. (*Reproduced by permission of the Raymond Mander and Joe Mitchenson Theatre Collection*)

Tyrone Guthrie with Toke Townley and John Mills, 1950. (*Reproduced by permission of Radio Times Hulton Picture Library*)

Tyrone Guthrie rehearses *The Highland Fair* at the 1952 Edinburgh Festival. (*Reproduced by permission of Pictorial Press*)

Harry Showalter, Judith and Tyrone Guthrie and Tanya Moiseiwitsch at Stratford, Ontario, in 1953. (*Reproduced by permission of Stratford Festival Archives*)

Between pages 208 and 209

Thornton Wilder and Tyrone Guthrie, Stratford, Ontario, 1955. (*Reproduced by permission of Stratford Festival Archives*)

Guthrie rehearsing *The Bishop's Bonfire* in Dublin in 1955. (*Reproduced by permission of John Sarsfield*)

The Tyrone Guthrie Theater Company, Minneapolis, 1963. (*Reproduced by permission of the Minneapolis Star and Tribune Co.*)

Guthrie rehearses *Hamlet* at Minneapolis, 1963. (*Both photographs reproduced by permission of the Minneapolis Star and Tribune Co.*)

Hume Cronyn and Tyrone Guthrie at Minneapolis in 1965. (*Reproduced by kind permission of Hume Cronyn*)

Between pages 275 and 276

Tyrone Guthrie, Alfred Rossi, and Stella Adler at the Jack I. and Lillian L. Poses Brandeis University Creative Arts Awards ceremonies, New York City, 1965. (*Reproduced by permission of Brandeis University*)

Scene from *The Three Sisters*, directed by Tyrone Guthrie, Minneapolis, 1963. (*Reproduced by permission of the Tyrone Guthrie Theater, Minneapolis*)

Tyrone Guthrie rehearses *Peter Grimes* at the Metropolitan Opera House, New York City, 1967. (*Reproduced by permission of United Press International*)

Tyrone Guthrie welcomes the acting company of the Tyrone Guthrie Theater at first rehearsal of the opening season, Minneapolis, 1963. (*Reproduced by permission of the Minneapolis Star and Tribune Co.*)

Peter Zeisler, Tyrone Guthrie, and Donald Schoenbaum outside the Billy Rose Theater, New York City, 1968. (*Reproduced by permission of the Tyrone Guthrie Theater, Minneapolis*)

Acknowledgements

The inspiration for this book came from Tyrone Guthrie, for which I express my gratitude. It came as a result of working under his guidance as an actor and his assistant in the inaugural season of the Tyrone Guthrie Theater, and, later, because of his advice, encouragement, and friendship, which I valued through the years.

The opportunity to be a part of the original Minnesota Theater Company was made possible through a fellowship awarded me by the McKnight Foundation, which subsidized a programme whereby theatre students pursuing professional careers could act, direct, design, write, and learn at the University of Minnesota and the Guthrie Theater. It was an innovative, important, and influential concept designed to bridge the worlds of the educational and professional theatres. As such, it was the galvanizing example for a number of related programmes in the United States.

I wish to thank the McKnight Foundation and the fellowship programme administrator, Walter N. Trenerry, for that opportunity. Also, my gratitude to the theatre professors at the University of Minnesota, who consistently provided me with creative challenges, especially my adviser, Kenneth L. Graham, who always gave generously of his time and helpful counsel; Frank M. Whiting, the man who did so much to bring the Guthrie Theater to fruition; and Arthur H. Ballet, a brilliant man of the theater who directed the Rockefeller Foundation's Office for Advanced Drama Research for all of its fourteen years. Naturally, I gratefully acknowledge the contributions of all those persons who were willing to share their memories of Tony Guthrie with me, those included in the book and the many others who aided me in various ways in making this endeavour a reality. They are Melissa Bakewell, James Bishop, E. Martin Browne, Douglas Campbell, Paddy Chayefsky, Eric Christmas, John Coe, Adrienne and Stan Cohen, Arthur Colby-Sprague, Patricia Conolly, John DeSantis, Martin Esslin, Laurence Evans, James and Louise Forsyth, Julius Gellner, Mrs Norman Ginsbury, Marius Goring,

ACKNOWLEDGEMENTS

Charles Gray, Rosemary Harris, Charles Landstone, Patrick Layde, Murray Macdonald, Joyce Redman, Auriel Sanderson, Dan Sullivan, Wendy Trewin, Diana Valk and her family, and my editor and friend, Anthony Whittome.

I want to make special mention of several persons whose deaths during the preparation of this book saddened me: John Gibson, Margaret Leighton, Henzie Raeburn, Nancy Wickwire, and a truly great actress and woman, Dame Sybil Thorndike, whose dazzling eyes and youthful spirit at age ninety I shall never forget.

To Robert Hardy my everlasting thanks for speaking with John Mills and Charles Gray in my place and for his unfailing interest in this project.

My gratitude to the Regents of the University of California for granting me a Regents' Faculty Fellowship in the Creative Arts, so that I could conduct research in London. And, at the University of California at Davis: James Meyer, Donald Swain, Lawrence J. Andrews, Robert Fahrner, Corinne Taylor, Shirley Vohs, Ninette Medovoy; and Rhonda Scott.

Finally, my appreciation to Dawn Nelson, my transcriber and typist, for her efficiency, enthusiasm, and friendship.

Introduction

astonish. v.t. to stun or strike dumb with sudden
fear, terror, surprise, or wonder; to amaze; to
confound with some sudden passion; to surprise
exceedingly.

William Tyrone Guthrie – knighted by Queen Elizabeth II, made a
Doctor of Laws of the University of St Andrews in Scotland,
appointed Chancellor of Queen's University in Belfast, called 'Tony'
by his friends – was a legend in his own lifetime.

That lifetime ended on 15 May 1971 at his family home, Annagh-
ma-Kerrig, in County Monaghan: he was the age of the century. And
rather fitting, too, in that there are many who thought him to be the
director of the century.

That kind of opinion is the stuff out of which heated arguments
are made. My intention is not to make a case for or against it, but to
allow Guthrie's colleagues and friends to speak for themselves.

Initially, the focus of this book was to have been on *process*, and
the reader will see that much of the following material adheres to that
intent. It is an informal record of Guthrie's directorial techniques as
recalled by many of the people with whom he worked in his long and
illustrious career (1924–71). For me, this is a natural extension of my
book, *Minneapolis Rehearsals: Tyrone Guthrie Directs Hamlet*,
which chronicled his creative work on the inaugural production of the
Tyrone Guthrie Theater in Minneapolis in 1963.

As I spoke with the people in this book (and numerous others), I
soon realized that the personal side of Guthrie's life was ineluctably
interwoven with his experiences in directing under many circumstances
and flags. The conversations were burgeoning out of rehearsal rooms
and theatres in the British Isles and North America, and into the pubs,
flats, apartments, houses, and the estate in Ireland to which Guthrie
retired after the work of the day or night. Also, most people could not

speak about him without *her*, his wife for four decades, Judith Guthrie, *née* Bretherton, a cousin who explored with him the environs of Tunbridge Wells as children, and, more than any other person, shared his adventures in the theatre and his life. And so, this book became more and more biographical.

I predict that nothing which follows will lessen the outrageously unique charm of the Guthries, or the myths and apochrypha – and more than a few *facts* – which have gone round the theatrical world about these two extraordinary creatures. The reason, very simply, is that this is a *memory* book. As such, the reader will have to determine for himself the accuracy of the quotes and weigh the well-intentioned attempts at recalling experiences – some of which took place as long as fifty years ago.

I'm reminded of Fellini's comments when asked about the experiences depicted in his autobiographical film, *Amarcord*: 'To remember is not exactly. People tend to remember not what *really* was, but what they *think* it was.'

Another consideration is neatly summarized in an observation made by Tanya Moiseiwitsch, Guthrie's long-time friend and collaborator. In speaking about the design of *Oedipus Rex* for the Stratford Shakespeare Festival in Canada, Tanya confided:

I don't think that struck me as being very strange at the time. It sounds rather awkward discussing it now. I think anything that is analysed either at the time or later tends to break it all down into some sort of chemistry that no longer exists. I think at the time it happened and it worked. But talking about it now to you, I seem to have lost something in the translation. Do you know what I mean?

Yes, Tanya, I do know what you mean. And, I trust, so will the reader. If one recognizes the limitations of human memory, then this collection of conversations can be put in proper perspective. I feel this portrait of Guthrie is worth the risk of an anecdote expanded, a hyperbolic quote, an 'I think he said', taken for true. After all, the very charm of a tall tale is its very tallness (as Guthrie wrote of *The Winter's Tale*), and the tales about Guthrie are among the tallest in the theatre world – but then so was he.

As Alec Guinness remarked in his address at Guthrie's Memorial Service, an old family friend had said of Guthrie's death, 'A great tree has fallen.' A rather apt metaphor considering Guthrie was the Johnny Appleseed of theatre – a man whose odysseys took him to four continents, many countries and even more cities, planting seeds and nurturing saplings which grew into some of the most respected theatres in the world: the National Theatre of Great Britain, the Stratford Shakespeare Festival in Canada, the Tyrone Guthrie Theater, Minneapolis.

The conversations herein, which create a mosaic of Guthrie, are with a cross-section of the thousands of people with whom he worked at various times. For every conversation included, I am confident several others could be found whose memories might contribute equally.

The chief areas of Guthrie's career in the theatre are covered: his artistic leadership of the Old Vic in the thirties and forties, including the war years when the Vic was based at Burnley; the commercial theatre experiences in the West End and on Broadway at various times in his career; the seasons at Stratford, Ontario, and Minneapolis.

There are comments about his brilliant successes; for example, the Victoriana *A Midsummer Night's Dream*, *Peer Gynt* and *Cyrano* after the war, the Guinness *Hamlet*, *Henry VIII* at Stratford-on-Avon, the epic *Tamburlaine* productions – one with Wolfit, one with Quayle, *Troilus and Cressida* and *The Matchmaker*.

Also, when he came a cropper: the Laughton-Robson *Measure for Measure*, the Richardson-Olivier *Othello*, *The First Gentleman* in New York, and the *Tartuffe* at the National Theatre in which, inexplicably, John Gielgud did not play the title role.

The monumental work on *Oedipus* in Ontario and *The House of Atreus* in Minnesota is discussed, as well as his richly textured, subtle handling of the Chekhovs in Minneapolis.

There are also observations about the key productions which influenced Guthrie in the development of the thrust stage: the Olivier *Hamlet* at Kronborg Castle in Elsinore and the enormously successful *The Three Estates* at the Edinburgh Festival.

Some conversations cover the whole of Guthrie's professional life and reflect deep friendships and loyalties; others are the result of a single experience under his theatrical maestro's baton.

Some people were treated to the Guthries' hospitality in a myriad of domiciles: the house in Burnley shared with George Chamberlain and Annette Prevost, cheap Greenwich Village hotels, the garret apartment in Minneapolis, Annagh-ma-Kerrig, and, of course, the legendary flat at 23, Old Buildings, Lincoln's Inn Fields, London, which, if one is to believe the stories, had both the comforts and aura of the stable in Bethlehem.

For the title of this book I must thank Stanley Baxter, with whom I had an illuminating, frequently hilarious visit. Many of those with whom I spoke were able to give a reasonable impression of Tony's voice and speech tonalities and rhythms, but none was able to hit the mark so accurately so often as the charming Mr Baxter.

Stanley reminded me of one of Tony's favourite expressions, most often said at the end of a long day to a rather harried thespian who just could not find a way to read that line, do that biz, figure out that speech. Tony would react with charming intolerance and say, 'Go home, think about it, come back, and astonish us in the morning.'

The expression seemed to bruit itself about my ears and memory to the point where no other title was even thinkable. And why not? 'Astonish' just might be the very best word to characterize what Tony did. Indeed, he astonished us daily with his invention at rehearsals, his infectious sense of play, and the joy of working together. Just as we were amazed and surprised exceedingly, and were *his* audience for a time paying daily homage in our astonishment, so, too, were the audiences – and most especially critics – stunned into sudden surprise, confounded, amazed.

The warmth and generosity with which I was received by so many people must be mentioned. Characteristically, one said: 'If you worked with Tony Guthrie, that's good enough for me.' I felt part of a special club with no other membership rule than that.

It's quite possible that Tony Guthrie might not have liked this book since he believed that the theatre was very much like writing on water – too transient to capture, hold, and analyse. However, this is not a work of dramatic art but, rather, an attempt to keep Guthrie's genius as an artist and his charisma as a man alive among those of us who had the fortune to have known him, and, most importantly, to share this special human being with you. I think we feel as Tony Quayle did when I spoke with him, and perhaps you'll feel the same.

It appeared that Quayle really couldn't end the conversation, so that, as we stopped in his office to look at a picture of Guthrie directing *Tamburlaine*, he had to tell me one more story. In the hallway another anecdote occurred to him, and yet another on his front-porch steps. Finally, he mused: 'I miss him very much. Well, maybe he was listening. He might have gotten a laugh out of it.'

Alfred Rossi
Los Angeles, 1976

Conversations

Anthony Quayle

ALFRED ROSSI: *How long did you know Tony Guthrie?*

ANTHONY QUAYLE: I first met him in 1931 or 32 when I was at the RADA and he came and saw me in a production of *St Joan*, in French. He was just about to run the Westminster Theatre at the time, and said he would like to have me in the company; but that didn't work out. Although he couldn't offer me a job at the Westminster he got me invited to go to the Arts Theatre at Cambridge which a friend of his was running. In 1932 he gave me my first job under his management in *Love's Labour's Lost*,* playing the King. Actually I think I was pretty inadequate; I was very young at the time, only about eighteen or nineteen. It was an enchanting production as I recall it, though I don't think it made theatrical history. At that time Tony was the forerunner of all the avant-garde young directors of today.

How did he approach the verse speaking in that production?

Tony never had a pedantic approach to verse speaking: that was not his primary objective. He was first of all a musician. He regarded a play as a musical score: its changes of pace, its modifications, its climaxes, crescendos and decrescendos were treated very much as a piece of music. He was keenly aware of rhythms – the overall rhythm of a scene rather than the clear carving of syllables. So there were often passages where he didn't care if the audience heard exactly what was said. He aimed for a general impression; the clarity of dialogue was comparatively unimportant. 'It's a dreary passage. Get on with it. Race it through.' So there'd be a great impression of brouhaha, confusion, noise, embattled opinion, out of which one vital line would emerge – bang! – like that, and hit you a wallop. He'd throw away twenty lines in order to achieve one which would slam you in the face. It was quite deliberate with him – in the same way as he would use movement.

*A list of Sir Tyrone Guthrie's productions appears in the Appendix, page 299.

19

He was a very, very good choreographer. To a fault he would create busy, swirling scenes in order to achieve the moment of arrested movement, which was then significant. He saw a play, both musically and in movement, as something to be moulded and wielded and made to find its own dynamic rhythm. Sometimes he would impose that rhythm. Sometimes he would half impose and half discover it. It was a very immediate working system. It was like a man working in glass rather than metal. He was like a glass-blower who has to blow it and keep it turning so that it is always in movement; because if it gets too thin it will break, and if it gets too heavy, it will sag. It is in the formative period of blowing a piece of glass that it has to be kept moving. And this is what Tony did with a play, always. He came with no static, preconceived idea. He had a general idea of what it should be and the rest of it was immediate, hand-to-mouth – like a glass-blower. He kept it moving, moving. And his use of the different ingredients – text, actors, design – this was always malleable.

Did you ever get the feeling he was imposing his half conception on you from the start, or was it more subtle?

Tony was a very authoritative, dominant man. It would have been impossible for him to be subordinate. He was never subordinate to anyone. He had in himself a creative originality which needed its own outlet and *had* to speak with its own voice. He could not help imposing his vision, his will, his concept of a play on the stage. It was his positive statement, as much as that of a master painting a picture. So he was always more interested in gifted young actors on their way up – actors who eagerly accepted his creative authority – than in established actors who are inevitably more set in their ways. Through all my formative years as an actor – years in which I was hugely influenced by Tony – I never had the slightest difficulty in going along with his ideas. They were always illuminating, and much better ideas than my own.

The only clash we ever had – it was short and sharp but not serious – was when I had become more or less established and had to take responsibility for my own performance. It was at a dress-rehearsal of *Tamburlaine* at the Winter Garden in New York, and he suddenly wanted to change something at the last moment. Right in the middle of the final dress-rehearsal. I said: 'I can't do it.' 'Can't do it? What d'you mean?' 'I can't do it. It's too late. And what's more, I think it's wrong.' Down in the stalls Tony said something like, 'Ugly scene, dear boy. Ugly scene.' But he didn't insist – he couldn't very well. That's what I mean. When you were young you'd do anything, anything he wanted, because it was so exciting. But when you came to have your own artistic responsibilities then there were times when you had to stand up for yourself – and there was the possibility of a clash. So I came to see why established actors didn't always get on with him – and why he tended to be intolerant of them. He was absolutely brilliant, but he had to have *his* way.

So, as I say, he was always at his best working with actors on their way up, and not with actors who had arrived.

How did Guthrie treat Olivier when he did Hamlet?

That's a long time ago, and my memory's not so vivid. I think he was beglamoured by him – and with reason. (Incidentally, Olivier was not on his way up. He was already a big international star.) I've never met a great man who was not flawed. Tony was a great man – and his flaws were part of his unique quality. I'm not trying to add up a plus and a minus in the balance account – I'm just trying to speak honestly of a perverse, complicated, brilliant and extraordinary man. Highly stimulating, and at times maddeningly provocative. At times you had to stand up and fight for your life, or he'd swamp you. But there were some young actors who, in Tony's eyes, could do no wrong. 'Nuggets', he used to call them – golden boys. And, as I recall, that's how he thought of Larry. And he was right too, wasn't he? Tony could be as indulgent of some people as he could be tough on others. It was part of his perversity.

What form did 'fighting for your life' with Tony take in your own case?

Simply that he had great intellectual power allied to a powerful personality, and if you differed from him in some concept – the interpretation of a part, or a scene – you were often hard put to it to defend your point of view. If you could persuade him, either by argument or demonstration, then he was generous in accepting it. But if you were tentative, if you didn't put up a fight, then he would over-whelm you.

Did he ever not allow you to try your own way?

Never. He gave actors great latitude. He would seize on their own creativity and develop it – set it off to the best advantage. Once he saw what you were after, and agreed with you, then he would start

21

adapting the production to suit the new reading. He would start to create other rhythms, other patterns – like crystals forming.

What about your experience playing Tamburlaine? That was certainly a star part.

Yes, it was. Probably the most demanding part physically, and the most vivid production theatrically, that I have ever been involved in. It was undoubtedly one of Tony's greatest productions, but it had a sadly short run in New York. But perhaps its shortness has added to its legend. Certainly I still meet people who tell that they came twice or three times to see it. Maybe it was ahead of its time. I don't know.

What were your first thoughts when he offered you the role of Tamburlaine in 1956?

I was thrilled – naturally – just thrilled. We had talked about the project for years, but had never managed to pull it off. I was tied up in Stratford, for one thing. But one day Tony said, 'Think I've found the situation. Think we can do it in Toronto and bring it to New York, and everybody will be happy. What about it? Are you on?' And I said, 'Yes, I'm on.' It was all quite simple when the time came.

Of course, he'd done the play with Wolfit in the early fifties. Did he ever refer to that, or did he indicate that there were other things he wanted to do with the production?

Not really. As he grew older he used to say, half-jokingly, 'Oh, I'm lazy now. It's so much work to find out how to make a play work – a big play like this. Now I can refine it rather than carve it all out again.' So I think he was glad to do another production of *Tamburlaine*. He saw how to get a polish on parts which had eluded him the first time. Plays that he liked he would do again and again – *Henry VIII, All's Well That Ends Well*. He was like a conductor with favourite pieces of music: he enjoyed going back and solving problems that had eluded him rather than embark on a new composer and a whole new work. . . . Though occasionally he did that too – the *Oresteia*, for example.

How did you and Tony prepare to work on such a difficult role?

If you mean, did we sit down and talk about it at length – we didn't at all. We had known each other for years, so there were no initial barriers to overcome. For my part, the only preparation was to learn it quickly. I was still the Director of Stratford-on-Avon and couldn't get away for the start of rehearsals. Tony started without me, and I had two weeks after I arrived in Toronto. It was just a question of fitting in and getting on with it, as professionally as I knew how. No bad method, either. Of course, I'd seen the earlier production with Wolfit, so I knew the mood of the whole thing and the scope of the production . . . a bravura mixture of violence and ferocity coupled with wonderful theatrical dexterity.

As you approached playing that role yourself, were you conscious of that performance of Wolfit?

Conscious, yes. Wolfit was a fine actor with great power, and he gave a great performance as Tamburlaine. But I don't think I was unduly influenced. It helped a lot to have seen the production and know some of the visual effects that Tony was after. Tamburlaine's death, for example, where he was like a big black bear, crawling about on the map of the world, yet hardly able to speak. This was vividly in my mind. It was like having seen a great Rembrandt from without – and then knowing the effect when you stepped into the picture and became part of it.

By this time you had a lot of experience and, of course, quite a reputation. Did he begin to treat you in a different way in this starring role?

Good heavens, no! Just the same. We were very old friends. I wouldn't be surprised, though, after that little row we had on the stage of the Winter Garden, if he had gone away and said, 'Dear old Tony – I'm very fond of him, but he's growing a bit grand these days,' because he referred to it years later. 'We had a nasty little altercation,' he said. 'I remember.' Oh, he remembered all right. He'd remembered that I'd dug my heels in.

I think this is a nasty question, but I'm going to ask it anyway. Did that contribute to the fact that you didn't work with him again?

No, I don't think so for a second. It's true, as far as I can recall, that he never asked me to act anything for him, but he made a number of flattering suggestions that I go and direct both in Canada and at Minneapolis. But I wasn't at liberty to do so. But there was no breach. On the contrary, when he died, I found that Alec Guinness and I were the only actors to whom he had left some personal memento in his will. But, as he died in Ireland and I was in England, I never got the memento. I dearly wish I had. I would love to have something of Tony's – no matter what – an old cracked teapot or one of those gaudy scarves he used to wear round his neck.

That production, of course, was absolutely stunning, from what I've heard from people who saw it. Do you remember how he worked on some of those spectacular scenes – the piercing of the man with arrows, and the leading in triumph of some of the kings you had vanquished?

The shooting of the arrows was simply a technical trick, but I could generalize about Tony's way of working. You see, directors work in totally different ways – and there's nothing wrong with that. Tony always got down into the arena with the actors – always. He would always come in working clothes – sandals, old grey flannel trousers, an old stained shirt, that vivid muffler round his neck. Most Bohemian-looking – except occasionally when he'd surprise you by turning up in a beautifully-cut blue suit, looking like a strange, elongated general with his clipped moustache and short hair. Perverse in everything, you see.

But in rehearsal the play poured through his veins. He would be there acting it with you, inwardly. Like a conductor, or a choreographer, it would surge through him. He would say, 'No, no, no. Stop!' He would always snap his fingers. Crack, crack, crack, crack. 'Back, dear boy. All back. Now then . . .' And up he'd get, and somehow – through his own body and voice, give you an often garish but very clear image of what he saw the scene to be. He was like a lightning conductor. He didn't sit back dispassionately and observe. He went through it all with you. He was a vivid part and parcel of the play until he felt that you had really got the feel of it. He wasn't really a good actor – he was too mannered and too eccentric-looking – but he knew the feeling of every scene, and he had a vivid concept of how each part should be played.

There are some directors who are violently opposed to such a method as Tony's. They feel that nothing must be 'demonstrated' to the actor, that every performance must spring from the actor's own thought and imagination. That their own function is to sit outside the hurly-burly and keep a watchful eye on it, stepping in only to stimulate the actor's imagination where need be. And that is a perfectly valid method too. But Tony worked the other way. The whole play – and every performance – flowed through him. And, since he was a vivid man, witty and highly intelligent, rehearsals were always the same – vivid, exciting. And his productions grew – they grew like plants. It was impossible to be bored with him for one second, because he could be so funny, so trenchant, so ironic – and so creative. He could mock the world – and himself – then howl with laughter. His zest for life was enormous. But with some people he could be provocative and cruel – even sadistic.

How could he be sadistic?

He would appear to take almost a pleasure in pointing out their shortcomings to some actors. He never minced his words. The arrows he shot could be mortal, and he often shot them with a certain relish. A very peculiar man.

I understand that there was an incredible reaction on the last night of the production in New York.

Indeed there was. I've never experienced a reception like that in all my life. We took endless curtain-calls, and then left the stage. I had gone up to my dressing-room in the Winter Garden and had started to change. Suddenly the stage manager came in and said, 'You'll have to come down again. They won't leave the theatre.' So down I went. And there, right down at the front of the stalls, were a faithful couple of hundred – still standing, and clapping, and cheering. It was very moving – because we were all participating in the untimely death of a wonderful production. It was real communication – but the audience had no words to express their sympathy and appreciation. Just this applause that went on and on. And that was the end of *Tamburlaine*.

The Henry VIII *production that you did in 1949 was rather significant, I think, in terms of Guthrie's evolving the thrust stage design which eventually he did at Stratford and in Minneapolis. As you recall that experience was there any discussion about why that staging concept was used for the production?*

No, there was no discussion – at least, not with me. He must have had a good deal of discussion with Tanya Moiseiwitsch. In fact she'd be the only person who would know if this particular staging had any bearing on the theatres they went on to build together. I saw the *Henry VIII* as a progression in the general way his thinking was leading him – had been leading him for some time – a tendency to simplify Shakespeare productions, to find a fluid yet permanent architectural setting, and to dispense even with the distraction of lighting changes.

LIBRARY
College of St. Francis
JOLIET, ILLINOIS

123,448

We did have many talks at that time about constructing a new theatre – the 'Tin Globe', he used to call it – but they came to nothing. Of necessity. You see, when I was first asked to take on the directorship of Stratford-on-Avon I was in considerable doubt about it. I had no ambitions that way. But two people influenced me strongly to accept the offer – my wife, and Tony Guthrie. Tony had quite a part in my going there at all. But a year later there he was urging me to build this new theatre he had in mind. To build it in Stratford. 'But what am I to do with the existing theatre?' 'Who cares? It's a dreadfully old-fashioned theatre. You can only do old-fashioned work there. Push it into the Avon!' It was rather like Henry II telling Becket to push down Canterbury Cathedral after urging him to become Archbishop. I simply couldn't do it. Perhaps the Stratford theatre was old-fashioned, but there it was, brick upon brick – and I was its custodian. So that was that. Tony took himself off and built the theatre in Canada. I think he was a bit huffed with me – but that's the way Tony was. There was this capricious, almost feline side to his nature. He was a man full of contradictions – which was what made him such a stimulating, captivating creature.

Would you call that production of Henry VIII, *with that kind of setting, innovative?*

Not really. Not in itself. There was nothing new in a permanent, architectural set or in a thrust stage. (Though the thrust at Stratford was a very limited one.) The setting was only innovative in the sense that all Tony's life was spent in moving gradually towards full expression at Stratford and Minneapolis. This was a final step along the path. Nor was there anything particularly innovative about the production itself. It was individual and idiosyncratic, but so was all of Tony's work. Every production of his bore his signature writ large. But this no more so than others.

I think that's what I'm trying to say: Tony had a perpetual freshness of approach in every aspect of his work, and this freshness, this individuality, gained him the reputation of being an innovator – especially in his youth. But if he was an innovator, it was innovation rooted in tradition. He was not an iconoclast.

A lot of people, I think, have a contrary opinion of that. Certainly the critics, on occasion, have lambasted him for what at the time seemed to be a daring approach to certain things, for example in Henry VIII.

'A daring approach'? – I don't know about that. He was often impertinent. He enjoyed nothing so much as puncturing balloons, cocking snooks at pomposity, making it manifest that the 'Emperor' had no clothes. But that is something more light-hearted and frivolous than 'a daring approach'. But he could go to great lengths – sometimes excessive lengths – in this urchin attitude. There was a scene in *Henry VIII* which revolved round one of the actors having trodden in some dog mess. It was this kind of facetiousness to which some critics objected. But that was Tony. He was extremely bold in all his effects. Sometimes he hit the target – usually he did. Sometimes he was wide of the mark.

How did he treat the sentimental scenes in the play?

Under his direction they were not sentimental at all. And they were wonderfully played by Gwen ffrangcon-Davies. But it's true that Tony could never have directed, say, *Romeo and Juliet*. Any demonstration of love between a man and a woman, or a boy and a girl, this embarrassed him. He couldn't direct such a scene, and he'd just leave you alone to cope with it.

Why?

I don't know. And who am I to pluck out the heart of his mystery? Perhaps his height had something to do with it. He was very tall – six foot six, I think. I once asked him if this had made him self-conscious when he was young, and I was surprised at the vehemence of his reply. 'I suffered agonies,' he said. 'It's as bad to be as tall as I am, as it is to be a dwarf. It was dreadful. Dreadful.'

But I should think there were all sorts of inhibitions in him which made love scenes embarrassing to him. As a director he had a tremendous range: 'pastoral-comical-historical-tragical' – in all these fields he was a master. But straightforward romantical floored him. And he'd be the first to admit it. It was the same with pretty women. They threw him off-balance, and he had a tendency to lash out against them.

Did that ever come out in any of the work you remember with him?

Not specifically. It was just a bias one couldn't help noticing. On the other hand he could be unexpectedly gentle and considerate. My own wife, Dorothy Hyson, was a very beautiful woman and Tony was never anything but dear to her. In the winter of 1939 – a bitterly

27

cold winter – she was playing Titania at the Old Vic, and had to lie for ages on an uncomfortable bank pretending to be asleep. At one dress-rehearsal she was lying there shivering when she heard a scrabbling close at hand, then a voice saying 'Psst! Psst!' She opened her eyes, and there, lying full-length from the wings, was Tony – pushing a hot-water bottle towards her. He was always terribly nice to her – perhaps because he was aware that she had poor defences and was vulnerable. But to any pretty woman who relied only on her prettiness to get through life he could be merciless.

If you had to characterize the quality or qualities that made Tony Guthrie the great director that he was, what would you say they were?

They were many and various, but they all added up to leadership. I don't list them in any order of priority. One was energy – dynamic energy of mind and body. He could go on pumping out provocative and stimulating work hour after hour, when everybody else was flagging. Next, a marvellous grasp of the patterns and rhythms of a play, of the interlocking scenes. A great appreciation of contrast – dark and light, fast and slow – in musical as well as visual terms. A great grasp of movement. With technical knowledge he could have been a fine choreographer: as it was, he was a superb director of opera. And, linked with it all, an authority, springing from his own energy and daring.

He was in himself a stimulating and challenging man – and a very amusing one. He lived life with zest, and imparted that zest to others. He was highly intelligent without being an intellectual – he was more instinctive than that, more emotional.

I think it was the very contradictions in his nature that made him so fascinating. For all that I've said about his being demanding and dominant, he was also enormously modest. He did not proclaim his pre-eminence. And he was generous – always giving things away. Time particularly. When I look back now and think of the amount of time he bestowed on us young actors – having us to meals at his home in Lincoln's Inn, talking to us, making friends of us – I am amazed at his generosity. He was generous too in the more obvious way – with gifts of money. He had no feeling for worldly possessions. They meant nothing to him. The art of the theatre was the only thing that really interested him. Nothing else. He was very pure in his approach to it. You were aware of his faults – I'm not sure, for example, that [his wife] Judy altogether shared his scorn of basic comforts – but his virtues so overweighed them that you were utterly beguiled by him. Oh, I would say the most enriching personality that I've ever worked with.

There were two sides in Tony which were at war with each other – very often the case in the most interesting people. One part of his blood was Irish – and very Irish too. The other part came from a line of eminent Scots churchmen – Dr Thomas Guthrie was his great-grandfather – all fire and brimstone and austerity. So there was a chop on the waves. They weren't all going the same way. They tumbled and conflicted. The great qualities were generosity, simplicity, single-mindedness, disregard of self – and vivid humour. The failings were trivialities – and served to make him human and fallible.

Since you indicated you started working with him very early, and he was a very significant man in your life and career, how did Guthrie help you most?

The most obvious help was by giving me employment. That is the greatest encouragement you can give a young actor – to invite him to work in the best company in the land. But he helped me most, I think, by the gift of his friendship – and in this Judy was equally generous. I learnt a lot about theatre – and therefore about life – simply by being with them, eating with them, laughing with them (there was always a great deal of laughter around the Guthries), talking with them. Their friendship was a rich and happy education.

What was so special about Tony's approach to theatre?

He didn't 'approach' the theatre any more than a plant 'approaches' the earth. He was naturally of it. It was his whole existence in an un-forced, spontaneous way. His great talents and imagination, backed by formidable energy and authority, flowered naturally in the theatre.

In so far as he had any conscious or deliberate 'approach' I think it was in choosing to work in a rather esoteric field. He deliberately chose to produce works of rare quality for a minority audience. He flirted with the commercial theatre, but it did not hold his interest or allegiance. He was interested in producing 'caviar' – and if 'the general' did not like 'caviar', so much the worse for them.

He was also a lifelong advocate of decentralization. He wished to see theatre flourishing outside the established centres of London and New York. And he backed his opinions with his actions – some would say too much so, and that he spread himself too thin on the ground.

Above all he regarded theatre as he regarded life (for the two are inextricably bound together) as a vivid and enthralling adventure. He enjoyed his life's adventure to the full, and he was eager to share it with others. He knew that he had something to give – he could hardly help knowing that – and his whole joy and fulfilment was in this giving, all over the world. His life was the spontaneous flowering of a genius which has no time for anything extraneous.

J. C. Trewin

ALFRED ROSSI: *When was the first time you saw a Guthrie production?*

J. C. TREWIN: He'd just taken over the Old Vic. It would have been 1933–4, and it was the Charles Laughton–Flora Robson season. They were doing major productions at Sadler's Wells, I remember, a most awkward theatre in those days. Awful side walls, completely bare and death to the acoustics. Guthrie decided to use a permanent stage set, a built-up central structure. You know these days it happens everywhere, but it was a sensation then and everybody talked about it. Afterwards articles on Guthrie's new staging were all over the place.

Do you remember some of the justification he used at the time?

Yes. I think the main thing he said was that it brought the action forward. In his interviews he said he had discovered that old-school Shakespeare sent you upstage all the time. He thought here that he would be able to keep the action – as he put it – reasonably within view and hearing of the audience. But, of course, he hadn't allowed for Sadler's Wells acoustics: nothing would have helped, in any event. The central structure became a nuisance when it had to serve for *Twelfth Night*, *Measure for Measure*, *Macbeth*. (For *The Tempest* Guthrie did have a practically bare stage.) Everyone was delighted when in *Henry VIII* he used some of the Casson–Thorndike sets that were first designed for the Empire Theatre production. Suddenly, with a bang, we were back in spectacular Shakespeare, as we knew it then, in the middle of Guthrie's severe new-style décor. He was also rather unfortunate that season because he was starring Charles Laughton, who had never played Shakespeare before, and frankly, except as Angelo, couldn't. I think he got the idea of Angelo all right – he was like a great sinister cat.

I'm curious about what you said about the severity of style that Guthrie introduced. Could you elaborate on that?

It was the change-over from semi-pictorial Shakespeare to director's Shakespeare in the modern manner. The Old Vic audiences were loyal to what they had been used to. Now they could not get used to Guthrie's pace. They found his setting bleak – I think that was the familiar word at the time. They couldn't get used to concentrating on the acting and dissociating it from its background. That was the great difficulty of the change-over: the scenic designer ceased to have the importance that he originally had. If a man just threw up a screen in the middle of the stage and said, 'That's all you're going to get,' well, the orthodox Vic audiences were alarmed. They said they weren't getting Shakespeare. One's memory of the period is of audience confusion. I think if we saw the same productions today we might feel that Laughton wasn't up to it. He wasn't really even when he came to Stratford in 1959. I don't fancy Shakespeare appealed to him very much. But of the Vic–Wells productions I think we'd say, 'Oh well, Guthrie knew what he was about.'

I've just recalled that I did see one earlier production of his – *Richard II* at Stratford in 1933, with George Hayes as Richard and Anew McMaster as Bolingbroke. He did that on a flight of steps much as Komisarjevsky would do *Lear*. That really, in its way, was quite spectacular. Stratford audiences – it was the second season of the then new Memorial Theatre, now the Royal Shakespeare – were even more conservative than the Vic's, but they accepted the production, thought Guthrie was a good boy, and liked him very much. It was in the following autumn at Sadler's Wells and the Vic that he started his new company, and I don't believe in that season that he got on particularly well with Lilian Baylis. He was doing things she had never seen done before. Even after Harcourt Williams, Guthrie to her was someone new and young and rather frightening, and Lilian Baylis didn't like being frightened. So at the end of that season Henry Cass – with, of course, Maurice Evans in his company – took over.

From your standpoint how would you characterize his first year? What did it accomplish?

I think it showed that he always managed surprises in almost every production, whatever you might have felt about the general impact. There was always something to make you sit up. I daresay everyone remembers Laughton after Duncan's murder. *Macbeth* was the last production of the season. Quite suddenly he came out of himself – the rest of his performance could be almost frighteningly dull – and he had a few sensational moments, right downstage, a man sobbing his heart out to the audience. I'm quite sure it was Guthrie's idea.

What are your recollections of the Olivier Hamlet?

Well, it was the big thing in the spring of 1937. I saw it innumerable times. I was working in Fleet Street and any time I could get away from the paper before seven o'clock I went along to Waterloo Road. It was the most startling performance I had ever seen, up to that time.

What was so startling about it?

Olivier. Young, handsome, at the height of his youthful powers, athletic. I don't say it was Shakespeare's Hamlet, but it was terrifically exciting, and Guthrie played up to him. It became an enormously exciting melodrama, a handsome hero doing all the things he should do. He had the Vic at his feet; I have never known an audience so overwhelmed. The scene at the stage door afterwards would be fantastic – the entire gallery out.

Guthrie had provided an extraordinary kind of up-and-down set. The actors were skipping about on Alpine peaks during most of the evening. At the end the Queen fell backwards from a high rostrum into somebody's arms. It was the late Dorothy Dix, and they say she was scared stiff every time; so would I have been.

Guthrie went on at length to do *Henry V*, a splendid production, the entire stage set in banners – they just opened and closed. I still believe that Olivier's performance was better than in the film.

Then, to Lilian Baylis's great delight, the company was invited to Elsinore to play *Hamlet*. The first time an English company had played there; most of the critics went over and the papers made a great fuss. There was to be a first evening performance in the court-yard of the castle – Kronborg. It began to rain about four in the afternoon; I'd never known such a downpour, and Lilian Baylis, who thought about the reputation of her company over everything else, was in great distress. I remember she went to the door of the hotel – Marienlyst, just outside Elsinore – and said in her most indignant matriarchal tones, 'This will have to stop.'

But it didn't, and soon afterwards Guthrie came round to the room where everyone was sitting and said, 'We're going to move to the cabaret stage in the ballroom.' He went on: 'I shall want volunteers to move the chairs in a semi-circle around the stage. I think the critics ought to do that. They haven't done anything at all.' So we all joined in and turned the place into an auditorium. About half past seven everybody began to arrive. It was still pouring, great sheets of rain sweeping across the Sound. I've never known such a night. There were some Danish royalties there, and they put them in the front row.

The company, without any kind of rehearsal, just started off. It remains to this day the most exciting performance of *Hamlet* I've ever seen. The actors seemed to be caught up in the strangeness of the setting; all the time they were playing – the first half especially – the wind and the rain were beating against the plate-glass windows around us. I think Olivier said afterwards that he felt it was the biggest challenge he'd had; in those days one hardly ever played on a thrust stage or in the round.

When it was over Guthrie said to George Bishop, who was theatre correspondent for the *Telegraph* – he's dead now – 'This has made me think – look what's happened tonight. Here is the kind of theatre we ought to use.' And you know what he did with that kind of theatre later on. Next night the same production, but in the Kronborg courtyard, a platform at one end and everything done normally, seemed almost boring by comparison; excitement had gone. The previous night was the first time Vivien Leigh had played Ophelia opposite Olivier – one of the few changes from the London cast. They were splendid together.

When you sat there watching it, did you sense that it was going to be a rather special event in the theatre?

No, I don't think so at first. We were all standing about at the back because the place was crammed. People who'd intended to come to the courtyard had to be packed into the ballroom; but somehow there were stacking chairs and gilt chairs for them, and the English contingent just stood or perched themselves anywhere they could. At the time nobody could have said why it was so exciting; the play just found some intimacy it never had before. In London we had got used to the proscenium stage down the years and given little thought to anything else – even though people like William Poel were doing experiments on the side. We knew this *Hamlet* was special, yet I don't feel any man there would have said, hand on heart, 'This is going to be the theatre of the future.'

As someone who has watched the theatre, not just in England but in other countries, develop over the last forty years, what would you say were Guthrie's most significant productions?

34

Well, first of all, that *Hamlet* at the Vic. I'd never known an audience and a company to come together like that. It was the swiftest performance I remember. His productions seemed to get quicker and quicker. You know, looking back, I can't remember a slow one – perhaps the late *Tartuffe* at the National – but towards the middle of his career they were generally at a terrific pace. That *Hamlet* just swept across the Vic stage.

Then, too, his work for the Olivier–Richardson season at the New from 1944. By then – and I suppose even earlier in his career – he had become a sort of elder statesman. Indeed I can't remember a man becoming an elder statesman so young. Everybody wanted to be directed by Guthrie. Everybody wanted to talk to him – sidling round, you know, so that they could get in his line; people writing and asking if they couldn't do X and Y and Z for him. Never was a man more courted. Not that it did anything to him; he went on as usual. Maybe I shouldn't say that these were landmarks in his career because the company then was so good. Richardson and Sybil Thorndike and Olivier in *Peer Gynt*, and Richardson, Guinness, Leighton, and Harry Andrews in *Cyrano*.

His next terrific production was *Tamburlaine* at the Vic – back in Waterloo Road then – in 1951. Marlowe's play hadn't been done in England for heaven knows how long. It was almost a première, and Guthrie put everything into it including the kitchen stove. So many crowd scenes, all entirely different; any Guthrie production had this extraordinary amount of detail.

After the *Tamburlaine* (with Wolfit) the next one for history was *Troilus and Cressida* in 1956. It split Shakespeare down the middle. By that time we had discovered that Guthrie didn't care much for poetry. If anything in the script amused him he would play up the fun and games, and *Troilus* gave him a wonderful opportunity to emphasize the satire at the expense of the love scenes.

Its success was due entirely to the invention. In those days we had got more used to the play – the Cambridge Marlowe people had been doing it continually, and there had been two or three Stratford productions, and the modern dress one at the Westminster just before the war. Still, we hadn't realized that it would go into a pre-World War One setting – this conflict of Germanic Greeks and Ruritanian Trojans was absolutely new. The evening went to a squeal of surprise; in speech after speech Guthrie found something fresh; he twisted phrases craftily to get a modern meaning. It was only when it came to

35

the parting of Troilus and Cressida that one had always assumed to be the peak of the play, that he scampered through it at an impossible rate. Simply because he wanted to get to the next bit of fun.

The last thing he did of any marked significance was the *All's Well That Ends Well* at Stratford in 1959. Modern dress, with Edith Evans as the Countess. Here he invented an entire Shakespeare scene, the Duke of Florence reviewing his army. The scene is less than a dozen lines long in the Folio, and with Guthrie it lasted ten minutes, a Crazy Gang affair. It was an odd position: one half of me angry – 'This doesn't exist! What *is* going on?' – and the other half laughing so loudly I couldn't hear myself think. Most of the critics were in the same state. But it was an expert production. I remember an elaborate dance at the beginning of a scene in the French Court; in the middle of it the chandelier began to dance as well. Typical Guthrie. After this he rather faded out theatrically; he was more often across the Atlantic than here. When he came back he had those unfortunate productions of *Tartuffe* and *Volpone* for the National. Neither of them worked.

What was the difference between those two productions that came off so poorly – by reports I've had from many people – and his earlier work?

In *Tartuffe*, for one thing, his invention seemed to have vanished. Sixteen or seventeen years before, he'd done Miles Malleson's version of *The Miser* for the Old Vic and made it a remarkably gay affair – it was almost a harlequinade. *Tartuffe* seemed to be slow and solemn, and it was miscast. It had been put into the programme because the National wanted Gielgud.

After all these years people still debate whether Gielgud or Olivier is the greater actor. And here was Gielgud coming back under Olivier's banner to be directed by Guthrie. It should have been a night of nights. But he was not cast for Tartuffe which went to Robert Stephens; instead he played the husband, Orgon, a relatively poor part. There was not much vigour in it, and – at least, as far as we could judge – he had no particular help from Guthrie. The piece just loitered along. Joan Plowright, who was the maid, carried off the evening; without her it would have been sad, and next morning's press confirmed it.

We thought: 'It's one of those temporary aberrations. He's going to do *Volpone* next. There he'll have a grand time.' He didn't. He used a full text – Sir Politick Would-Be and all the scenes usually cut – but from the first there wasn't the old light, there was no surprise. Probably that's the answer. It was extremely restless and without any of the compensating virtues. Though you might agree that the average Guthrie production could be over-restless, he always came out in the middle with some exciting flash of originality. No originality at all in the *Volpone*. Better than the *Tartuffe* – but anybody could have directed it. You could have come out of the Vic and said: 'Who's the director? I didn't get a look at his name.' You'd never have said that in the past. Even after secondary plays, you came away saying, 'What a night! . . . Guthrie, of course!' So now when you had to leave a theatre, forgetting that he was the man, there could be only one response: 'This is it, I'm afraid; it's getting towards the end.' Everyone was upset.

How would you rank Guthrie with the other directors of the twentieth century?

I can speak only from my own experience. There are always five directors I think of (and really I ought to add one other, Robert Atkins). The Russian Komisarjevsky showed that there was no need to use the funereal pace of the Edwardians and the early Fifth Georgians. He might have been capricious but he was stimulating. He held that Shakespeare had to be rethought every time you looked at the text. Bridges-Adams, at Stratford for fifteen years, was the finest of the absolutely direct, scrupulously faithful, civilized men. And I'd always put with him, in later years, Glen Byam Shaw.

Apart from these there were the two exciting 'mad dogs' of direction, if I can call them that admiringly, Guthrie and Peter Brook. After any production by one of these you could go home and argue for hours. I remember session after session: 'Well, even if he was crazy in the second scene, look what he did – how the play rose! Yes, he may have messed it up in the fourth act, *but . . .*' I always believe in the man who can make you argue, get back to the text, flip over the pages, read speeches aloud – Guthrie was one of the few men who inspired us like that. I'm sure most people who had anything to do with him, or who just sat in the audience and watched what he gave them, would call him one of the most exciting directors they'd ever known. Even when he maddened me, I did feel: 'Thank heaven I've been here tonight.' Just to think of him now is to be taken back to a dozen plays. And are we really going to say that of today's directors?

There is a generation of actors and directors in my country, and I think here too because I sense it from what I see and have heard from people

I've talked to in the theatre, that either (1) have never heard of Tyrone Guthrie; (2) if they have heard of him it's in vague terms; or (3) if they do know his work fairly well, they tend to dismiss it – in that what at one time was incredibly innovative for the English theatre is as passé now and as Establishment as the kind of theatre Guthrie was rebelling against. Was Guthrie right for that certain age and could he have done top work, at the zenith of his form, in today's theatre?

Yes, he could. The answer may be that every decade looks back with a certain amount of horror on the decade immediately past. I was speaking of Bridges-Adams just now. Many people today have never heard of him. But Guthrie's fame has lasted for forty years; the name still means something to a great many, even to young people in their twenties. I'm perfectly sure that if it were revived now, that 1956 *Troilus* – capricious though it was – would excite a younger audience just as much as some of the productions by modern young men at Stratford. Indeed it might excite them more. I know the young men have their qualities; perhaps because I'm one of Guthrie's generation, I'm inclined to think of some of their work as freakish. Anyway, I'm certain that Guthrie at his best – if his work could be reproduced – would be received with the kind of surprise and delight that, say, a Stratford *Pericles* gets now.

Annette Prevost

Annette Prevost was Lilian Baylis's secretary at the Old Vic in the thirties, and later, during Tyrone Guthrie's tenure as Artistic Director, worked in various capacities for him. She and her husband George Chamberlain were the closest of friends of Guthrie and his wife.

ALFRED ROSSI: *Did Lilian Baylis ever talk about her successor at the Old Vic?*

ANNETTE PREVOST: She was very worried about the whole thing, and actually she felt that Tony Guthrie would be a suitable person to take it on, *if* he was prepared to do the slog, which was an enormous slog. I mean not only being the director, but also doing the donkey work as you might call it. I think she suspected that he would want to move on to other things. The ballet was so firmly under Ninette de Valois' control and the opera had a committee that looked after that. But we never had anyone permanently attached to the drama company.

Did Miss Baylis ever broach this idea to him?

She *said* that she wanted to retire. She was a fairly sick woman. And she said, 'If only I could get the companies fully established and with people to look after them, I could retire in peace of mind,' and, you know, go *right* away, because she knew if she was anywhere around, she would be running the show.

After she died, how did he get appointed?

Tony eventually was asked to become Director of Drama at the Old Vic and very soon thereafter became Administrator of Sadler's Wells and the Old Vic organization.

Later, at the beginning of the war, he was the person who kept the thing together. At that time the theatres were all closed and Sadler's Wells was commandeered by the local ARP people. Then we had the blitz, and we had about a hundred bombed-out neighbours living there. And, actually, I was in charge of the theatre at the time, and Tony and Judy moved in here. We all did a bit of looking after these people and trying to do our own work. And we had companies out on tour. And we couldn't keep in touch with them because you could never get a telephone call out beyond Manchester, and they were all in the north-east. So we took over the Victoria Theatre at Burnley, and had some little offices up there, and we moved up there as our head-quarters. And we used to come down to London on a rota, you know, one person was down in London for one week and the others were up there, etc.

Tony and Judy and my husband George and I all shared a house up there in Burnley, which is where we all got to know each other pretty well. Anybody who needed somewhere to stay when they were up there just used to come and be dossed down and looked after. And we did work very closely together then. We had our offices all rather cooped up in a funny little cottage outside the stage door. And then when we came back to London we went on working together. Of course, Tony was with us. I mean he organized these tours, you know. *La Traviata* was done with screens and half the singers acted as stage staff and the other half acted as wardrobe and that sort of thing, and going round to the munition works, and gradually building the whole thing up again. Then we had the seasons at the New Theatre and the Prince's, which is now the Shaftesbury.

Why did Tony want to go to Burnley?

To get to the other side of Manchester, because nearly all our touring was being done in the north-east or Wales. I mean, twice I had to go up by car, using precious petrol to deal with a crisis up there. Because the telephones didn't work. It was just after the blitz moved out of London and into the provinces, which was rather unfortunate.

What was his attitude towards the work in Burnley?

You see, we only used the theatre in Burnley very occasionally. We used to do seasons there and otherwise it was road shows in those days, coming in weekly. But we all had to take our turn with the fire-watching duties. Tony, of course, couldn't be put on to the fire-watching rota, as we could never guarantee where he would be on any given night.

We were always on the go, because we had the opera company and two, sometimes three, drama companies, and then we had the Playhouse Theatre in Liverpool. And seasons going on in London at the same time. It was just roller skates all round, trying to keep up with them.

But then, when things got easier, we moved back to London at the end of 1942.

What was it like sharing a house with the Guthries?

Oh, great fun. We divided the house into two, more or less. We had a mutual bathroom and a mutual kitchen which I didn't use very much. Judy was a terrible – what we used to call – spudler. She used to love just messing around, doing things, you know. Not an ideal lady to share the kitchen with, but we managed. And, again, you see Tony was away half the time and my husband was away half the time, and Judy used to come down to see her parents in Kent. It was very Bohemian and a *very* open house. I mean sometimes I was alone in the house, or *thought* I was, and I used to go in at night and find people in there. 'We've come to stay. We've brought you ration books.'

'Go over there, Prevost will look after you.' Never bothered to tell *me*.

So then when you came back to London you were working with him at the New Theatre?

Yes, Tony got Larry [Olivier] and Ralph [Richardson] and Johnny Burrell together to form this company just before the end of the war and to do these seasons at the New Theatre. But up till then we'd also been playing there with the opera and ballet. Bronson Albery was the director of the theatre that is now named after him. We took the Prince's as well, and we also did a season at the old Playhouse. There was never a dull moment.

When you went back to London in that New Theatre season, that season with Olivier and Richardson, was there a great sense of expectancy and hope?

The result of the war was more or less known, so Tony was able to get them out instead of kicking their heels and waiting for release. And then by the end of the war we were all absolutely dog-tired and dead on our feet. And Tony felt, you know, that he would have to have a break soon. He thought that we'd got this triumvirate now who one hoped would be able to take on and give it continuity. And we'd still got the theatre up in Liverpool. So there was this carrying on forward. And then Tony, to everybody's great sorrow, gave up. He'd worked himself out. I mean, we were all at each other's throats by then, out of sheer exhaustion.

Do you think his work in that season was some of his best?

Yes. He had, of course, such good material. And, of course, in those days it was something that just didn't exist in London, and it used to be that you practically had to have armed bodyguards to get the artists out of the stage door. Well, you know the stage door at Wyndham's backs on to a little court on to the stage door at the New, which is now called the Albery, and so you couldn't drive off, as you might say, from the stage door. We used to have to arrange for them to go through the front on the last night, because you just couldn't move, it was worse than a football game. And it really did fulfil an enormous need.

I suppose of the three companies that went all through the war, the one that made the most progress was the ballet, because it was escapist. But Tony didn't care for ballet at all, didn't understand it as an art. I don't think he thought it was a sensible art form. I think he thought it should be saying something that it wasn't saying. I remember having great arguments with him on the subject of *Giselle*, and hearing Tony saying, 'Well, have you ever seen a performance of *Giselle* that meant anything?' Because he was a great one for Freud and those people. Well, he'd just wipe the floor with you because you couldn't answer the question. And I don't know whether that's right or not. But he didn't want to accept it as pure entertainment.

That's interesting, since he had such a fantastic eye in his own work for movement, for colour, for pictorial beauty, I would have thought that he would have been able to appreciate the technical expertise of form and line and colour.

I think he found it artificial, you see. Because he never did direct a ballet in all his life. And I think that if it had interested him he would have done it. He was very musical, you see. He loved opera, and he knew a great deal about it, and he knew quite a good deal about painting. But he definitely had got this blind spot with the ballet.

John Gibson told me that they used to have a devil of a time getting their digs, because they needed such a big bed for Tony.

Yes, six foot five he was. And so self-conscious about it. I mean a great many people hadn't got much shinbone left from being kicked by me for saying, 'Aren't you tall?' when they were first introduced to him. People used to say that to him and – I don't know why, because he had the *presence* to go with it – of course, Judy herself was about six foot, and so they made a rather splendid couple together and one just didn't notice. I must say there were two rather frightening moments here when I heard that awful crash which I knew meant he hadn't remembered to bow his head. We've got two funny little attic rooms at the top of the house, and they used to have those as what we called 'The Suite'. Well, they first started coming to us when Tony's mother died, which was in 1956. In the beginning of 1957 Tony suddenly said to Judy, 'We must give up the Inn [Lincoln's Inn] and go and live in Annagh-ma-kerrig, so you'll just have to get everything packed up into a container and arrange for it all to be taken over there.' And poor old Judy, you see, was being uprooted from her only married home and was sort of minding desperately about this. And he was immediately off to Israel or somewhere, so we used to go over there as often as we could when Tony was away to try and cheer her up.

Why did he want to go back and live in Ireland after his mother died?

I suppose partly because she'd left the property to him and he felt he just couldn't only use it for popping over to, and partly because he felt a sense of responsibility to the staff and that sort of thing. I mean, he didn't want to go there and be the landed gentry. I don't know what else he would have done with it except sell it, because there wasn't anybody to take it on. You see, the sad thing was that they had no family. And his sister only had one child, a daughter, who is married and lives in America. And his sister already had their own place down in Kilkenny.

Did you ever visit them there?

Yes. The first time I went there was when his mother was alive, and we had breakfast on the card-table in front of the fire in the drawing-room. It was a wash-up breakfast with Tony in charge in the pantry at the sink. We all had to help and·had to know where things lived in the cupboards. Great fun. And I was left to clear the table, and so I went out to the pantry, and asked Tony: 'Please, what do I do about the crumbs on the baize?' And he said, '*That* is a village in Gloucestershire.'

He was very fond of the estate, very fond of it. And it *was* very lovely. It was originally a farmhouse, not enormously pretentious but very nice, and the front of the garden sloping down to this lake which was a mile long and half a mile across. A lot of the property was pieced off to the Forestry Commission which was the only way they were able to keep it going, because they paid minimal rates for it, but they maintained it.

Judy was depressed about moving to Ireland. I mean, only because it was done over breakfast on the day he was going away. Rather like one time in September 1939, up at the Wells. I went back to the theatre on some sort of assignment and Tony met me and he said, 'Oh you've got to do this, that and the other, because George and I are going off to join the Pioneer Corps.' And I said, 'Oh dear, oh really? And what's going to happen to Judy?' And he said, 'Oh, Judy must get a job,' just like that. The Corps was a sort of home guard. I think all they were going to do was to break up the road so that the enemy couldn't pass over. It was for people who were too old or too infirm to join up. But then the Pioneer Corps didn't get mobilized, and he got rather interested in a problem that was happening to one of the companies, and no more was said about it.

It was rather like that over giving up the Inn. Mind you, I think by then the benchers were rather wanting it for legal people more. They had originally got in there because the idea was to have it a mixture of the profession and interesting intelligentsia people. They were turned out of it once. It had to be torn down and rebuilt. But they were allowed to go back again. That was their home, you see, when they married in 1931.

Judy always said that the only reason Tony married her was because he wanted somebody to take it out on when things weren't going well in rehearsal. But they'd known each other all their lives, you see. Tony's father was the family doctor and Judy's father was the family solicitor, down in Tunbridge Wells.

It's quite interesting, because if you go to the Inn, and you're walking down Chancery Lane you go in through a wicket gate in a big oak-studded gateway which is kept locked and a porter has to come and undo it when anybody wants to get in there. Otherwise you have to go and come in through Lincoln's Inn Fields. And then you go up this terrible little wooden spiral staircase twisting around – you know the ones where the steps go up to nothing, so that if you're carrying anything you'll be inclined to fall down and you have to be very sober coming away again after a party. And they lived up on the top floor. And they never really gave it up, until 1957.

Anyway, Tony decided to go to Ireland, and she was rather disconsolately sort of trying to pack everything up, and saying, 'Well, it's no good my taking . . . there isn't any electricity down in Annagh-ma-kerrig.' And it suddenly occurred to me – and we, thank heavens, had just got possession of the whole of this house, because we'd had to have people living in the top part after the war when they couldn't get accommodation – so I said, 'Well, you'd better let us have Tony's bed, and anything else that you particularly want to have over here, and then you can always come and stay with us.' Which they did, all the time. And, again, of course, it was much more fun for them, because they didn't like what I would call orthodox living. It was much more fun to have your meals as and when you wanted them or have picnics in the garden. And they always used to, if they could, take breakfast up to bed. Empty the coffee pot into the sheets. I loved them so much, I was able to be longsuffering.

Then they came and visited you on and off for how many years?

Well, Tony practically died here actually He was over here doing a show for the Phoenix Opera Group – *The Barber of Seville*. So he came over alone as he often did, and he was with us for two or three weeks. He obviously wasn't in good shape. I mean, we knew that he hadn't been well, because he'd nearly died ten years earlier. And he had been told to take life easily, and he just said he couldn't. He'd rather bust than turn into a vegetable. And, again, wasn't too careful about what happened to poor old Judy.

But, anyhow, he was here for this time, and it was obviously more than he ought to have been doing. And I got rather worried about him. Although we were here most of the time, we couldn't entirely reorganize our lives around his being here, which meant that sometimes he came back to an empty house with something on the low gas in the oven. And I said to him, 'Why doesn't Judy come over?' And so then we rang her up and asked her. They'd had a series of guests over there, which is partly why she'd had to stay. So she came over and she was more able to try and bully him a bit. She would go to rehearsals with him and that sort of thing.

He was obviously not at all well, and used to look a dreadful ashen grey colour. He had lost a bit of weight then, but not enough. He was still much too heavy. And that's why none of our furniture has got any springs in it, because I remember him coming in and flopping – he never sat in a chair, he always fell into it – and saying, 'I had no idea you lived up such a steep hill.' And he'd done it so many times.

He enjoyed walking. And I had a row with him about it. I said, 'Well, surely you could bring yourself home in a taxi, even if it's only from King's Cross. And I'll hand you out the money to do it with, if it's necessary.' He was so generous to other people, but so mean to himself. He used to get a bus part of the way, but it involved him walking up from King's Cross which used to bring him up through a short cut, where he had a very beloved, overgrown Alsatian dog called Buster who was very fond of him. It belonged to a garage, and it was rather sad, because when Tony was here and then went back – how he knew I don't know – Buster used to come to our front doorstep and look for him.

When he was here the last time, which I assume was the last time he came to London before he died in Ireland, did you ever have any talks with him about the fact that he was ill and that death might be near?

Oh, not specifically, but we did talk quite a bit about death, I think. He had rather a John Barleycorn attitude towards it, that you take an ounce of the earth and then you put it back again and the cycle goes on. He was very philosophical about it. And didn't quite know what he really believed or what he didn't. But certainly believed in some sort of continuation. I don't mean as a person, but just that you've taken out and you've given back, and so it went on, and that's what we all have to do. That was partly why he didn't approve of cremation. He was buried in Annagh-ma-kerrig, at their parish church, which is I suppose a mile and a half away from the house. It's very unpopulated country. Dougie Campbell was awfully good about going over when Tony died. He and his wife, Ann Casson, both went over and dear old Alec Guinness went, and various people.

Did he finish the work on The Barber of Seville?

Yes. And he should have gone down to Brighton on Saturday for lighting rehearsal and dress-rehearsal on Sunday. You see, they were finishing their rehearsals at Morley College, and he went just to see if everything was all right. Andrew Downie, who lectures at the college, brought him back, and Tony was looking rather ghastly and said he simply hadn't been able to carry on with the rehearsal. So we got our doctor, who fortunately was just over the road there and had looked after him before, and he came and gave him some prescriptions and said he *mustn't* go down to Brighton again, but must stay in bed and keep absolutely quiet.

However, Tony *did* go down to Brighton on the Monday for the opening, and then went from there to stay with James and Louise Forsyth at Anstye Cross. And I think paid a visit back to Brighton from there. Then went on and spent the night with Mrs Robin Fox at Cuckfield, who'd recently been widowed, and then flew back to Ireland. He was there for just a week, and then snuffed out. I think poor old Judy had lived with it for a very long time and it did worry her. But it must have been a horrible shock.

Did she talk to you about his death?

No. Part of her trouble was that she tried to be too brave. The postmistress, Mrs McCabe (whom Tony mentions in his autobiography), actually rang us. She rang the closest, most intimate friends, so we would know before it was on the news. And we sort of put it round and about to people. And then I rang Judy in the evening, and she was *far* too calm. Then when she came over for the memorial service – I hope it was a spanking one, I think it was – I had to organize it so it was difficult to know whether it was or not. Poor Judy was most beautifully serene, but too totally withdrawn.

Alec was absolutely splendid in his little talk. It was a *happy* occasion. I mean, one sort of felt that Tony was there too. Oh, I still get dreadfully cross with him even now because I can't ask him something or other, you know, which only *he* would know.

Obviously, even though he knew he was ill over a number of years it didn't seem to prevent him from doing anything he wanted to do.

Well, you see the first time he was ill, he collapsed under an absolutely simple operation. He had this trouble with his sinus. They'd been staying with us, and they went to Belfast on the way home – and he was going to have this operation. It was supposed to keep him in the hospital overnight or something like that. He got off the boat and went in and had the operation the next morning. And in the afternoon I had a telephone call from a friend in Belfast who said, 'I'm just ringing you up to tell you that Tony's not expected to last the night.' And I said, 'Well, don't be so silly. Yesterday he was in spanking form.' But he was very ill then. It was some sort of cardiac collapse, and then he was told to take life quietly. And he had to cancel a couple of productions he'd got in mind. And then soon after that he wrote another book which kept him occupied, and which he rather enjoyed doing.

You have so many memories of him and Judy over a long period of time. How would you characterize their relationship?

Well, Judy was very much *behind* him all the time. I mean, he was so busy getting on and doing the creative work, and she turned up with a thermos of hot coffee and looked after this and that. But he was a very ruthless person, even to Judy. When I say ruthless I don't mean unkind, and I don't mean unaffectionate. They were obviously devoted to each other. But he was ruthless to himself. I suppose what I'm trying to say is that I don't think he ever put himself in the other person's position to look at something. He looked at everything from the outside, so to speak. I mean, I think the two examples I've given you – the one about, 'Oh, Judy must get a job' and the one about moving over to Annagh-ma-kerrig – if he'd felt that she would have minded about it, he would have been distressed. But it was beyond his tolerance to think that that might be the case.

What is the most characteristic memory you have of Tony?

Well, one thing I would like to say about him was that he had enormous humility. It wasn't humility to *him*, but it appeared to be humility to other people. I can think of him now, down in our little kitchen, busy doing the washing-up after a meal or something. Well, I mean, he shouldn't have been. He should have been up here sitting down and resting. 'Oh no, you got the meal ready. I'll do the washing-up.' In little odd ways it came out. Nothing was too small for him to be glad to do.

One of my splendid pictorial memories of poor old Tony was of him sitting in the stage door at Sadler's Wells during the blitz with a telephone draped round his neck, trying, as I say, to get through this dreadful trunk exchange in Manchester, because there was a crisis on with one of the companies in the north-west somewhere, and at the same time, trying to feed a very reluctant two-year-old baby, giving it its dinner – this child took an enormous fancy to Tony, and it was supposed to be spoonfed. The parents were people who had been bombed out and were living there. And he came on the potato-peeling rota just like everybody else and making the porridge and all that. He was mean to himself, but he was so generous to other people.

I've heard that he took care of a lot of old actors.

Yes, but I mean one wasn't to know. One time he made me very angry, because he wrote to us when we were both working long hours at the Vic, and George was the secretary of his company, you see, and looked after his professional work. He wrote and said, 'Would you please issue a contract to . . .' – it doesn't matter who she was – 'for a book she is writing called *The House in Malone Road*, which I want to give advance royalties to, because I think it might possibly turn into a film', or something like this. 'Send a contract to her with an advance royalty cheque of £200.'

So poor George and I who weren't used to doing contracts like that – generally it was done through the agent – sat up all night with the contracts file and eventually got this damn thing done and sent it off with the cheque to the lady. And got this letter back saying, 'Thank you very much for your letter and very kind cheque. I've signed the contract, because I know and love you, but can't understand what it's all about, because I should never dream of writing a book in my life.' And we found it was simply Tony thinking up a way of giving her £200.

Drat him, and bless him – why couldn't he have *told* us what he was up to!

—

Tanya Moiseiwitsch

ALFRED ROSSI: *What was your first acquaintance with Tyrone Guthrie?*

TANYA MOISEIWITSCH: I went straight from art school to become what was. known as a scene-painting student at the Old Vic. This particular year, 1933, was Guthrie's first year there, and it became known as 'The Laughton Season'. I was privileged to watch dress-rehearsals, which was really part of the duty of a scene-painting student anyway, because you had to make notes and see what needed touching up and repainting.

And because of this I sat absolutely enthralled, very aware that these were rehearsals quite different from anything I'd ever seen in my life. Electrifying, I think, would best describe them. And not exactly plaintive criticisms of what the actors were wearing, but, 'Oh, isn't this hat too big?' 'Yes, rather Edwardian. Take it off.' And this character was a cardinal in *Henry VIII*. Well, of course, a cardinal's hat *is* rather big.

Years later I was asked to design *Henry VIII* at Stratford-on-Avon. And Tony – I don't think I called him Tony for years – I don't remember calling him anything for a long time – explained *Henry VIII* to me. And I could see it was going to be *quite* different. We were going to *ignore* the proscenium arch. We were going to design together. I was never allowed out on my own as it were. He designed the ground plan. And that's *right* I think; a director must know where he wants people to be. And the plan showed an asymmetrical setting of stairs going up to a platform above with alcoves below. There was plenty of level space, but a lot of it was taken up by very wide, very shallow stairs. So that, obviously, grouping could be made, and nobody was going to mask anybody else. But, in fact, on the fore-stage, there was a masking problem. And I well remember Anthony Quayle as Henry VIII – this is the 1949 Stratford-on-Avon production – sitting on his throne and saying, 'Tony I can't see that front row seat. I imagine the person sitting there isn't going to be able to see me,' because there was this quite enormous henchman carrying a spear or halberd, or whatever it was, standing with his back to the audience and making really quite a barrier. Tony went down, sat in that seat and said, 'Can see perfectly. On.'

What was the first production you designed for him?

It was *The Alchemist* at the Liverpool Playhouse, which the Old Vic was running during the war. He proposed to do it in modern dress with a wartime situation: people leaving London because of the bombs, instead of, as written, because of the plague. And that made perfect sense. And he also pointed out to me that the disguises that everyone keeps putting on and off, should be done in full view of the audience, so that they get, as it were, a backstage look at what is happening, so it became fairly three-dimensional. There were three doors because, he said, with a farce you have to have plenty of ways on and off, so that people can scuttle through and make wild reappearances looking totally different. And it's more fun if you can see how they are arranging these disguises, which helps the plot along.

And also he had an idea – to me it was revolutionary – that for a few days there should be no setting planned. I'd been brought up that you really had to have your ground plan absolutely stabilized before you got to the first rehearsal, so that the actors would know just where the furniture was going to be. Well, he thought it would be rather a lark if, because it was so complicated a plot, everybody should have a say in where they thought all the various episodes should occur. It was fairly fluid for about three or four days, and then I said, 'The carpenters are getting a little bit anxious about knowing how much they have to do.' And so he said, 'Well, I think it's time we settled.' And from then on I realized how reasonable he was, how considerate for other people's working situations. You can have changes of thought, you can have last-minute ideas – obviously everyone will rally and do that, but basically people who are employed, as it were, with the pencil poised, or the saw, or the needle, must be allowed to get on with it. Otherwise it will be a most frantic rush.

And from then on I realized, that although there were going to be changes and pretty basic changes sometimes, on the whole it was tremendously well planned from the start. And we used a kind of shorthand which served a perfectly wonderful purpose of saving time. After twenty years, we did *The Alchemist* again and somehow we seemed to have done a lot of prep. for it, without being able to say exactly when and where, though I did remember it was Liverpool. It seemed as though the play came much more readily. I guess I'd got a lot older and had more experience in translating or interpreting, or call it what you will, an idea.

How did he communicate his ideas about the design of a production?

Tony quite often drew pictures, and I thought rather too well for my comfort. He drew very clearly and explicitly, and, at the same time, they were just wild line drawings, often with his left hand, although he wrote with his right. I've seen him use both. And he would explain by means of drawings, some of which I kept, because they were far better than anything I could do. In fact, once I traced one, and acknowledged by signing his initials in the corner. I remember that he also tended to explain things by means of musical dynamics – *piano, forte* and so on, some not quite as obvious as that. The contrasts between scene and scene were essential to keeping, not only the story line going, but keeping the attention of the audience, because one could go on droning on a monotonous note in both colour or speed, or lack of speed, of the general tone of each scene. He tended to work in contrasts. At least, this is something he rather drummed into me.

How did he do that?

Not in a dictatorial way at all. He always said, 'Now this is an idea I've got. If you don't like it, you must contradict it, or you must tell me where you think that we should think about it again.' And somehow I always took this invitation very seriously and really meant to – well, not argue, but perhaps present another point of view if I had one, but somehow his was always the dominant one. And it followed through; it was seen from start to finish, an overall picture. Now that was something I appreciated and wanted and needed – that guidance. I don't know, of course, how he worked with other designers. But I know that for me it's important, it's essential to have these guidelines and this kind of map to follow in order to *read* the play. I read a play just like a novel. I don't see it in space, and I don't see how it's going to work at all, so I need this directorial point of view put to me. And it's never been put to me so explicitly – not in full detail, but an overall picture – as by Tony Guthrie, who I always felt had a tremendous grasp of the *shape* of the play.

There are some critics who have said that, on occasion, he disregarded

*the author's intention and went off on his own flights of fancy. What's
your feeling?*

I simply can't endorse that. Because I know, from working with
him, that he paid unfailing attention to the author's shaping, phrasing,
colouring of scene, as it followed scene. And this, in turn, would have
an effect on the colours that we chose to dress people in and the background against which they were seen. And I discovered that colour
meant a great deal to Tony in the effect that it had either on one's
nerves or one's senses. That low-tone, low-key colouring appealed
to him, and his work has been called 'Rembrandtesque'. Well, that
really implies a lot of dark lovely rich surroundings, and possibly a
blaze of light where the action is. And these contrasts, again, one felt
were very characteristic of Tony's work, although he wouldn't say,
'Let's do it in the style of Rembrandt.' Well, yes, he *did* say that on
occasions, too. Painters were named – Holbein, of course, for *Henry
VIII* and Van Dyck I remember he mentioned rather firmly for
Twelfth Night, partly because of the hair-style and the fact that one
could have long hair and be a girl or a boy, which worked very well
for Viola and Sebastian, who looked remarkably alike. And Franz
Hals, I remember, was the jumping-off ground for *Cyrano de Bergerac*.

How did you approach the work on the Oedipus Rex *production in
Canada? The only production of Tony's, as you know, which was ever
recorded on film.*

I seem to remember the first thing I was told was that it would be
in masks and the actors would be much taller than they really are, in
pretty uncomfortable boots. We were doing this in the tent in Stratford,
Ontario, and so I had to ask myself, 'How do you make masks that
aren't boiling hot to wear, and boots that they aren't going to break
their ankles in?' So it was all experiment time for me, much helped, I
may say, by everyone who worked on it, and chiefly by the actors who
were incredibly cooperative and enthusiastic and adventurous,
because it can't have been easy. In fact, I know now that it was far
from easy and extremely hot, but so rewarding. So rewarding to be
more than life-size and to be acting in a play that was more than life-
size.

And I realized that we had gone through a quite different process
of planning this time. I think the first thing was to discover that metal
and stone and wood were our basic materials. That doesn't, of course,

mean that they were literally made of these things, but we had to somehow suggest them – an oversized version of gold and wood and stone. And, indeed, bird's eggs for Teiresias.

I often wonder what would have happened if something Tony dreamed up had really happened. I *know* he wanted Picasso to do the masks for *Oedipus*. I don't know who got in touch with him, but I don't think any answer came, and therefore it didn't come about. I felt necessarily very humbled and fairly frightened at dealing with the mask situation when I knew what the real aim had been. And there was no question of doing anything 'in the manner of'. So one just started out hopefully trying to interpret thoughts of kingship and making it clear which were the chorus interpreters and which were the protagonists.

From that, but many years later, we faced three times as challenging a project in *The House of Atreus* which was the agreed title for the *Oresteia*, when it was done in Minneapolis at the Guthrie Theater in 1967. And this, because it was three times as large, took not only three times as long to prepare, but really it *seemed* like a lifetime of preparation. I remember this time Tony made even greater demands on the actors, and he wanted Apollo, for instance, to be nine feet tall, and he made certain specific plans for the moves which I thought, 'Well, that's absolutely impossible in masks.' But there again, given practice masks of lighter weight and better-able-to-see-through masks, all of which was wonderfully interpreted and carried out by a fellow designer, Carolyn Parker, somehow the actors did, I think, fantastic feats of endurance and strength and in spite of all that, not seeming to be in great pain or danger. I've never seen anything like it before.

What were the rewards in working with Tony?

Well, the contrasts of the plays that one worked on with Tony were, I suppose, the most rewarding things of all. Because, compare *The House of Atreus* with, say, *Uncle Vanya*, both of which we did at the Guthrie Theater, in the same season, both of which we enormously enjoyed, and agreed and discussed how much we'd enjoyed them. And 'enjoyed' is just a loose term for meaning it had been a wonderful working time. Possibly even more enjoyable in the planning and rehearsal than in *fact*. Once the play is on both the director and the designer tend to go off to do other things. Although you sit and enjoy it with the audience and that is, of course, one of the best things in life, it is the planning and the working on it that sticks in your mind as the most enjoyable part. And *Uncle Vanya* was a great favourite both of mine and of Tony's.

We did several Chekhov plays between us, which he himself had translated with his great friend Leonid Kipnis who translated from the Russian pretty literally, and then Tony put it into working English. And also the actors had quite a hand in that. Several lines, I think, were changed in rehearsal, to be spoken more comfortably.

Then another great contrast was *Peter Grimes* at the Met with miles and miles and miles of fishnet and vast windy seascapes, very unrealistically aimed for. We did it first at Covent Garden, when a real fog came in on the first night and practically obliterated the singers – it went down their throats – it wasn't very popular, but it did give them a *marvellous* effect from our point of view, but not to be repeated. And then twenty years later, we were asked to do it at the Met where it all fitted on to various astonishing hydraulically arranged trucks and wagons. And indeed at the dress-rehearsal we took our picnic lunch to eat, as it were, on the seashore. But we were way, way, way back, miles away from the curtain line. And as we were finishing our sandwiches we all realized that the ground was moving under us, and the whole seascape was gliding forward into its position for the opera to start, and we had to scurry off before the singers all got into their allotted places to begin the dress-rehearsal. *Peter Grimes* was practically all black and white and grey with here and there very modest colour introduction.

Another time I was asked, and thrilled to agree to do, Thornton Wilder's *The Matchmaker*. And for this Tony, again, came up with the idea and I wholeheartedly agreed with it, that it should look flamboyantly 1880s-ish, with painted backcloths and all the theatrical artifice that one could conjure up for the proscenium stage. And the colour range there got brighter and brighter as the evening went on. I remember in the last scene I don't think we left a single colour out. When the play was on tour before it got to the Edinburgh Festival, he would stand at the back, partly because they were still doing rewrites and making alterations, and partly because he thoroughly enjoyed watching the audience's reaction. And he said to me on one occasion after a particularly hilarious house that, 'It's wonderful to watch the audience *swaying*, like a field of corn in the wind.'

One of the things that I want to stress, because I was so impressed with it, was the fact that Tony always seemed to be working on three projects at once, probably more. I think this was his normal practice, that there was always something in the melting pot, something in the planning. There was something which he was working on at that very moment, and also something far ahead, long-range, usually with several designers. In time I came to work on two plays with him at once, but as a rule it was one at a time. But his brain was busily engaged on at least three. And one had to rather, well, make appointments, make sure that we didn't all overlap and get in each other's way.

This was often made much easier by the fact that he would invite whoever was working over to Annagh-ma-kerrig in Ireland where there was, almost, peace from the telephone, because the telephone didn't ring very often. And when it did it was an event. And it didn't always work anyway, so you couldn't always hear what was being said. And there was not a feeling of isolation at all, but a feeling of marvellous work surrounding. And with outdoor activities such as, 'We'll all go and pick up logs and twigs for the fire', or 'We'll all go and sweep the leaves.' He would – I wouldn't – saw down a couple of branches that were getting in the way of the view. There was always something to be done, which, in fact, probably helped the landscaping, but it also, I think, had a very relieving effect on the brain, because you can sit and ponder over a design or production thing for just a little too long, and you become sapped. I think he realized that, and it was quite deliberate. It was to get some oxygen into the lungs, and one would get back to it refreshed.

And other things happened there which there wasn't leisure to do in London. He read aloud a great deal. He read aloud either the play you were working on, which made much clearer to me what it was about, or he read aloud short stories by Irish authors or by Chekhov. And on Sunday he would quite often read the lesson in church, and it was as though it had been newly written. It made such tremendous sense. I haven't heard anyone, really, read with such *clarity*.

If we were working on an opera, then that was a wonderful excuse to play the gramophone, and play the opera in question, not once but again and again and again. But the most favourite music on that not very hi-fi record-player was Verdi's *Requiem*. He had an absolute obsession about it. He played it in various versions, that is to say, there were, I think, three or four recordings. He would choose, 'Now shall we have this, now shall we have that', and it wasn't in a way to compare. It was simply that different interpretations gave different delights. And it was such a moving work. We followed it in the score.

And I won't say that we sang with it, because you can't compete with a recording, but Tony *did* sing a great deal. He sang a lot at his work. And I think everybody who ever worked with him noticed this – he sang between scenes. This may, again, have been a form of rehabilitation between work sessions but I think, of course, if we were working on an opera that was a marvellous opportunity for a great deal of singing.

It seems significant that the last production he directed was an opera.

Yes, we worked on it together. It was the Phoenix Opera Company's *Barber of Seville* for the 1971 Brighton Festival. I do remember that it was a rather frenzied getting together of a production. I suppose I was very unobservant, but I didn't really see how overtired and over-worked he was getting. I admit now that, looking back, I should have seen it, but in fact it seemed that we were doing splendidly.

Both he and Judy had arrived back from Australia in what seemed to be robust health. And with a great deal of enthusiasm and excitement about their visit to Australia. And in fact, when I arrived for Christmas, just after they got back, I stepped in the doorway and Tony said, 'You must go.' And I thought he meant – I had just arrived – that I must leave immediately. And I thought that was a very odd thing to say. And I said, 'What do you mean, I must go?' And he said, 'You must go to Australia. You'll absolutely adore it.' And I suppose I laughed and said, 'Well, chance is a fine thing.' And now here I am in Australia. And a few nights ago I went to see the Octagon Theatre, which is one that Tony inspired here. These thrust stages really are proliferating. At this moment, I'm working on a proscenium theatre again and loving every minute of it. But I really am wedded to the kind of stage that we worked on together, because the audience–actor relationship is very important and, to me, it's Tony's biggest contribution to the way theatres have been going.

Alec Guinness

ALFRED ROSSI: *When did you first meet Tony Guthrie?*

ALEC GUINNESS: Well, I suppose it was in 1935 when I did that interview about going to the Old Vic. I was only considered for very small parts, things like Boyet in *Love's Labour's Lost*. He'd done it before at the Westminster Theatre, which was a very joyous, gay affair. But I was there for the whole of that first season and then I went back to Gielgud for another season and then I went back to the Vic again, at Guthrie's invitation, to play Hamlet in modern dress. I became very friendly and close with him. He was marvellous with young people anyway, as you must know. I think Gielgud, who really sort of set me going, was a great disciplinarian. Although it was wonderful to be working with him, I think young people, certainly someone like myself, could get tied up and knotted and then suddenly to go down to Tony Guthrie's work, which was enormously free and encouraging – to a certain extent too much so, maybe. I mean if something amused him you could go over the top. Or, indeed, if something touched him. Although I think it was wonderful, to have that breath of fresh air going through one's life, it was also necessary to remember that there were other disciplines in the theatre to face up to. But I owe him an *enormous* debt.

Did the fact that he asked you to play a Hamlet right after Olivier had played the role for him affect you?

No, I wasn't so concerned with that. I mean, I'd been in Gielgud's *Hamlet* – no one has greater admiration for Laurence Olivier than I do – but I don't feel that Hamlet was his forte at all. It *was* Gielgud's. His was definitive at that period. I mean I was in *the Hamlet* that he did in London in 1934. And I was very much under the influence of Gielgud's manner and diction. Tony's production was called modern-dress but it wasn't – I mean no one smoked cigarettes, no one fiddled around with glasses. It wasn't that, it was sort of *fin de siècle* with a modern touch, pointing up the social standing of people and the time of day or night, if they're in dressing-gowns or night-gowns or things which very often get totally lost in a period piece. He was very much influenced by Dr Ernest Jones and those Freudian things which had been incorporated in the Olivier one which he'd done.

Did he bring this into your production?

No, because I was thinking, 'Oh I'm going to have a lot of that, I suppose', and you know when I even tried to mention it he became evasive and said, 'Don't let's worry, just let's do it.' Which made me feel as if he just sized me up as to what went on inside me, and he thought that either he does or doesn't do it, but it's no good trying to impose it at all.

How do you feel about the work on Hamlet? *Now, thinking about it so many years afterwards?*

Well, it was a marvellous production, and my performance was nothing. I was twenty-four and very innocent theatrically, and I think Tony wisely let me go my way, in so far as I didn't attempt to do what was impossible for me to do. It remained in a very minor key; it was no good then, or indeed now, tearing off an enormous strip, because it would just be forcing the issue, and Tony never tried to force me.

The only thing where we did differ was very minor, and had to do with my suit. He'd seen me wearing a light grey suit around the place, with a sort of chalk stripe in it – very much in this period, 1937–8, and he said, 'Think you ought to wear that', and I was determined to be in a dark suit whatever happened. I said, 'This is certainly not going to work with a Prince of Denmark. Surely the whole thing ought to be elegant, whatever we do.' And I personally think I was right; however, he didn't quarrel with that. He finally said, 'All right, be comfortable', but he wanted me to wear the grey.

I don't think I ever worked with Tony without having a bit of friction along the line somewhere, funnily enough. We had quite a row when we did *Cyrano de Bergerac*, in which I played de Guiche with Richardson as Cyrano. It was a rather good production, but I didn't awfully like the translation we were doing, and I wasn't very happy about it. I couldn't really believe in it. He wanted me to play the third act very operatically, and I had said, 'Please, Tony, no. That's Cyrano and other characters but de Guiche must come in surely like a piece of cold steel and puncture things – a semi-villainous sort of situation, or at least that's what the audience thinks.' And in front of the whole company he said, 'No, no, you've got to take the stage, you've got to sweep the whole thing up.' And so I did. But I'm afraid I just gave it a little extra which made everyone collapse with laughing and then I said, 'Was that what you meant?' And he replied, 'You know perfectly well, I didn't mean that.' And he was very angry and didn't speak for a day or two, and I got back to doing it my way.

What kind of notes would he give you?

I think the actors were left very much on their own in one way – the development of a character I think he left very much to the actor. There might be the briefest possible references to how one was going to tackle something before one did it. He hardly ever said anything other than the sheer practicalities of speed or positioning or the tightening up or the elaboration of some passage. I can't really remember any kind of notes of a fine nature, other than in a general discussion.

When I first did Hamlet I went to Annagh-ma-kerrig and worked alone with him. It was on my honeymoon actually. And there again I think he was only seeing what he'd bought, having suggested that I should go and play Hamlet, and what I might contribute myself in the way of originality. If one did strike anything original, I remember him always becoming very serious and saying, 'Interesting. Keep that.' But there was hardly ever anything beyond that. When it came to the actual rehearsals I used to do the soliloquies away from the rest of the company, at night usually, up in a barn of a room at the Old Vic. He had a mania for speed and I used to have, in those days, a very swift easy diction. And he used to take pleasure in just that sort of technical thing. He used to ask people up, to my astonishment and rather embarrassed horror, now and then. Like Ruth Gordon I remember coming up. There was some dim light, just a dreary old dirty light bulb burning somewhere and me rattling away at speed among a whole lot of theatre baskets, old props and stuff. There was hardly ever any, what you could call, a deep discussion of anything. I think he must have gone on the principle that if people were going to be alive, that they were going to provide their own form of life.

Can you tell me your recollections about the first season at Stratford, Ontario?

Well, Tom Patterson, as you know, came over and solicited Guthrie's help, and Guthrie went out to see what it was all about. They showed him a little tiny shell, not bigger than this dressing-room, something for a tiny band or a singer. And he just laughed at that and said, 'You're just wasting your time and money and my time and everything. Either do it or don't.' And he obviously charmed them, and he *liked them* very much. And, you know, money started to be raised and then he came shopping around for who would be prepared to go. And, I think, I was the first he asked and 'Would I?' And I was enthused by *his* enthusiasm, but we were full of trepidations. Frankly, three weeks before we opened we both said we were not going to open – we were going to withdraw. We both felt we were being treated in a rather cavalier fashion. Both of us had said that if the play was going to open on a certain day, the theatre must be completed by such and such a day. Quite a reasonable and professional request, two weeks before or something. We must also be able to rehearse in the theatre. Well, it was nothing like that, nothing happened. I arrived before Tony, and the theatre was a hole in the ground less than the size of this room, about six feet deep and ten feet across.

So you were really taken aback by your first impression of what they had planned for you in Stratford?

Well, Tanya Moiseiwitsch had been invited to design the whole thing, and Cecil Clarke went out there interviewing actors a lot. I liked the actual setting but if you're mostly in the hands of amateurs, as we were, you know how nervy you get, if you're a pro.

What were your thoughts about the actual productions?

I thought the effect on the people at that time was what was so fascinating. As I said at Tony's memorial service, they were a very divided community – the Anglicans and the Presbyterians and this, that and the others – and they had very little to do with each other. And suddenly they were unified. Whether they still are is another matter. I don't think any of these things last terribly long. And Tony I think was full of warnings about that at the time.

How did you decide upon the season?

He wanted to do something he had not done before, and *All's Well* was a play he was unfamiliar with and we decided on that; it was a mutual decision. He didn't want me to go and turn in a Hamlet which I might have been getting a bit old for anyway, and I also thought it should be left to a Canadian. I'd never done *Richard III* and we thought that a kind of riproaring melodrama might be a suitable opening. And with it we also felt we'd both like to tackle something we didn't know. Well, that was rather difficult, to find something with which we'd had no association or were totally unfamiliar with. And I'd always liked reading *All's Well*. I thought he was marvellous on that, because it was exploring the text as well as the fantastic invention going on all the time. He was at his sharpest and most helpful, because he didn't dare fly away on his own fantasy. *Everything* he had to discover, although all the actors did discover the play together.

Was there a particular suggestion that Tony made at the outset of rehearsals that guided you?

I can't remember, because we didn't work quite like that. We were very intimate friends and one would sit up in his flat in the old building in Lincoln's Inn or wherever, discussing various oddities and he would suddenly say with that hawk-like look – and you never knew whether he was quite serious or whether he was just testing one out – 'Think it's all about' (some particular play) 'Jay' – which was always the word he used for jealousy – or 'Think it's about . . .' And one didn't want to be thought a fool, so one would nod rather gravely and say, 'Oh yes', or 'Oh is it?' and so on.

The first time I worked with Tony I learned a valuable thing. When I was a young actor it was the custom to mark our books, the moves, etc., and doing Shakespeare one had these little Temple editions. I'd worked with Gielgud and a lot of older actors, and it was the thing one did for entrances and exits and odd movement, down left or up right or whatever. I was marking my book one day and he said, 'What are you doing?' I said, 'Oh, marking in my moves.' And he said, 'Don't. If I give you a bad move or suggest a bad move to you, you won't remember it. And that's a very good thing. We'll think of another one. If I give you a good move, you'll remember it.' And I have never marked a move or anything ever since, in a script. And he was right. When I have directed myself, I have always tried to persuade actors to do that.

Didn't you refer, in the memorial service address, to a disagreement with Tony about a prop in Richard III?

Yes, it all had to do with Hastings's head. And oddly enough it was a thing I had mentioned before we went into rehearsal in discussing how we were going to tackle it. I said, 'I hope we can do without a realistic presentation of that blood-soaked stuff, because I would like to try and act the blood-soaked thing, but with, perhaps, an ordinary linen bag with something in it.' I experimented with this during rehearsals and I thought it worked all right. We had several dress-rehearsals. And when I went to the prop table to collect the fake head I suddenly found the whole thing had been covered in artificial blood and stained and gooey and messy and it became something quite different. And I said, 'Why has this happened? It has always been understood that there was going to be a plain bag on the stage.' And the assistant stage manager said, 'It's Mr Guthrie's instructions that it should be like that.' And so I talked to him about that. Now, mind you, it seemed rather minor in a big opening – but it was important to me. And he said, 'Can't be bothered with things like that', and I was very angry. And I think for four days I rather drew aside.

I was exaggerating. I felt that he'd overridden what we'd discussed and were trying to do. Then I think it was on the last dress-rehearsal, he was wandering around with practically no clothes on except a raincoat and he had a bag of cherries, which he very gravely offered me. It was a gesture of peace, and I think I said something like, 'Even a bag of squashed cherries doesn't look like a Hastings's head.' And he was still not speaking much. And on the first night, when I got down to the prop table there and found that the correct bag had been restored with no blood, I was so moved that I dried up for a moment, when I came to the prop onstage. Never could get it right from then on. To say it was a love-hate relationship is excessive, because there was no hate on either side. I think he felt very proprietory towards me.

Because he helped you so early in your career?

Yes. He never claimed that, but he did. I think he did feel a bit proprietory, and I always acknowledged his help, I hope. But I think the fact that I went off and made films and a bit of a name for myself didn't please him.

Did he ever speak to you about your film work?

No, I don't think he ever mentioned it. 'Film star's coming to tea,' he would say – or, so I'm told.

Did he think you'd got a bit grand after you'd achieved a certain prominence?

He pretended to think so. I mean, I never have at all. I might have been terribly grand when I was about twenty-four and playing Hamlet and that had gone to my head. But not later at all. He met me at Liverpool when I first arrived back in England, having been away in the war. I had been in command of my ship and was dressed as a very minor naval officer. When he'd last seen me I'd been dressed as an ordinary seaman, but he knew *perfectly well* that I'd been commissioned and was in command of a tiny craft. Had a bit of gold braid on my arm. 'Officer class, I see.' And he meant it rather nastily, enough, you know.

He didn't quite laugh at certain things. This has nothing to do with the theatre at all, but ten years ago, I suppose, I was in Ireland quite a bit and I went up to spend the day with him and Judy and they produced some wine. They liked their 'tipples'. And it was absolutely *revolting* wine. And Judy was saying, '*Not bad* from the post office for three shillings and sixpence.' And it was like red ink. I couldn't quite make out whether they were drinking it for my sake, or whether they actually did like it. However, I made no comment. I just drank and thought how ghastly it was. I had a friend in Dublin, who owned a very good wine shop, and a week or two later when I was back there I thought, 'I'll send them a present', and I sent a couple of cases of very nice wine. And never heard a word, never heard a word. Checked up to see if it had gone. 'Yes it had gone, been received.' And then I finally phoned Tony, ostensibly about something quite different. Talked for a bit and then I said, 'By the way, did you ever get some wine from me?' 'Yes.' That was all. Because he knew, although I'd tried to disguise it, that *my* wine was a comment on their wine. It's funny – for all his marvellous generosity and bigness of heart, he had a puritanical streak. Of course he was aware, very aware, of people's personal weaknesses, as well as their strengths. He did delightful and wonderful things for me, as well as for many other people.

John Gielgud

ALFRED ROSSI: *How did Tony Guthrie approach directing someone of your renown and talent?*

JOHN GIELGUD: Well, as he had known me all my life, I think he was fairly gentle with me. But when he worked with Marie Tempest, who was a terrific old martinet and old-fashioned comedy star, he was very rude to her once or twice, and they had a real upper and a downer, and finally she gave in and said, 'Oh, you'd best show me how to do it.' He rather enjoyed keeping people who thought they were great stars in their place. I think Ralph Richardson had rather a tricky time in *Cyrano*. Sometimes I had the feeling that he liked to put the stars downstage in the corner in the dark, while the extras were having a jolly good time picking their noses and scratching their bottoms, because he had a love of grotesque byplay which was very amusing and very lively.

And certainly in spectacular productions like *Tamburlaine* he achieved a wonderful sweep. He had a marvellous talent for filling the stage one moment and emptying it the next. But even in the modern-dress *Hamlet* – the first one with Alec Guinness – which I admired very much indeed, there were whole bits of the play that I felt he'd neglected because he was looking towards making wonderful effects in the main scenes. There was the famous thing of everyone under umbrellas in the graveyard scene, and he had the play scene done in full Edwardian court dress, trains, feathers, and long white gloves for the ladies, and Hamlet put his hand up Ophelia's skirt, while he was lying at her feet. There were sensational things like that which had obviously been fascinating and attractive for him to do. But then there was an important scene like Polonius' letter with the King and Queen, which I suddenly felt he'd not bothered to rehearse very much, because it didn't interest him tremendously. He loved movement and action, and he was a terrific pioneer. It was the idea of a new stage, a new world to conquer.

Unfortunately, I never worked with him on a very exciting scheme, so I don't think I ever saw him working at his very best but, of course, off the stage he was so amusing. He chose to live in a punt on the river one year when he was working at Stratford and in that extraordinary flat in Lincoln's Inn in London, where you ducked under an avalanche of socks that were hung out to dry over the doorway, and there were dead plants and kittens and a very bad lunch, because his wife couldn't cook for *nuts*, but they were both so sort of Irish and endearing. And his comments were always very, very funny, you know, a sort of boy scout way of rallying people's morale which was terribly amusing. I think he liked best to have new people whom he could bring out in a way they perhaps didn't know themselves, particularly the small people in the companies.

Did you feel that he purposely left you alone to do what you wanted when he was directing you?

Oh no, I think he was very determined to have his own way but I think he got awfully angry if people thought that they were to stand upstage centre and everybody else was to keep away from them. I gather he and Donald Wolfit, who was a very effective but a very selfish actor, didn't see eye to eye at all. In fact, Wolfit left in the middle of his season at the Vic because he quarrelled with Tony. But I don't know how Athene Seyler and Laughton and Flora Robson and that company at the Vic in the 1934 season got on together. However, it was an enormously exciting season; though Laughton didn't make personal successes, he did give a wonderful Angelo. But he *would* play Prospero and Macbeth (instead of Caliban or Falstaff), and I believe Tony made him play Dr Chasuble in *The Importance of Being Earnest*, instead of Worthing, saying he gave the play too decadent a flavour.

Of course, he caused terrific umbrage with the Old Vic regulars, by having so many well-known actors there, and I think that he fought continually and with a great deal of relish against a certain amount of backbiting and criticism that he was apt to receive. I think everybody in the theatre respected him enormously as a kind of exciting pageant master of the theatre. He was supposed to have done a splendid *Six Characters in Search of an Author* at the Westminster Theatre before the war and also the most beautiful production of *Love's Labour's Lost*, but I never saw either of those productions. Tanya Moiseiwitsch, who nearly always designed for him, was a marvellous ally. You felt that they saw everything the same way and that they exchanged their mutual ideas with enormous pleasure. I would love to know what she felt about him, because they were so terribly close, but perhaps she would be reluctant to criticize him in any way; though she must have known all his faults as well as his virtues.

How would you characterize the kind of rehearsal atmosphere that Tony used to create?

Oh, very schoolboy, in a way. He loved getting everybody together and being very jolly and very funny. Sort of a schoolmaster technique.

He was quite an entertainer, wasn't he, in his own right?

He always longed to be an actor. I think it was a great disappointment to him that his great height and general appearance were too odd.

What did you think of him as a young actor?

Oh, I don't think I thought very much of him. I don't remember really. He was in two plays with me, but he was a great character rather than an actor; he was too strange and idiosyncratic. I suppose he could have played things like Epihodov in *The Cherry Orchard*. He did a beautiful *Cherry Orchard*, by the way, at the Vic. I would think that he would have been an ideal director of Chekhov, because his sense of humour was so great, he would never have sentimentalized the plays. He didn't like sentimentality, and I think had a good deal of contempt for sort of conventional teacup comedies like the play he did for Marie Tempest, which was just a little boulevard comedy by Robert Morley, which I shouldn't think interested him very much. He did it, I suppose, just as a job of work, to show he could do that too amongst other things.

But I think he did prefer the classics, and he also loved things that were not well known; before anybody else (before Peter Brook even) he did *Troilus and Cressida* in Edwardian costume, and a modern-dress *Hamlet*, which was much better than the *first* ever modern-dress *Hamlet* which had been done by Barry Jackson in the twenties. Guthrie's was a beautiful production, and he did know marvellously how to treat Alec Guinness who is a very modest actor, and shy. Tony brought him out in a very marvellous way, and he was devoted to Tony too. He worked with him a great deal more than I ever did. But I would think that Alec appealed to Tony probably more than any other star he worked with because of his humanity and sweetness. Of course, they were together in Canada in other exciting productions.

I think he knew that I was determined to go my own way. He was always awfully sweet to me about it; I've got some charming letters he wrote to me about performances I gave, not under his direction. He was a very warm audience, an enthusiastic and generous creature. But he was, to me, always eccentric, and I was always frightened that if I were to work with him, he would go off on a tangent in a way that I wouldn't dare to dispute, whereas with Peter Brook I knew I'd be able to argue it out with him. Tony's was a *wayward* talent, for all its brilliance.

Several people I've talked with have indicated that they often would genuinely disagree with him about some particular thing, but somehow his way of presenting it and his supreme confidence seemed to make people who should know better not argue with him. Do you think this fair or not?

It all depends on the actor, you see; you never know. I mean if I take on a job with a director I don't get on with I would either leave, or I would make myself go his way. I was in a production two years ago of a Shaw play in England in which I found I didn't like the director's conception at all, but as I had put my shoulder to the wheel I wasn't going to walk out and leave everybody in the cart, and so naturally I made the best of it and one has to do that on many occasions.

Working with Tony I was *slightly* irritated with his kind of quirkiness. The first scene of *Tartuffe*, for instance, I thought he overdirected absurdly, because he was so determined to make it funny, I felt sure it would not amuse the audience. But it was no good my saying so. He had an actress I didn't admire (but one that he admired very much) playing the most important character in the first scene, and comic business which he invented for her I didn't think was funny *at all*. But naturally, I didn't open my mouth, because one can't be destructive, once one has agreed to appear in a production. I think Guthrie had taken on the play, and then found it wasn't cast as he would like, and he just had to make the best of a bad job; so I tried to do the same. Sometimes an actor and a director have to do that.

What is so bewildering is that after a play has failed, you say, 'I knew all through rehearsals, I knew when we read it, I knew the casting was wrong.' But, sometimes, when you feel like that all through rehearsals, by some extraordinary miracle at the dress-rehearsal things suddenly come out right. So that you never can know for certain.

Just as when you think you've given a good performance one night, and they come around and say you were dreadful, or you think you've given a very bad performance, and they come round and say you were wonderful. One often has to make compromises in the theatre in order to carry out one's obligations to the author and the other actors and the management. Of course you occasionally get mad, crazy, temperamental people who walk out or make terrible rows or resign in the middle of rehearsals, which I think a really professional person would never do. I'm sure Tony would never have done it. If he took on a job he'd finish it. Even if he found in rehearsing that it didn't work out very well.

Sometimes I found in working with him in Minneapolis that the performance was almost anti-climactic.

Well, I should think so. He wasn't one to sit in front every night and gleefully watch the audience's reactions. I would think he would most enjoy the actual physical job of working with the actors and creating the ensemble. He had a terrible illness a few years ago, and I don't know whether that tired him out. He didn't seem to have changed much when he worked with me on *Tartuffe* at the Vic. I was delighted to find he seemed so exactly the same as I had always known him.

He had suffered a heart attack before he worked in Minneapolis. And then, of course, came back and did the two productions in London in 1967, Volpone *and* Tartuffe.

Oh yes. I never saw *Volpone*, but they said that wasn't good either. You see we all have peaks; one has to face the fact that after a certain age it's rather a question whether your talents are really still at that peak. Musicians seem to last the best. One has the terrible feeling in the theatre that the moment perhaps comes when you shouldn't do so much or you should only choose exactly the right thing to do.

The two times he directed you were about thirty years apart, weren't they?

But I found very little difference in his personality or in his treatment. But, of course, in both cases it wasn't entirely under his control. I didn't discuss *School for Scandal* with him (although I was presenting it myself), and I didn't discuss *Tartuffe* with him either. I just went down for rehearsal prepared to admire and fit in.

Is that normal for him, or for you – that you wouldn't discuss what you were going to do with the director?

I should have been more cagey over the Molière. I was excited at the prospect of going back to the Vic after many years and I was rather haphazard over the *Tartuffe* engagement. I think I was in America before we started, and I know that there was an awful lot of muddle over it – who should direct it and all that. And, having chosen it rather vaguely, I began to think, 'Oh, Molière's never any good in English.' Years before, at the Vic in 1929, I'd done *Le Malade Imaginaire* and it hadn't been much good.

Funnily enough, Molière had nearly always been more successful in America than in England, until this last *Misanthrope* at the National (which was marvellously good in a brand-new translation and for which Tanya did the décor); it was brilliant, really, the sort of thing Tony might have done himself – beautifully cast and wonderfully staged. I think it's the first Molière I've ever enjoyed, really, either as actor or audience. But in America several of the plays have been a success – *School for Wives* for instance, two years ago, which I thought was simply awful. But certainly this *Tartuffe* of ours was no good at all; though it went very well with the audiences it seemed, I thought it was miscast. However, Guthrie did do a splendidly arranged last scene.

That's what's interesting. You know when you get a man as good as that he may do quite a bad job on the whole play, but there *are* often certain excellent things in it. He did the love scene and the final scene with the king's messenger most marvellously well. They were beautifully placed and grouped and timed and everything. But the main part of the play seemed to bore him. He couldn't find any life, but then he hadn't very interesting actors (including myself) to work with in those scenes, and so nothing seemed to come out right. And we had this awful rhyming version of Wilbur's that I thought was fatal. All the critics said it sounded like a Christmas pantomime, and it did. And the set was not a help either. I think it's awfully bad for a director to have to accept somebody else's set already designed before he is engaged. The entrances weren't in the right place, all that. It was really, as can sometimes happen, a rather confused affair all round.

Didn't he direct you just for a couple of weeks before Granville-Barker came when you did Lear *in 1941?*

Yes, but he didn't do much work on that and Barker scrapped nearly everything which he and Lewis Casson had done before he arrived. I always remember it was the first time Barker had ever been to England without his wife. We never could get him away from her when I worked with him at the Vic once before. She used to come to rehearsals and take him off to the Ritz at lunchtime and he never came back. So when we got him to come over this last time – it was the beginning of the war – he was staying at the Athenaeum Club alone, and we thought, 'What a marvellous opportunity.' Guthrie and I and Casson all arrived on the first morning to take him to the Vic for the rehearsal and Barker came down the steps in his business suit and said in rather querulous tones, 'Who sent me freesias?' Of course, it was Tony who had sent the flowers to the Athenaeum. It was charming of him and rather ridiculous and didn't suit the occasion at all, but it was very typical and endearing.

What was your reaction to the modern-dress Hamlet?

I loved the modern-dress *Hamlet* when Guinness did it at the Vic between the wars and he was frightfully good in it. Tony had found just the way to direct him. (When Alec did it a few years later directing it himself, it was a great disappointment.) But I didn't like the *Troilus and Cressida* at all. I admit I saw it with one of the understudies playing a principal part. It was a great success and had wonderful critical reaction, but I found the play so hard to follow, and I felt it was confused by being given in Edwardian dress. That was the kind of thing that used to annoy me about him because I felt he was enjoying all that so much (Helen of Troy playing the piano in a hobble skirt, etc.).

I'm rather old-fashioned about Shakespeare out of period. I think it can be-done in any period *before* Shakespeare but, to me (in every production later than Jacobean, at least), it confuses the actors by their having to dress and move in one period style and speak lines that belong to another and I think it's quite difficult enough to speak even dressed in the proper period. But I confess I *did* like the modern-dress all-male *As You Like It* very much, to my surprise. It was just the kind of thing Tony would have done marvellously himself.

What kind of notes did he give you?

I don't remember very well. I only know that Komisarjevsky only gave one vaguely general feelings about character. And Michel Saint-Denis went into a great deal of detail, which I was inclined to rebel against. Granville-Barker, on the other hand, criticized in great detail, but I always felt that he was absolutely dead right, and I agreed with every word he said. Tony I don't think said much to me personally either in *Tartuffe* or *School for Scandal*, as far as I remember. And I don't remember much of what he said to the other actors either, except that he sort of spurred them on, pinched them and pushed them about and said, 'Oh, you're like the governess in *Jane Eyre*, and can't you be more amusing?' You know, things like that which were sort of quirky and amusing and quite true. But, of course, not being an actor he couldn't get up and show anybody. I never saw him do that.

You never saw him demonstrate anything?

No. Zeffirelli used to get up on the stage and act whole scenes for me which drove me out of my mind. But it's very difficult to remember afterwards what people say to you in rehearsal. Of course in a big repertory company there are usually quite a lot of people miscast, whereas in a West End play one can usually cast very carefully, which makes the director's task rather different.

The School for Scandal *was a West End production, wasn't it?*

Yes, but it wasn't quite rightly cast, because I had a repertory company of players and Leon Quartermaine, who played Sir Peter, was much too sweet, and the Lady Sneerwell was rather old-fashioned and ham. Some of the other performances didn't harmonize well. Alec played a small part, Snake, beautifully, but the balance wasn't very good, and except for getting a lot of extraneous fun out of the play, it didn't seem to me that Tony had really examined the balance of the two stories and the whole relationship of the different acts. But there wasn't time to do that, as Tony was acting in a film at the time, *The Beachcomber* I think it was called, with Charles Laughton and Elsa Lanchester. When I directed it myself only a few years ago at the Haymarket I found it was a play that needed *endless* care in rehearsal, but I think Tony gave us only about five or six rehearsals and the rest of them I think I had to take because he wasn't there. Then I found he had devised and ordered rather impressionistic scenery; he had the picture scene, for instance, played in a front cloth, using the audience for the pictures – stunts like that, which I didn't like at all. So in the end I just shut my eyes to the production and tried to play my own part of Joseph as well as I could.

Then I remember he took immense pains (and it was typical of him) with the curtain calls. We spent about three hours arranging very elaborate calls, in which some of us appeared from behind the screen and popped out, others took calls in twos and we all finally danced up and down the stage. One of the critics said the production wasn't very good, and that in the end it looked as if the whole company had gone to join the Russian ballet. I suddenly developed a terrible hate against stunt calls. If the play has gone well it's all right, but if a play hasn't gone well and then there are very elaborate curtain calls it doesn't work. But a dance (in a Shakespeare or Restoration play) is always a success with audiences and is a fairly safe card to play.

I know he spent a great deal of time on the calls in Minneapolis. I think he felt that in some respects they were almost as important as the performance.

Well, of course, they are, but in an open theatre it's rather difficult to arrange them, because there's no curtain to come down. And at Chichester when I was there I felt that they had taken a great deal too much trouble in two or three of the productions. The scene shifters worked very often in front of the audience, so the changes were rehearsed very carefully, but when I did *Caesar and Cleopatra* there, so much was going on – young men doing somersaults and gymnastics – to cover the changes, that they became almost more important than the play itself. You know you must be so careful. What will get a round of applause or a big laugh is not necessarily the best thing for the play. You can do the obvious and that isn't good. But, of course, the obvious in Shakespeare is sometimes very necessary. I remember in the Guthrie *Henry VIII*, which was rather a wonderful production, he suddenly changed from a completely realistic style to all the courtiers pretending they were walking in the streets and birds shitting on their heads and stepping into imaginary puddles, and this didn't belong at all to the rest of the production. It was amusing and the public loved it but it seemed to me to stick out like a sore thumb because it completely destroyed the dignity of the rest of the play.

Do you think he didn't select enough from his own imagination?

I do. Like many Irish talents, it was a rather untidy talent. I think the Irish are very untidy, in their acting and their writing and in their personal characters (though not Bernard Shaw!). They are wildly endearing, but you know if you go to Ireland you feel a very curious mixture of wild enthusiasm and a sort of helpless kind of haphazardness. Of course, perhaps we're *too* orderly in England. We're rather stiff upper lip and prissy, but the Irish are a bit over-impulsive, warm but a bit crazy, you know.

Suppose you'd had a choice of three roles in which you could have been directed by Tony Guthrie, what would you have picked?

I don't know what I would have chosen, because after *Tartuffe* I don't think I would have risked it again. Yet I think that his *Peer Gynt* with Ralph Richardson was an enormous success and brilliantly done. I wouldn't have known what he'd have done with the rest of Ibsen. I don't care for his plays very much myself. I would have done a Chekhov play, I think, if I'd had a choice. He might have done *Ivanov* much better for me than I did it for myself, because it was a rather difficult play. I had seen a Komisarjevsky production, and thought I could do better, but neither my direction nor my own performance was very good. And he would have done wonderfully the version of *Crime and Punishment* that I did in 1946. Anthony Quayle directed it rather well in London and Komisarjevsky directed it in New York, with a cast of about forty people, and I'm sure with all the vivid melodrama Guthrie would have made a wonderful thing of it. I never trusted him really in Shakespeare, because I thought he was too fancy, except in the modern-dress *Hamlet* which I did admire very much. All his *Twelfth Nights* were black productions emphasizing cruelty and madness. They always told me that *Love's Labour's Lost*, which was the first Shakespeare he did in London – I think it was at the Westminster Theatre – was a great beauty done in an extremely simple setting just with two tents. It's a play I've never been able to understand very well, and I've rarely seen it. I should like to have seen his very much. I don't know how he altered over the years, whether he changed much. We none of us know how much we change, or how it goes.

I think it's interesting that you didn't feel that there was any difference, essentially, in his way of working over thirty years.

No, not at all. And I hoped so much that *Tartuffe* would be a success. But I was very stupid over that play because the minute I began to rehearse the part I knew I should never have taken it on. What I should have done was to get out of the play, and I should have realized that before I accepted it.

It was a little curious in that I think some people expected you to play Tartuffe.

Well, I thought so too, and then everybody said, 'Oh no, we need a younger man,' so naturally I hastily blushed and said, 'I'm sorry to have suggested such a thing.' But it was all originally fixed with Roger Planchon's idea of a young Tartuffe (he was engaged to direct it and dictated the settings before Guthrie, but was prevented at the last moment) and when I began to rehearse I thought there was no part in the play for me, except possibly Tartuffe. Maybe I'm too old for it, but I'm sure I could, etc. But of course I couldn't say that with another actor already asked to play it.

How would you compare Guthrie and Brook?

I would say that Brook is a genius (a pocket genius, perhaps) and Tony Guthrie was only a brilliant man, both remarkable talents and with a certain amount in common. But, to me, Peter has a kind of integrity, a sort of solid quality, that I think Tony lacked. But Peter's gone very much to another world now, and one doesn't see him any more. The four times I've worked with Brook have been enormously important to my career – I had a new start, almost, working with him. And that gave me so much pleasure, and naturally I've always longed to work with him again – I'd do anything for him. The Seneca *Oedipus* which I did with him at the Vic was extraordinary. I never saw any of Tony's Greek productions. I never saw the *Oedipus* (in Canada) with the masks, which I should have liked to have seen, because he might have found a way of breathing life into those old plays. Of course, Brook's never done a Greek play, but the *Oedipus*, especially the orchestration of the text, was an extraordinary production. It wasn't altogether good for me, and he more or less destroyed everything that I felt I could do, instinctively. He wouldn't let me do any of the things that I thought I knew I *could* do. He wouldn't let me use my voice the way I wanted, he wouldn't let me do anything very emotional in any sort of way that I was used to being emotional. So that I broke completely new ground with it. It was agony, I was miserable, I wasn't very good, I didn't get very good notices. And yet I went into *Forty Years On* the following year, which was a kind of light revue (in which I played the dotty old headmaster of an old-fashioned boys' school) and I walked on the stage and felt absolutely relaxed, because I'd done this *wicked* work with Peter – it was very like going into the army, ten weeks of *hell* – and I can't imagine Guthrie ever bothering with all those tremendous physical exercises and improvisations and limbering up. Not that I really *approve* of that, but when Peter does it it can have marvellous results. And I'm glad I did it that once though I don't know that I'd ever do it again.

What's your fondest memory of Tony Guthrie?

Well, the fact that we had known each other all our lives – his mother was my mother's bridesmaid and they were so fond of each other – gave me a *basis* of affection, you know, which never ceased, and we were always delighted to see each other. I don't know whether he ever *asked* me to Minneapolis or Ontario. I would rather have loved to have done that but maybe I was too grand and West End at the time or didn't want to leave England or something. When I became a sort of manager and director as well as a leading actor, I rather wanted to stay in London and do things my own way. I think probably I would have learned a lot from pioneering with him and enjoyed it very much too. But it's too late now, alas.

Robert Morley

ALFRED ROSSI: *You once said that Tony Guthrie was the only person you were ever enamoured of to the point that you would do almost anything for him even when you thought he was wrong. Could you expand on that?*

ROBERT MORLEY: Well, I think my feeling of admiration for Guthrie must go back to the days when I wrote my first play, *Short Story*, which he directed. It was put on by a very commercially oriented management, and in those days Guthrie was more commercially oriented than he appeared in later life. He was, in those days, like me, ready to try his hand at anything. And he tried his hand at that play which he would later in life never even have read, let alone directed.

It was a play I wrote with Marie Tempest in mind. She was a great star of our youth, a dynamic leading lady of five foot six, who lived in the style in which leading ladies lived in those days. She dressed not only for dinner, but also for rehearsals in the evening. I'm not sure that Guthrie ever dressed for dinner or rehearsals but the rest of us *certainly* did. We rehearsed from about seven till ten and then broke for supper, at the Savoy, returned to the stage at half-past ten and rehearsed again until half-past twelve or one o'clock. We also rehearsed in the mornings and in the afternoons, while Miss Tempest slumbered.

But what made the play so peculiarly difficult for him to do was that the original conception of the play was written about an actress who had been a failure and decided to go back to the stage to the astonishment and later the despair of the dramatist who had persuaded her to do so. But when she got the play Miss Tempest said, 'It's quite inconceivable that the public would accept me as a failure. I must have been a great star in those days.' And so the whole plot of the play went out of the window, but I was left with a cheque for £100 which she gave me when she accepted the play.

I rewrote the play, partly with Guthrie's help. Guthrie in those days was a dialogue director of a film being made by Carol Reed. He didn't take his duties very seriously as a dialogue director and he used to sit about on the beach with me, striving to get some sort of coherence into the play. Eventually either he or Beaumont, who put the play on, decided that the only hope for it was to have it all star cast. They engaged Sybil Thorndike, Margaret Rutherford, Rex Harrison, Isobel Jeans and A. E. Matthews to support Miss Tempest. And the play then only managed to run three months.

Guthrie had an original idea in directing the play. It was rather dull and he wanted something, obviously, to sharpen his fangs on. He was a very merciless man in many ways. He had a curious streak of sadism in him. Perhaps sadism is too strong a word. But I remember at the dress-rehearsal, when the curtain came down – and Miss Tempest had studiously ignored all the directions he'd given her; although they began in the role of mutual admirers they ended in the roles of mutual antagonists – I remember Guthrie in that very extraordinary voice of his, saying to me at the end of the rehearsal, 'Very common little woman. Will you tell her or shall I?' The idea of telling Miss Tempest *anything*, let alone that she was a common little woman, seemed to me so appalling. I'm not really sure that he measured up on that occasion to the dragon himself. But, nevertheless, he directed the play as well as it possibly could have been directed and breathed a little life into it.

Then when I wrote my next play I took it to Guthrie and asked him if he'd direct that. By now his stature had increased somewhat, so there was a subtle difference between us. He was absolutely delightful. He accepted the play as a sort of old pals' act, I think. It was a play called *Goodness How Sad*. 'Do you want me to read it to you?' he said. 'Or will you read it to me?' I said, 'I'd rather you read it to me.' So I went up to Burnley where he was directing, and he and his wife were in bed as I recall, and he read it to me. He read me the whole play, absolutely beautifully, playing, as he did, all parts extremely well. And I never said anything except, 'Thank you very much. Well I'd better go on to bed now too.' And he went to sleep. And that was the end of any collaboration between us. But he understood what the play was about, and he directed it marvellously. It didn't catch on very much. It was the sort of play that actors like acting in but the public found rather a bind to watch. It was a backstage story which doesn't traditionally do well in this country, unless it's *Trelawny*.

He had that curious quality which my mother-in-law, Gladys Cooper, had, which was high spirits. It was the greatest of all the gifts he had, and it was great fun to be with him, always. This is what made the rehearsals so peculiarly enjoyable. He did, indeed, direct me in a play. He made a mistake in casting, which wasn't by any means un-known with Guthrie. And he then decided to throw the actor out. And got me in as Higgins on ten days' rehearsal. I played Higgins with Diana Wynyard at the Old Vic. He hadn't much time to direct me because I joined the cast rather late and I had to learn the lines. He came round at the end of the first night, into my dressing-room, and he said, 'Yes, it's very dull now, but I'm sure it'll get better.' Not in any way was he ever capable of offending anyone. He was always funny. And if he did think a performance was dull, he was perfectly ready to take the blame for it.

He had this extraordinary gift of giving everybody a good time and having a good time himself in the theatre. He never went on with the actors rehearsing after a certain time. Nor did he ever give the im-pression, as some directors do, that rehearsing is the greatest possible fun and should be pursued far into the night. Personally I think some actors like rehearsals and some don't. I don't, really. I use it as a means of learning the lines, and if the director is there, I suppose I listen politely and think of something else. Guthrie was not the sort of person who allowed actors to have their own way. He was a brilliant director and as far as I was concerned, in thirty-five or forty years in the theatre, I have never found anyone with anything like his approach, his charm, his gaiety, his genius, his gallantry or his sense of saying, 'You do it my way, and if it's a failure we'll be there together.' He wasn't the sort of director who walked away from a disaster. Every-thing that he did he considered worth doing to the bitter end and there were bitter ends.

I did another play with him, *A Time for Laughter*, which I also put up the money for. It was an absolutely unmitigated disaster. Guthrie said to me, 'This isn't one of your common plays, and you will try not to rewrite it. It's written by a dedicated and enormously religious Roman Catholic.' Guthrie had taken an option on the play for America, and I had the play for England. It never occurred to me that Guthrie would want to direct it with me in it. It was my intention to change it substantially. However, I did ring him up when I thought it was courteous and said, 'Actually, I'm doing the play that you're directing in New York.' And he said, 'Oh I might as well direct it for you.' Well, nobody ever said no to Guthrie, I don't think. On the other hand, although it wasn't entirely as I'd planned it, I was very grateful to think that even if it wasn't going to be all that great a success – because I knew that he'd had an entirely different idea about the play

79

from me – it would be much more fun to do it with him than to do it on my own.

So he arrived, and also he'd brought Ruth Gordon, who was an ageing lady in those days and not the sort of actress I can work with. I don't care for the dedicated members of my profession. Miss Gordon had wrapped herself every evening in a shawl of misery and, I presume, concentration, and was unapproachable from the wings. I don't like that sort of thing. I like people to level with me and slap me on the back just before I go on and if necessary on the stage too. I don't think unless you amuse yourself in the theatre you're capable of amusing the public. I know a lot of actors don't like amusing the public. And here, of course, is the difference between me and the next generation of actors who were not trained as I was primarily to please the public. They were trained, and indeed are still dedicated to the proposition that a performance can be perfected at any given performance, even if there's nobody in the house at the time. Once they have, to their satisfaction, perfected a performance, even if there's no visible reaction from the public, or no different reaction from what it was the night before, they then grow tired of the role. For me there is no such thing as perfection any more than there is any such thing as finally settling with the income tax. You go on every night with a different audience, every year with a different accountant. It's your job to keep your audience amused and content, preferably by looking at them. Now Guthrie was a director who wanted very much to impose his style on everything he did and he was the only one who ever managed it, as far as I was concerned, successfully with me.

The theatre is a jungle in which the director, actor and playwright fight for supremacy, sometimes even with the manager. And I've always managed to keep on top. But I didn't, I don't think, want to keep on top when Guthrie was about because I ascribed to him, I'm not sure really whether rightly or wrongly, a sort of superhuman integrity. I don't think I was right, really. I don't think he was a particularly honest creature, any more than anybody else. But he was an enormously amusing man, and so his wife was too, an amusing man herself, for she was more like a man than a girl really.

They were an extraordinary couple. They seemed to entirely counterpart each other. She had great devotion to him. She was the sensible father figure in the stalls with the chicken sandwiches and the beer, and there was a bottle there for us but the first glass naturally went to her husband. The only other woman I ever knew who devoted so much public approbation to her husband and kept him constantly on a pedestal in front of his friends and admirers – because I think if you were a friend of his you were also an admirer, and if you were an admirer you were probably also a friend – was a fellow called Martin Harvey, whom his wife always referred to as 'the GM' even in his presence. And when you asked what GM stood for of somebody else they said, 'It stands for the great man.' And Judy in her way, also, rightly, thought of Tony as the GM. And so he was. He was a wonderful director. I remember going up to Stratford and seeing him with a company directing a Shakespearean production, and I saw the same company a week later with another director and I couldn't believe it was the same company I'd seen. He could mould clay to make it look like china. And he always, I think, was particularly careful – I'm sure everyone else has told you this – to see that it was a team he was directing. And if he thought that some of us were too big for our boots or were likely to lean too heavily on the cast, he would take great trouble to cut us down to size so that everybody felt they were entitled to a fair crack of the whip under his direction.

Is that what he did with you?

'I don't want any of that old-fashioned stuff,' he used to say to me. 'This is not 1938', or something, and I'd say, 'Well, I'm sorry, but I'm a 1938 actor, you'll have to put up with it, *won't you?*' This was when we were doing the last play that we did together in which I begged him to let me get my hands on a script. It was a play about religion so I don't think you can say who was to blame about it, because 'Religion', as somebody who came round to my dressing-room the first night said, 'is a subject which always leads to unpleasantness'. It never led to unpleasantness with Guthrie and me all through to the end of his life. Indeed, a week before he died I lunched with him. At the luncheon I'd said, 'My dear Tony, if I didn't have you to direct me I really wouldn't need anyone. I mean, they're all the same, their names all start with Peter, and I don't really know which is which. And you are the only director in my lifetime for whom I've stood when he came into the room.' And Judy said, 'You're the only actor who's ever made my husband blush.' I don't think it was true but I was very proud. And I think it was really rather significant that when he died his bailiff approached Judy to tell her that Guthrie died unostentatiously reading his letters. He used the phrase 'the great tree has fallen, m'lady'. And then on the day of his memorial service, a great tree in the churchyard of St Paul's, Covent Garden, fell down too. I don't think there was any significance in it, but it made a good end. And Guthrie was always very good with curtains; it was one of his fortes.

What did Guthrie think you needed as an actor?

I suppose in a way he said, 'You can do better than that,' which was his attitude about it all. And most actors if told they can do better than that very often do. I think that was his approach, that he always believed that with a little more effort you could achieve a little more. Most directors in the theatre today like to make the effort themselves and shrug their shoulders at the effort of the actor. More or less saying, 'Well, I'm stuck with him, I'd better put him downstage upside-down and see if his teeth come out.' Guthrie believed very much, I think, in letting the actor struggle to do better for himself. He had implicit faith in actors, and he liked them.

Directors today – a good many of the avant-garde directors – give the impression that they are the intelligent ones, and the actor is the fool. This is always unfortunate, particularly if they are both idiots. A film director really only savages the meat. It's difficult to know whether a stage director does much – a film director does a great deal more. I've seen productions which I thought were jolly well directed. But more often than not, it was because they were jolly well acted. You might argue that the director is responsible for the acting, but I don't think this is very often true. 'How do you get on with directors?' I once asked Ralph Richardson. And he said, 'Well, I usually give them a couple of days to find out if they know more than I do, and if they don't I take over.' And a director asked me the other day, 'If I put you in this play do you think you could give up your tricks?' And I said, 'No, I don't, nor do I want to, dear. I mean it is an impertinent suggestion, and one that you'd obviously made after you decided not to offer me the part.'

But I think Guthrie acknowledged our tricks and tried to encourage us to explore parts of our repertoire which had not been extended, which I think we rather enjoyed doing. He never, I think, snubbed the actor. He didn't like them coming in late. He was rather a disciplinarian. If he got bored or we got bored – and this I think was the great thing about him – he stopped the rehearsal. You see they lead rather deprived lives – directors. They're only showing off for a limited period, about a month, before the play opens and after that their little hour is over, and we're left to do the work and also to get the acclaim.

So a director likes increasingly to direct more hours a day really than he should. Some directors, like Peter Brook, work unceasingly at it and indeed now have dedicated themselves to a proposition where they won't allow the actors to be seen except by obscure nomadic tribes in Africa, so happy are they to continue working in a vacuum.

Stanislavsky in many ways harmed the profession by blowing up the role of the director and his method – the Stanislavsky method – has been more grossly misunderstood and misquoted than almost any, and was responsible indeed for the Method in America, which had no connection with it at all. If you talk to actors who have ever worked with Stanislavsky or indeed children of actors who worked with Stanislavsky, it was always absolutely clear that all the experimental part, all the stretching and the getting into the part, the improvisation, took place before rehearsal started as a matter of casting the part. He had a great many actors to choose from and not knowing which was best for a part or at least not making up his mind about it, he used to send them home to think about the character he'd asked them to play and see if they could come up with anything which would enhance what the playwright had written. And when they came back and said, 'I think he had venereal disease and a squint,' if Stanislavsky liked that, he gave him the part. It wasn't written in the script that the man had venereal disease and a squint and as soon as he started rehearsals the actor was promptly reminded that he hadn't got either. But at the time, it was a method Stanislavsky used to cast the plays. It was carried, I think, to ridiculous lengths, but on the other hand there's always a contradiction to everything one says. And that curious actor Marlon Brando, who is a product of the Method, is probably the best actor in the world today, so you really don't know, but I think he would have been the best actor if he had never even heard of the Method. Anyway, when I was young there wasn't much talk about acting. We talked about bridge and girls and people never talked much about rehearsing and acting. It was considered a necessary thing like going to the lavatory, but I don't think anybody of my generation ever seriously considered the art of acting. And, indeed, I have never considered it an art. To me it's always been a craft A very useful and highly rewarded craft, but a craft.

Do you remember any specific things he suggested to you in terms of your writing, when you worked together on your plays, as opposed to your actor–director relationship?

The first play presented great difficulties to him and myself, and I think he did help with the basic construction of the play, to try and get it on the stage It wasn't an easy problem. The best idea he had for that play was that, although he was using the same set three times, he changed round the angles of the room so that each time you saw it from a different perspective. I never quite understood the idea, but I thought it would be extremely amusing to do. I don't know whether he ever did it in any other production. But this was a play that was sort of a drawing-room comedy, and he did a drawing-room set. But he had the designer do three versions of it, so that one moment you were looking into the garden and the next moment you were looking into a fireplace and third you were looking into a desk, I think. However, this was all thrown out by the manager who said he wasn't really sure the play was going to go, and anyway that three sets on this occasion were sort of not better than one, so the idea was abandoned. It was – looking back on it – a very skilfully directed play. If indeed it was a play at all, which by the time we'd altered it and finished tearing it apart I don't think it was. He was very clever at the technique of concealing faults in poor plays.

He wrote a play himself, or several; one was called *Top of the Ladder*, which John Mills did. It was a pretty terrible play, but it was a subject about which he knew nothing whatsoever, which I think was big business. And had he written about the theatre I think he would have written extremely well. He wrote a number of books, all of which I thought were disappointing. The gaiety, the gossip, the fun, seemed to be lacking in the books. There seemed to be a more serious purpose. I don't think the theatre has a very serious purpose. Certainly the theatre which he lived in hadn't. It was either to show you something for the first time or to show you something you'd seen before and were asked to look at in a different way. The essence of everything he did, I think, was to *entertain* the public.

He was a little bit of a schoolmaster in some ways. Politically, he, and I think rightly – I don't use this as my own idea, I think I read it somewhere – would have liked at one time to have been allowed to interfere in the political situation in Ulster. I think one of the reasons he returned to Ulster so frequently is that he always thought that he might be given the job of taking over and running the country. He would have done it extremely well. There is certainly a case to be made for people like Guthrie, who was a born leader, who founded theatres all over the world, who understood the problems of civil authorities, and benevolence, and generosity, and guilty consciences, and who, if he wanted to, could get money for anything. There's a lot to be said for a man who is a natural leader not spending his entire time in the theatre. And I think we were all perhaps rather sorry that he didn't spread himself around more. He did go into jam making in Ireland, but I don't think it was a serious attempt.

Well, I think it was serious, but it didn't work out very well.

He did a rather touching and splendid film on the B B C, a profile of his life. It was sad but interesting. There was a great deal about a railway station in his childhood memories. I suppose we all have childhood memories. We all want to belong somewhere. Guthrie, I don't know whether he ever really quite belonged. His parentage, his background, his family, were something he never discussed. Underneath everything else was a deep religious conviction. I remember the last time I met him – I think it was a fortnight before he died – I said, 'You don't really go to church, do you?' And he looked at me as if I was a new subaltern that had joined the regiment and smoked the wrong sort of cigarettes, and he said, 'Well, of course I go to church. Good heavens . . .' And couldn't visualize, I think, anyone not going to church. He liked to go to church to sing the hymns, he said. I don't know why he went to church.

That's interesting, because every time he had a chance to satirize the church on stage, he did.

He worshipped, but he criticized. And I suppose in essence that sums him up. He worshipped the theatre, but he always criticized it.

What was your impression of the Lincoln's Inn Fields flat?

Well, you couldn't believe it when first you went there. And then afterwards when you'd been there a bit you thought, 'Well, it was the only possible place for them to have lived.' As far as I remember, the iron bedstead when I knew it had gone through the floor. It was propped up perhaps with books. It was enormous and it took up one room. In those days there was not much attempt to decorate the kitchen-dining room. In fact, I remember there was a gas stove – it used to rub shoulders and indeed almost take part in the conversation – and Judy would reach over to it without getting up to pass the beetroot, which I was never fond of, but I used to eat it when I went to the Guthries'. For some reason they were very fond of beetroot.

They lived incredibly sparsely. The question arose whether they were economical, mean, or were not well off. I never could decide. They had that ascetic thing about them, that food meant very little to them really. And comfort nothing at all. They lived, as I say, in a slum. There was no other word for it. It was like a dreadful set of a Sean O'Casey play. But, it suited them very well, and they were happy there and we all went and worshipped there. It was sort of humble. Be it ever so humble, there was no place as humble as the Guthries' home, I think you could say, to paraphrase the quotation. I think this insistence on asceticism, on economy, on cut out the frills, in his private life, was equated in his production by putting in as many frills as possible. He was never happy unless he could find someone to ride a donkey on the stage or, you know, divert attention from the star. I mean, he was wonderfully good at inventing business for actors who really couldn't act. But there was no extravagance in his own life at all. And I'm sure he was perfectly capable of working for nothing, if he felt that the people he were directing were not well off or not able to afford him. He was a doctor in every sense of the word. Not only a doctor who was made a doctor, but I think he regarded everyone as his patient, to be cured eventually. I think this was his approach to life. He certainly thought he'd cure the playwrights and the actors. And I suppose he lived in the hope that one day he'd cure the public.

Sybil Thorndike

ALFRED ROSSI: *When was the first time you worked with Tony Guthrie?*

SYBIL THORNDIKE: That was in *Short Story* by Robert Morley in 1935. Marie Tempest was in it, and he was marvellous with her, because you see she'd never been under such strict direction before. She was behaving abominably. And he was never afraid of anybody, you see. He said, 'Miss Tempest, why are you being such a bitch?' And she was astonished. Nobody had ever said such a thing to her before. At any rate, she laughed and said, 'Well, come on, let's get on with it.' And then Tony did a very clever thing. Rex Harrison was being very clumsy over a bit of business he was doing, and Tony said, 'Can't you do that?' And Rex said, 'Can't, my hands are full. I can't do any more.' And he turned round to Marie and said, 'Miss Tempest, would you mind showing Rex how to do that?' She was awfully taken aback. But she did it beautifully. Technically, she could do anything, you see. And they became friends after that. And he was right for her, too, because he made her more realistic than she ever was before.

Oh, he was wonderful in that way. He saw people's tendencies and corrected them. It was Margaret Rutherford's first real show in London, and Tony had an awful difficulty there, because Marie was beastly to her. She was resentful of anybody else who got such big laughs. She was kind to me, because she knew I was younger and my laughs helped her laughs. But with Margaret Rutherford she jumped on every laugh she got. Tony used to be furious. He'd come round and say, 'Marie, you're killing Margaret Rutherford.' He watched the shows, you see, saw where we were. And he saw me one night when I bonked Marie Tempest on the nose with a pineapple. It was her fault. She was in the wrong place. I had to wave the pineapple round. It was just before the curtain. I waved this pineapple, and I bumped her right on the nose. The audience rocked with laughter. The curtain came down and I said, 'Marie! What have I done, I've killed you.' She said,

'It's all right, dear, I was in the wrong place.' And she was. She was generous like that. Oh dear, I bonked her on the nose good and proper right there. But Tony was wonderful with everybody. Marie never underplayed, she overplayed, so he toned her down and he beat the others up. Oh, Marie was an old bitch but a darling. I adored her, absolutely adored her.

Tony directed you and your husband in Macbeth *during the war, didn't he?*

Yes, we did it in a strange new way, because we were touring it in the coalmining towns. We started at Newport on the border of Wales, then played in all the Welsh coal valleys and up the coast, finishing at our home in Portmadoc in the north. My husband was a Welshman, you see. And it was Tony's idea, with Lewis, to play Macbeth rather like Hitler. He had a make-up like Hitler. He and Tony were very original together, because Tony took a lot from Lewis and Lewis took an enormous lot from Tony, but they were devoted friends. They were candid to each other but admiring of each other. They would criticize each other, because Lewis was better on speech than Tony. Being a Welshman, he was a lovely speaker, a natural speaker. And Tony was *wonderful* with him. I thought, 'Oh, Lewis will never stand anybody producing him in *Macbeth*. He's so violent himself.' But he and Tony got on very well. He would take things from Tony that he wouldn't have taken from anybody else.

How did you approach Lady Macbeth?

My conception was the same as I've always had of her. I think she was a wonderful person, you see, and adored him, but she had no scruples. When I played it with Ben Greet, Ben said, 'She's a wicked woman.' I said, 'She's not. She adores her husband and is pushing him for all he's worth.' Tony and I were quite agreeable. Where Tony helped me was taking me away from theatricality, because I'm awfully apt to be theatrical. From my training, I suppose, and from my dislike for conversational acting. I dislike it so much in Shakespeare. Not hearing the words properly and taking everything down to realism, which is ridiculous in Shakespeare.

What were Tony's ideas about, let's say, the sleepwalking scene?

Oh, it was just a very straightforward scene. Shakespeare has done it all. And you only had to speak it in a dream. There was nothing original about that, he had no tricks for it. Such a lot of people have tricks in that scene. He played it absolutely realistically – a woman sleeps with something on her conscience.

You know some people have said that Tony was guilty of a lot of tricks. But it sounds like when he worked with you he didn't take that approach at all.

He had to stop *me* being tricky. No, I don't think he *was* tricky. I think a lot of modern people call it tricky when they're asked to be big, and they don't like being big. They like to be conversational. And I think this conversational acting has ruined the theatre. Oh, I think it's ridiculous. There's no large size at all. You get large size in Johnny Gielgud and Ralph. Not so much in Larry, because Larry is always apt to be conversational, but he's a very fine actor.

What was the reaction to the Macbeth *in some of those small coal-mining towns where they probably hadn't seen too much Shakespeare?*

Well, when Lewis told the people who sent us out, the Arts Council, that we wanted to do *Macbeth*, they said, 'A tragedy? For those poor Welsh people?' Lewis said, 'I know my people. They like tragedy.' And I remember in one coalmining place in the south of Wales, one of the coalminers came round at the end and said, 'This is the play for us. It kindles the fire.' And what could you want more than that – to kindle a fire? That is what the theatre exists for.

Did Tony go with you on the tour?

Oh yes, he came down and saw us when we were going over the edge. Because I go over the edge quite easily. In a way I've always been used to good direction. My husband – I've always loved working with him – was merciless with me. And I think I've always been a good girl in the theatre and did what the director wanted, because I love acting more than anything, except music, and I always wanted to do the best. And so, unless there was a director who was conceited – and that would drive me potty – but I've only found that in a film. But, with Tony, I would have taken anything he said, because I knew his criticism was right, and good for me.

Was there anything remarkable about your experience in King John?

We had a very stylistic King John, Ernest Milton, and Tony had to do away with mannerisms. I remember Ernest saying to me, 'What is this extraordinary creature who's directing us?' I said, 'He'll take your tricks away, darling.' He said, 'But my tricks are me.' I said, 'But they aren't. Your tricks are something you've imposed on yourself.' And he used to know that – Ernest Milton was very mannered, but if you took away his manners, he was a great actor. His Hamlet was wonderful, but it was full of mannerisms.

Did Tony direct you in Medea?

No, my husband did. Oh, Lewis wouldn't have let anybody do the Greeks but him. He was trained under Gilbert Murray, you see. Tony thought that I was extreme with Medea. But you can't be extreme with the Greeks. You can't be too extreme, because they *are* too extreme. They're so huge, so much greater than realism. But you have to have realism too, or else you don't move people.

What did Tony say to you about that Medea *after he saw it?*

Oh, he said, 'You're enjoying yourself now, aren't you?' But he didn't say anything *else*. I *was* enjoying myself too.

Tony was always helpful even when other people had produced things. He could come in and say, 'I think you're doing this too much', or 'Not enough there', and 'I think you've misinterpreted that.' I know he helped me an awful lot in *Arms and the Man*. I was playing the mother.

Did the other directors appreciate that?

Oh, the director wouldn't know.

Why did Tony do that?

Because he was interested. He'd come round to see us and he'd say, 'I loved your show, but I think this . . .' Which everybody is entitled to do, if you're friends. And a director wouldn't notice, because you wouldn't *tell* the director.

I know that you and your husband were both very close to Tony.

Oh I loved him very much. I remember the last time that I saw him. He was lecturing at the University of London in Hampstead. I had dinner with him first, and I was sitting with Judy. His language, the four-letter words that came out! I can't think why, because it wasn't a young audience – I suppose he did it to shock them. Judy said to me, 'Really, he's using some words tonight, isn't he?' I said, 'I think it's ridiculous. Why is he doing that?' She said, 'I don't know.' It's just he was shocking them, I think. I think they were a little bit fusty, those fuddy-duddy professors, and so he used as many four-letter words as he could. And I think it was very good. I think people want shocking. He shocked them into awareness. *He* was a very aware person himself.

Is there a role that you wish Tony Guthrie had directed you in?

No. Because all the things that I wanted to do Lewis directed me in. And Lewis taught me more than anybody I know. He was so musical. Tony was musical too. Tony and Lewis got on very well like that. They were very much the same, except that Lewis was much more violent tempered than Tony, because of Lewis being a Welshman. It was terrible. Tony always knew how to get you with humour. Lewis was too violent and used to get people on the raw, because of that. But that's Welsh, part of the make-up.

That's part of the magnificence of the Welsh people – the musicality and the passion.

And a big scale. And yet Lewis himself could play the most realistic roles; he was very realistic too, but if you weren't heard, he'd kill you. And Tony was the same. Tony and Lewis were awfully at one, although Tony had more tact than Lewis. He was very tactful, as you can see, with Marie Tempest, asking her to show Rex Harrison, now that was a real bit of tact. When we were doing the Welsh tour of all the industrial towns, if Tony wanted Lewis to do anything different – and Lewis was apt to go further than Tony wanted – he would always come to me and say, 'Look, don't let Lewis do this.' And it was so very difficult for me, because I was in the middle.

You were asked by Judy Guthrie to be a part of Tony's memorial service. It must have been a very emotional moment for you.

I don't know how I got through it. I've got a letter from Judy in my Greek Bible that I always use to keep my place. I was with Tony when I started Greek, during the war. I'm not very good at it. I only really do Bible Greek, which is very simple Greek. Would you like to read that letter?

Would you read it?

'Dearest Sybil, I think you know how much your reading of that sonnet meant to me. You will know what I'm going to say now is not meant lightly. It was so wonderfully inspiring. When you read you also spoke to the trumpets which sound on the other side, which is, isn't it, what the sonnet is mostly about? That the trumpet should speak in a young voice. When Tony broke me the news of Lewis's death, I rather selfishly thought, "I must do something nice for myself" and I went and read this sonnet, cried like a drain and felt a hell of a lot better. And when you were reading yesterday I felt that you and Lewis and Tony and I were all together somewhere. With loving thanks, God bless you, dearest Sybil.' Isn't that a lovely letter? Oh, she's a wonderful person. She was so wonderful that day, at the funeral. We had lunch together, and she wouldn't let anybody be solemn, because she said Tony wouldn't have liked it.

Alec Guinness told me that when he gave the speech people were laughing, and it was almost a gay occasion.

It was, it really was, and we felt that Tony was there laughing with us.

Laurence Olivier

ALFRED ROSSI: *The 1937 production of* Hamlet *at the Old Vic was a first for both you and Tony Guthrie: you playing the title role, and he directing that play. How did you work with him on it?*

LAURENCE OLIVIER: I imagine he was much more authoritarian with a younger person, like Alec Guinness, who played it three years later at the Old Vic, and was, at that time, only twenty-four. And I think Tony worked with him on his experience of having done it once already, and perhaps was more outlining in his approach to it with him, I daresay. I was, what, twenty-nine I suppose, but much more experienced than 'Little' Alec, as we used to call him. It was very much of a partnership I'd say, discussing what would be effective. I wanted to be terribly gymnastic, I remember, and I remember him not persuading me out of that, but *circumstancing* me out of it. After the play scene I had a terrific idea about playing the lines:

> For thou dost know, O Damon dear,
> This realm dismantled was
> Of Jove himself; and now reigns here
> A very, very, peacock.

On the words, 'very, very, peacock' I wanted to leap off the top platform, bounce on to something, catch hold of the pole that was to cross this sort of proscenium arch, swing twice round the pole – one on each 'very ... very ... peacock' – leap towards the astonished audience and land in the footlights before their blanched faces. But Tony was awfully serious, he never said, 'That's ridiculous!' or anything like that. And God knows it *was*. And he said, 'Well, what do you want?' And I said, 'Well, I want something to bounce on.' And all the carpenter could think of was having a box with some three-ply over some chicken wire which would give a little bounce, and that was what he thought I could leap down on. There wasn't any pole or any proscenium arch, so I was going to have to leap off the top, then

93

bounce on that and then jump from there. I'd have broken every ankle that anybody ever thought of! And so I tried it from a small height first, and it didn't work at all, and I said, 'It's no good, is it?' And he said, 'Then I think we'll forget it, shall we?' It was so sweet the way he'd arranged it, so that I wasn't going to make that much of a fool of myself.

That type of flamboyant action is the kind of thing that Tony himself directed a number of times, so he might have been worried about your safety.

We were both after achieving effects. We were both young enough to make that the prime object in our existence. 'Make a fine effect,' as they used to say about Edmund Kean or someone. And we were both trying for the most dramatic and startling effects all the way through. Also, we were both making effects of versatility, i.e. following *Hamlet* with *Twelfth Night*, playing Toby Belch. Then when the coronation was coming I said, 'Well, don't you think we ought to do *Henry V?*'

Those roles were suggested by you?

Yes. And that cheeky little bastard Dickie Burton has to copy me inch by inch and do Hamlet, Toby Belch, Henry V, one after another and then Coriolanus, what's more. Saucebox! Anyway, I remember once Tony came to my dressing-room which is number eight – I dressed there quite a lot in those days – I had parted my hair down here and grew it long in a full swoop like that – a bit girlish – and I put white inside the lower ledge of my eyes to glisten them up a bit. And he came and leaned his huge length against the door there and looked at me and said, 'Every inch a Hamlet. Think they're going to fault you about your verse speaking, about your lyrical quality. However, do your best. Good luck, dear boy.' And he'd *never* mentioned the lyrical quality before. Just before I went on the first night. I think he *must* have mentioned it before, but I only remember that time. I don't think he mentioned it to me in rehearsals at all.

Was he a stickler for verse speaking?

No. The first letter I ever had from him was after Romeo when I was totally birched by the press for not being able to do Shakespeare at all. And he wrote me a perfectly charming letter. This was way back in 1935. And he wrote me – I'd never met him, didn't know what he looked like, I knew he was tall – and he wrote me a perfectly charming letter of appraisal about my Romeo saying how he really admired it and it was intensely real and all sorts of things that it had never been before, and so on. Then he said, 'Think they're right to fault you about the verse speaking.' I remember that phrase. Now, I don't know, people say, 'Did you get the press round to you or did the press get round you and make you different?' I don't know, I really don't know. Presumably I learned to speak verse to most people's satisfaction somehow. Whether they got used to me or I got used to it I'll never know.

But obviously in terms of what Tony was trying to do with you in that production of Hamlet, he wasn't inordinately concerned with the verse.

No, he was just trying to *set* me. He was just trying to give me a good setting. All we leading men always used to say you're really lucky if you've ever seen – he'll cover you up if he can. I remember one scene I had – it was during the exhortation to the players, 'Speak the speech I pray you' and all that. And I was busy talking to a couple of them and I heard a snapping of fingers, and I looked up – it startled me – and there was Tony telling one of the players on the other side of the stage to point at me behind his hand to one of the others. And I said, '*Tony!* – If you don't mind, I'd like the audience to listen to this. And in the second place, no player, the lowest thing that crawls, would do that – his head would be rolling in the sawdust, before he knew what was happening to him, if anybody saw him. And in the third place, Hamlet's being so sweet to them, it's so ungracious. For God's sake, cut that out.' He said, 'Oh very well, I'll cut it out.' I knew why he was doing it, of course. He was building round me all sorts of biz. He was always inclined to mask the central important business with all sorts of extraneous rubbish all around, I must say. And as a leading man you had to keep an eye in the back of your head, I can tell you that! But we always got on absolutely marvellously, and I was terribly happy working with him, always.

What did he think you needed?

We never got very deep in conversation about my acting. He obviously liked it, because he kept on casting me and trying to get me to do things with him. And he obviously realized that I recognized *his* qualities. Except that I was awfully unkind to him once – I didn't mean to be – when I said, 'I'd like to do *Macbeth* and I'd like Michel Saint-Denis to direct it.' Then again, later, I was going to do *Oedipus* and he didn't want me to do *The Critic* on the same night after it and I said, 'Sorry, boy, sorry, I won't do *Oedipus* without *The Critic* – I'd hate it.' And whether I was right or wrong, or whether it was good show-manship or vulgar showmanship, anybody else could say but me.

Do you recall the performance of Hamlet *at* Elsinore *that was moved inside the hotel ballroom because of a storm?*

Very much so. Tony was terribly busy with the business end of it, and said, 'Larry, go to the ballroom and rearrange it for me.' Left it to *me* to arrange all the entrances and where every scene was to be played. And he was that loose about it, that easy. I remember I'd put Torin Thatcher, who was playing the Ghost, to be up on the little stage, I think. I'd brought everything else right down into the audience. And I never appeared up on the stage, which was the best central position, of course. Tony came round after the first act and said, 'Thought this was just going to be a joke. Thought we'd just do one act and apologize, give everybody a glass of champagne and send them home, but every-body's taking it *far* too seriously, we'll have to go through to the end.' And then after the show I said, 'Wasn't it wonderful? Torin Thatcher finding himself in that king position as the Ghost, with me *leaning* up, crawling up the stairs in a prone position having to gaze completely dead upstage to him, and he had the whole thing to himself?' And Tony said, 'Yes, it was absolutely lovely, I never enjoyed anybody else's pleasure like that. It flowed through the hall like warm strawberry jam.'

That night, apparently, from what he later wrote, was a very significant event for him.

Oh, for everybody, for the world.

It's changed the design of so many theatres, and you can see this chain of events. Did you ever think past that event at the time?

No. It happened and there it was, and I saw it could be done and it was quite good. But I didn't think it was going to transform the shape of the theatre or anything.

I've never got beyond that sort of shape of set. My own production with O'Toole, the inaugural one for the National, was vaguely spectred by his production, you know? And indeed the film probably was influenced by his production. Certainly the film of *Henry V* was influenced by him. In fact, I copied outrageously. It was so funny, when he didn't like the film. I was making up for something at the Old Vic, I think it was *Richard III*. He came and stepped into my room and said, 'Saw the film, thought it was vulgar.' It was funny, because if you saw the film now, one couldn't say it was vulgar . . . it was *too* tasteful for words.

Do you think that he was a bit put off that you had pinched some things?

I think that he was a bit. He was only human.

Did he take an anti-heroic approach to Henry V? *He's written an anti-heroic essay about it.*

Oh yes, he would do that. I had thought of being very cynical on 'Tell me, my Lord Archbishop, is it true or is it not that there is any reason why we should not fly hence and pinch the French crown?' And I suggested this to Tony. When we came to it and the bunting started to go off for the coronation, neither of us had the guts to go through with it. It really had to be heroic and he insisted on it. 'Don't think this is going to be suitable.' And I said, 'I couldn't agree more and it isn't. We'll have to do it straight.' It's the one thing you *can't do* really to Shakespeare, you can't really slant it, you know. And he knew that.

You don't think he ever did?

A little bit. But I think he always *questioned* it. You can't slant it psychologically, because Shakespeare will always defeat you, always trip you up some way, so you can't do that. I mean I once saw Michael Redgrave have the courage to do Richard II as an out-and-out pussy queer, with mincing gestures to match. But there comes a time when Shakespeare says, 'This is the last act now, you can drop all that, and become St George like everybody else, can't you?' And that's what you have to do. Characterize Hotspur till you're black in the face, or Richard III, and Shakespeare says, 'Sorry, you're St George now,' in the last scene. He won't tolerate political slants, psychological slants. He won't stand a very strong light thrown across the work. He'll trip you up, it's funny. It'll stand it, Shakespeare will *survive* any treatment, somehow.

There's a story you've told about kissing Ralph Richardson in an Othello *rehearsal . . .*

There again it was Tony and I who were really rather conspiring between ourselves and Ralph was oblivious to what we were trying to do. Ralph would have none of the talk about Iago being in love with Othello at all.

What was Guthrie particularly after in your creation of Iago?

Well, whatever it was, the poor fellow didn't get it. I made a most miserable flop. I think we played it completely wrong. I played it as a young charmer. I'd been talking to Laughton about it. And Laughton couldn't bear Clark Gable and thought that Gable was Iago, because Gable was such a man among men to all men who would do the same sort of wink and throw of the head and grin to stage hands as he did to the director. Laughton didn't trust him at all. And Laughton could sense, probably exaggeratedly, that Gable was making friends and influencing men against Charles. It was probably Charles's suspicious mind, to a large extent. But he thought Gable was trying to win *all* the men on the set who would favour him with lights, and all that sort of nonsense people talk about in Hollywood – I just don't believe it *can* exist; I've never seen any evidences of it anyhow – I've often noticed my leading ladies being frightfully sweet to the boys but I supposed that's in case there might be a row and then one is on her side, I don't know.

Anyway, I was influenced by the idea of playing it all for charm, an absolute charmer so that everybody would say 'honest Iago' with complete conviction. But actually I think it's quite wrong and I think that the NCO Iago is right. And Othello didn't have him because he wasn't the right man for the job, he wasn't sufficient for Othello, who needed support of class very much, being a blackamoor. You can call it what you like, you can call him Negro. We hear towards the end of the play that he came from Mauretania, which was right on the *blackest* east coast of Africa. And some people have it that he's a Berber Moor. A blackamoor doesn't mean a Moorish Moor at all. A black man was a blackamoor. He was a *black* man. And all Shakespeare cared about was the idea of a black man strangling a white girl.

But we tried to justify Iago's evil by making it a psychological impulse, that he didn't himself understand, rather like Hamlet and the Oedipus complex, that absolutely subconsciously Iago was in love with Othello. And it couldn't work, because you couldn't express it. So there I was being a charming young blade with a beautiful under-graduate's accent and not making any sense at all. As far as I remember

I was every bit as classy as Tony Quayle who played Cassio – so the only interpretation that makes sense is the NCO. And you can hear Othello saying, 'I don't think so. I think I'll have this young Florentine,' you know, with his splendid graces and airs and that. And Iago, like a gnarled NCO soldier, would hope to Christ he was going to get into the officer class and when he failed he was going to react like everybody I've seen in any service I've ever been in, which was only one, the Navy. And when you are in a service, then you *understand* Iago.

When you're in the service you'll be eating and a hand will come over your shoulder and you look at the wrist and see how many stripes are on it before you look up. When you're in *that* sort of set-up and somebody is expecting an extra half-stripe and doesn't get it, you see him eating *into himself*, in the mess, you know. Absolutely white and grey with shame and betrayed hopes. And when somebody younger has got the half-stripe more than they, and they've just been shown once again that they're not quite the right class, to be a lieutenant commander, you know. I was ridden by one of these men, an NCO class man, who *did* get a half-stripe, and as soon as he got his half-stripe he'd start taking it out on me: 'How's our film star today?' All that sort of thing. And I let it get me down, and I really got into the fantasy class of hatred of this man and I used to walk about the aerodrome saying, 'How can I get him, how can I get him?' One day walking across the field, I stopped right in the middle of it and said, 'Of course, he's married. Christ, Iago!' Because in his moments of expansiveness this fellow had said, 'You must come and call one day at my farm. It's only four miles down the line and my wife would like to meet you.' And I thought, 'Christ, I could *kill* him. Murder! I could *be* there when he wasn't expecting me, and I could sort of get up rather quickly . . .' And I thought, 'Thank God I played Iago and now I not only understand him, but he's teaching me to avoid this situation.' You know, it's astonishing really when you think of the cast of that first *Othello*. It was first of all Tony's production. Roger Furse's setting, Anthony Quayle, Andrew Cruickshank, Martita Hunt, Ralph, myself. It was an absolutely solid cast. *It cannot fail.* There never was such a crashing flop.

When that happened, how did Tony react?

Oh he would always wipe things off like that. 'Rise above.'

Did he ever listen to the critics at all?

He'd usually giggle. Usually snicker, with this rather schoolboy snicker, used to do that and say – his favourite expression about the critics – 'Cheek.'

In Minneapolis when he directed Hamlet, *there was a vitriolic critic who wrote for the* Chicago Tribune – *Claudia Cassidy – and she gave the production a very bad review, and he said, 'Think I'm cheeky enough to think I know more about Shakespeare than Claudia Cassidy.'*

That's Tony.

Was his invention even more fertile in a comedy like Twelfth Night?

Oh yes, he loved that, the farcical business, he *adored* that. And I was a match for him, I'm afraid, you know, at that sort of outrageous comic invention. He loved all that! Didn't matter *how far* we went, he loved it more and more. It was *disgraceful*, how far we went with Malvolio and Maria, you know, 'get thee behind this box' and all that. And Aguecheek was Alec Guinness, caught outside you see while he turned round. He was pretending to be a statue, I mean *that's* sort of far.

Just listening to you now, I sense there must have been a great rapport, an exciting give and take.

I never was conscious of a difference with him, never. I never felt the slightest bit out of tune. I mean if he came back and said, 'Much, much, much too much, dear boy,' I'd know it was right. And certainly I'd feel guilty about it if I'd given an outrageous performance. I used to have Jessica Tandy in hysterics – it was really awful of me. He'd say, 'Very naughty.' And he was damn right, it was worse than very naughty. But there was *one* thing he said, out of all the years of not really saying anything, he absolutely saved my career once. I had opened in *Arms and the Man* – you probably know the story, I've told it a dozen times. I always feel inclined to give him great tribute for this, because God knows what I owe him for it. He'd only say a line like, 'Think they'll fault you for lyrical quality.' That sort of comment – just that much. Never, 'I will take the clay and I will mould it' with me at all. He may have done it without my knowing it, but it was never consciously rolling up his sleeves and starting to push you about, *never*. And never very *perceptive*, even, except this one time. I opened with Ralph in *Arms and the Man*, which John Burrell directed, before we came to the Old Vic for the *Peer Gynt* lot. A week or two before we opened, we paid for the production in one big week at Manchester. Ralph was Bluntschli and I was Sergius. And Ralph and I went down to the theatre together and we had a beer in the pub opposite the stage door and on the way back Ralph bought a paper. And I remember walking down to the hotel looking over Ralph's shoulder and seeing, 'Mr Ralph Richardson a brilliant Bluntschli; Mr Laurence Olivier on the other hand . . .' And I thought, 'Right, I'm going straight back into the Navy. I'm going back and I'm *not* going to take any more of this. I'm *never* going to take this again. I'm going back in the Navy. This is my give-up.' And I said as much to Ralph. Tony hadn't been to the first night, and he came to the second night and I was sulking away. And passing under the canopy at the Opera House, he said, 'Liked your Sergius.' And I said nastily, 'Oh, thank you very much.' And he said, 'Why, don't you like it?' I said, 'Christ, if you weren't so tall I'd hit you, how could you like a part like that? Are you insane, you bloody old fool?' And he said, 'But don't you love Sergius?' I said, 'Tony Guthrie, if you go on making these inane remarks I shall really never speak to you again. What do you mean, how could you love *a bloody awful part* like that!' He said quietly, 'Oh I see, well, of course, unless you learn to love him you'll never be any good in it, will you?' Wow! By the end of the week I was loving him so much I was the hit of the show and when we opened in London I got the best notices.

And that's influenced you ever since?

Absolutely and, God, through me, hundreds of other people, hundreds. Of all the priceless remarks, to have that one from Tony. And the *only* one that has saved I don't know how many careers through me, through repeating it. It was in this same season he taught me another *priceless* lesson. In practicability. He was too canny to be caught out with too intense a sense of idealism about his own work. Too canny for that. And this is what I admired about him *most*. There was some bit of biz in *Peer Gynt*, and I wish to God I could remember what it was. An element of scenery, a truck with something on it. It was very late in the evening before the opening and it had to be done and something had to happen and it was there and it was a transformation, very cunningly done and it took a certain amount of rehearsal. And in his opinion it was obviously taking *too much*, or *might* take too much time. The rehearsal might get hung up on it and everybody might get tired and it would spoil the first night. Something like that.

He never explained it but I could see all this through what he was doing. And it was a marvellous lesson in practicability. He cared about it. He made preparations for it, spent quite a lot of time at ordinary rehearsals, in rehearsing it and making it happen like that. On the one and absolutely only dress-rehearsal which we had in those days, he tried it once, he tried it twice, 'Right. *Out. On.*' He loved this idea. And I don't know any other director who wouldn't have gone on for at least half an hour, trying to get it right. I thought, 'Boy, I admire you more than I can say.'

A great sense of not getting too concerned with one tree in the forest.

Yes. 'How much does it matter? Is it worth making Ralph tired?' You know. That's saved my neck several times.

Tony Quayle said that he thought that Guthrie was enamoured of you, in the sense of being taken with you as a talent, a charismatic man-animal-actor on the stage, so that very often he would give you your head. Do you think that's a fair statement?

I daresay so. Ungrateful as I am I never appreciated it quite in those terms. Perhaps it's just as well I didn't. I might have let it go to my head, I suppose. But I thought he *liked* me, certainly. I didn't recognize that he gave me my head any more than he gave anybody else theirs, but I think probably that is *true*. I think he did trust me with a lot of invention and did enjoy, as you say, very kindly enough, my versatile talent and liked to deal with it.

Why was he so special?

He had a tremendous intellect. He had terrific resilience. Fantastically inventive. Did you see his production of *The Tenth Man* in New York? Did you see his production of *Pinafore*? He was a bloody genius. He was absolutely inimitable, when he was on form. Nobody like him. Nobody could come near him. He made mistakes, he repeated himself, he got boring on occasion but he was a fascinating man to work with, to watch his work. And as a companion, couldn't be more happy, joyous and funny, lovely to be with. Oh God, he was marvellous to rehearse with, *so* funny! What a lovely man. Oh, I miss him terribly. It's awful that we weren't closer during the last fifteen years or so.

He said something to me once; I've never forgotten it. He said, 'Are you enjoying your job at the National?' I said, 'Yes I am. It's really lovely.' He said, 'Good, I'm glad.' I said, 'How long have you been at

Minneapolis?' He said, 'I'm not at Minneapolis any longer.' 'I thought you were still there.' 'Good God, no, dear boy. I never keep these jobs down for more than three years.' I said, 'Don't you?' He said, 'No, it would make it so impossible for the succession, you see.' And he must have seen my face because I felt awful. I'd held this one for five years and had every intention of holding it down for five more if I could keep it. And he came to me a little while afterwards and I said, 'I say, you made me feel terrible back there. Do you think I ought to go?' And he said, 'Don't, for God's sake. I could have bitten my tongue off when I saw your face after what I said. Don't be ridiculous. Of course, you're absolutely right to stay.' And that's the last talk I remember having with him.

Coral Browne

CORAL BROWNE: During the war, I suggested that Jack Buchanan, who was a very well-known musical comedy performer and a great star, and myself should get together and do a revival of *The Last of Mrs Cheyney*. I always loved a good director, so I asked for Tony Guthrie, which was sort of unheard-of, because Tony Guthrie was not a man who was ever likely to do anything like *The Last of Mrs Cheyney*, which wasn't in his sphere at all. To my amazement he said he would be delighted to do it. I'd never worked with him and I'd never met him. We found out that the reason that he did it was that he needed money desperately, not for himself, because he never needed money for himself – he needed it for the Old Vic. They were very short of funds at the Vic. He did it for a percentage of the gross, two and a half per cent I believe. All of that money, I understand, he put back into the Old Vic.

After I got to know him a bit, sometimes I'd go and have dinner with him and Judy at their flat and play with the kittens – with any luck you might have got one for dinner. At that time he said to me, 'You know, it's so ridiculous. You're wasting your time in these plays *The Man Who Came to Dinner*, *My Sister Eileen*, etc. when you should be in the classical theatre.' When Guthrie eventually took over the Vic with Hugh Hunt, I got a call from him saying would I join the company? I was terrified but also fascinated.

So my first jump in was as Emilia in *Othello*. Tony got Michael Langham to direct it; his first job, I think it really was, more or less, from the time he came out of the prisoner-of-war camp. He was very young and looked very ill, but Tony gave him this big break. It was a difficult play, but he did it frightfully well. Towards the end of the season, Guthrie said, 'I've got something absolutely lovely for you. You're going to play Lady Macbeth and *A Midsummer Night's Dream* in Africa.' So I said, 'Oh, lovely, the company's going out there.' About twenty-four hours later, Hugh Hunt came into my room and he said, 'Oh, you're going to play Goneril or Regan, whichever you fancy, starting with Rotterdam and you'll play seven countries in seven weeks and finish up in Finland.' I said, 'This isn't what I've been told by Tony.' I went to Finland. But it was extraordinary that the two people who were joint administrators of the theatre at that time obviously had never got together on it. That's odd, isn't it?

ALFRED ROSSI: *When Tony directed you in the West End piece, do you recall his approach?*

He always put you in the *right* light at the *right* moment and it was up to you to do the rest. He assumed you were employed because you could act, if not, he was willing to *show* you how to act. But he always seemed to shy very much against anything to do with lovers. He hated love scenes. Oh, they seemed to bore him a great treat. So we got to literally within three days of opening *The Last of Mrs Cheyney*, and we had never done the last scene, Jack Buchanan and I – I mean, *at any point*. We were not gritty, but a bit worried. I was sitting on the table in the middle of the stage, with my legs dangling. And Jack and I said, 'What are we going to do? How are we going to do it?' And Guthrie said, 'I think it looks lovely, very unusual sitting on the breakfast table. You do it there.' And it was marvellous, since it was extremely unusual. That was the way it was done. He saw it in Blackpool, which is where we opened before we came to London. We opened in London, but he didn't come to the opening night, and I don't think he *ever* saw the play. We had dinner with him about three or four weeks later and said, 'When are you going to see the play, it might need pulling together.' He said, 'Oh, I'm sure it's lovely.' We had a very jolly dinner and that was the end of that.

Do you have any idea about why he didn't handle those romantic scenes?

It must have been something deep inside himself. Nobody really knew his relationship with his wife, which was obviously very deep. They were very much the same person. People all used to giggle a lot and say, 'Has he married his sister?' As far as one knew, he was not a man that ever had anything to do physically with anybody. There was no talk about him pinching anybody's bottom or giving anybody a cup of tea or banging on the bedroom door on tour or anything of that kind with anybody. So maybe it was something very deep within himself that perhaps was part of his own life that bored him, or might have embarrassed him.

When Tony offered you the role in Tamburlaine *why did you accept it?*

Well, I had seen Guthrie's production with Wolfit at the Vic, and
it had influenced me enormously, because I thought (and I still do) it
was the most beautiful thing I had ever seen. I don't think I've ever
seen anything that excited me more. All the arrows, the cruelty, the
costumes, the extraordinary settings. It was a production that I was
proud to be associated with when I was asked to be in it. I've never
been one of those people who cared very much if I had played the
leading part or the lousiest part. I've always been terribly keen on
what the thing was as a whole. I've never been an actress who skimmed
over a script and said, 'That's fourteen pages. I'm not playing it. I
want to play that one that's fifty-eight pages more', or something like
that.

But the *real* reason I went was because I'd done a play at the Haymarket, which had been a failure. It was the first failure I'd been
associated with. I couldn't stand the barrage of lousy notices. I
thought, 'Well, the place for me is not the theatre. Get out of this job.
You'll never be able to do it again.' I think I'd been out of work something like nine months, and it was obvious that I wasn't going to work
ever again. Guthrie found out, and said, 'What is this I hear about your
not going on the stage again?' I said, 'I simply haven't got the nerve.
I cannot face another first night in London. I'd rather be dead, finished.'
And he said, 'This is ridiculous. It's a great waste, and you're being a
silly girl. But I can see your point and if that's the way you feel, how
would you feel about trying something in another country?' I said,
'In another country I might be able to do it.' And he said, 'Will you
come with me to Canada and be in *Tamburlaine*? If you're away from
all these dreadful horrors of the press that you're so afraid of, then
come with me where it won't be like that.' So I went into *Tamburlaine*.

I was very diffident about it, being in a state of nerves. I felt nervous
being in a strange country. They were marvellous actors, and they had
all come from universities, and they weren't actors as we know them.
They were very dedicated people who had made up their minds to go
into the theatre, like Donald and Murray Davis, Barbara Chilcott, and
all the university boys, like Bill Shatner and Lloyd Bochner who have
gone a long way. I was overawed at this marvellous approach that they
had and their great vitality. I thought, 'Why have I been brought over?
What am I doing here? Oh, I'm terrible.' And Guthrie was always
asking me to do things which I found very difficult, which he seemed

to think that anybody could do. Things like, 'Make your body rigid, and then you'll be lifted up by these men and carried across the stage.' I kept saying, 'Do you want an *adagio* dancer, or do you want an actress?' He said, 'You can do this. I'll show you. If they can lift me, they can lift you.' He fell back and these great big men lifted him up. I was never very comfortable on this bit, I can tell you that. I was always being lifted or being carried on poles.

So I said to Guthrie at rehearsal one morning, 'I feel like a fish out of water. I don't know what I'm doing. I really don't know what I'm doing *at all*. And don't tell me you're putting me in the right light at the right moment.' And he said, 'Aren't you funny? I always thought you a man, and now I find you a mouse. You amaze me.' And I said, 'I'm a mouse, all right.' He said, 'Do you want to know how to play the part?' I said, 'That's the idea. I'd like to know how to play the part.' 'Well then, I'll help you. Would you give up your lunch today?' And I said, 'Certainly.' He said, 'I'll give up my lunch too.' So the company all went off to lunch. I sat in the corner with a dunce's cap on. He took me over it word by word, line by line, like a child. He said, 'You raise your voice here, and you come down with a cadence there, and I want to hear twenty-eight words on that one breath there, and then you'll move two steps there, then you'll move one step back.' And he did it *absolutely* for me. I knew that I had to have something, or I'd have a nervous breakdown, or burst into tears. I was miserable. Whatever 'it' *was*, wasn't coming. In every play, when you have this terrible uncertainty, you *wait* for the breakthrough to come, then it starts to move forward, and when it starts to move forward, you go forward with it, but this wasn't starting to move *anywhere*, except, I thought, it was just going back. It was absolutely marvellous of him, and he fixed it gently, sweetly, and in about half an hour.

Do you think he was a good actor?

Yes. I think he was a wonderful actor. He would have been a wonderful actor had he not been ninety-two feet tall and not been like a *windmill*.

His complete disregard for ordinary conventions was the most marvellous thing. He was always getting off aeroplanes. He always flew Air India, or some *extraordinary* line. And I think his *entire* luggage consisted of something like a very small string bag. He was always ready to go somewhere, like Tel Aviv or somewhere with a string bag. He would absolutely fascinate me. I went to dinner one night, and I *swear* that that dinner was a tin of Kit-E-Kat. I swear it was. I know it was. Judy bustled it up in the frying-pan and put some peanuts on it. He never knew what he was eating or what he wanted to eat. Food meant nothing to him. I don't think he spent any time about that. On another night I went there to dinner. It was a room filled with books and kittens. There were rags and things that the cats sat on, and the kittens everywhere. There was the eternal frying-pan, and the most extraordinary things among his books, which he absolutely adored, like old socks. Old socks hanging down – stiff and everything. The *Lunts* had been there to dinner the night before. I thought, '*How* did they talk to this extraordinary Bohemian?'

I think that the facts of the Lincoln's Inn Fields flat have become myth, the legend of that place seems to have grown like Topsy.

He was playing the piano once and I don't know how, but we got into bull-fighting. I think it was about three years running I'd been to Spain to see the bull fights. He stopped playing and he said, 'That's disgusting. Absolutely disgusting.' And he went on playing the piano. Then somebody said to me, 'Oh, isn't so-and-so attractive?' And I said, 'Oh, no. I don't think he's attractive at all. I don't think he's had a bath for a month. I like all my men scented up, perfumed and put into the water and taken out and absolutely lovely.' And Guthrie stopped playing and said, 'You're the most degenerate woman I ever met in my life. This is quite terrible, since God gave everybody these wonderful odours, this great *smell* that belongs to them alone. The thing that you should love is their smell and everything about their bodies and their perspiration. You're just degenerate with all that scent you want to put on everybody.' And he was cross. It was the only time personally we crossed swords about anything, not that *that* was crossing swords exactly. It was the only time I ever saw him ruffled. That he should get ruffled about that, and yet everything else in his life he took in his stride. People would get drunk, fall down, be sick, but that didn't matter to him. The mere fact that somebody thought people ought to be bathed with lovely soap, that he thought was really the end.

Bringing you back to the Tamburlaine *for a minute. After he had given you that kind of acting lesson, did he give you much direction?*

No, no, because it was absolutely right. He made it fall into place for me, so that I knew exactly what I was doing.

Did you find that that was the type of thing he did with other people?

I never heard that he did it with anybody else. No, because he always assumed that they could do it themselves. But he was extraordinary, because I remember on the morning of the first night of *The Alchemist* in London, which he directed, a great friend of mine, Charles Gray, who was in the company, rang up and said, 'I hope you're not coming tonight.' And I said, 'Yes, I am. Why?' He said, 'Oh, the curtain went up last night on the dress-rehearsal. I don't know what I'm doing.' You see, Tony made the rehearsals so marvellous and everything such fun and such a pleasure to go there for wonderful hours. I never heard anybody complain of being tired or overworked or anything like that. But when the curtain went up, you were absolutely alone, because you didn't have this perpetual marvellous voice, saying, 'That's lovely, dear. Little bit more over there. Oh, lovely, oh that's *very* funny. Oh, yes, we'll *enlarge* on that.' And the curtain went up and one found oneself so terribly alone, without the fun. It suddenly became serious when the audience was there. It was something one was not prepared for, because he was always on the stage. He was always jumping up on the stage or jumping down or improving this or doing that. Suddenly you had to do it without any interruption. And Charles phoned up and said, 'I feel absolutely dreadful. I don't know if I can go on tonight.' I went to the performance, and he was better than any other time in his life. Tony got this wonderful performance out of him, this magnificent performance, which he got out of him day by day by day.

Did you feel that way?

I certainly didn't feel that way in *Tamburlaine* because, God knows, he was there all the time, and he certainly was on the opening night in New York. That was as funny as anything I've known, because they had a very strange wardrobe mistress. I don't think she knew anything about the wardrobe. She had decided, for the opening in New York, that she would *wash* my wig and do it all herself. At the half I was about to get into my wig, struggling like Cinderella and the glass slipper. And then the tears started to come because I couldn't get this thing on. It had shrunk into a *peanut*, and there was no gum. Tony had come in to wish me good luck, and saw my predicament. He shot out of the theatre, saying, 'It'll be all right. It'll be all right.' He ran to a drugstore somewhere, got some gum, came back, and I got the wig on. He cut it up the back with scissors; he did it himself.

That sounds like a high school director who has all these students he has to take care of personally. It's charming. Do you remember any directions he gave you as Helen in Troilus and Cressida?

He explained what he wanted, which was the remnants of a good-looking woman – full-blown, drunken, ridiculous. The whole point of the play was the futility of fighting over a woman not beautiful any more – a woman who for seventeen years had been drinking *steadily*, with big tits and the hair all dyed blonde. She was always chewing her pearls. When she wasn't chewing the pearls, she had a cigarette holder a foot long. It was a divine conception, because there was Paris, the lover, who was as tight as a tick under the piano. He was out like a light. It all took place in this mad summer house, this terrible little conservatory. There was this drunken lady singing on the piano with Pandarus playing and an atmosphere of champagne in everybody's shoe. She was a wild sort of Mae West – this very full-blown rose. They saw that I was dressed in coral-velvet everywhere, with the breasts coming out – one or the other was always coming out. The legs were crossed, and there were these awful shoes that were laced up the leg. It was such a wonderful idea, and in that scene he made the whole point of the play – the futility of war – fighting over this good-for-nothing drunken broad.

Was he a special director in any way for you?

There's never been anybody who has made it the fun that he did. There were laughs all the time even in the middle of the most tragic death scene. 'Look at Miss Clever today. What does she think *she's* doing?' And you're off. I'd just love to have done anything in the world that he wanted me to do. I would have walked over broken bottles to be with him.

Stella Adler

ALFRED ROSSI: *You said that on the first day of rehearsal for* He Who Gets Slapped *you were a bit late and* . . .

STELLA ADLER: He thought I was being starrish. I wasn't. I'm not usually late, but it just happened. He, however, thought that maybe I was playing the star, so he put me in my place. I walked in and he was explaining the set; he stopped and said, 'Don't do that again, Miss Adler.' And then continued speaking about the scenic design.

By the time you worked with him you had worked with Stanislavski and been a member of the Group Theatre. Did those experiences come in conflict with the way Tony directed?

Not at all. He simply gave it to you and made some theatrical suggestions. He never criticized, he didn't bother. He said, 'Go there,' and when he said 'Go there,' a miracle happened. Anybody who saw the production, or evaluated it, could see that the staging was of the utmost importance. He was not a director who bothered the actor, and he certainly didn't bother me. He couldn't get very far with Dennis King, because Dennis gave him exactly what he could give him, so he didn't bother with Dennis.

He was very upset with the *ingénue*, and he finally threw her out. I was very impressed with his patience with her, until one night he asked the cast to rehearse a bow. And he said, 'Miss Adler will lead the bow.' And this little girl – I don't remember her name – was reading the paper while he was giving the direction. And he jumped up from the audience and snatched the paper out of her hand. That was the only time – he was not a man to lose his temper – he did anything like that to give her a warning. I went through the full two periods of rehearsal after his first reprimand and never sat down, never missed a moment, never gave a rehearsal which wasn't a full rehearsal until one day he said, 'Please, Stella, don't give me this much.' He realized that I was being a dedicated and disciplined actress, and wasn't reading the paper while the scene was going on. We'd rehearsed the scene twice all the way around, so I knew he was changing things for other cast members, not changing things for me. I felt I helped him by setting the tone that he had created already and wasn't slacking just because he was re-directing.

I remember that he gave you a lot of room to do what you wanted. For example, he'd say, 'I would like you to do this scene around the table.' But *how* you did it was very much what he respected in the actor. And he let it go even if it was bad. He felt mostly that an actor knows his job, and if he doesn't know his job, then I've made a mistake in casting. He had a very professional attitude towards that. He didn't expect perfection, so if he couldn't get what he wanted, and even if it wasn't good, he'd say, 'Let's settle for that.'

How would you compare, if you can, Guthrie and Stanislavski?

Tony was interested in visuality. Stanislavski was interested in it being all different kinds of theatre, but he was basically interested in the actor. He did such a variety of productions but always finding how the actor could interpret that particular style. Tony assumed, when he engaged the actor, that he would *know* that style. Whereas Stanislavski would *work on* the style with the actors. He was more a teacher. I think when you see the repertoire of both men you realize that they both risked a lot, because their range was so vast. For instance the *Oedipus* that Tony did was incredible. Also *Six Characters* and *Tamburlaine*. That production in England was one of the greatest productions I've ever seen. They messed it up here terribly. It just didn't work. I saw both productions, and I never saw such a difference. His work did not go as well here as it did elsewhere, both because of the economics, and because of the difference in acting experience here. He could depend a great deal upon the actors in England who were used to repertory, who were used to characterization, used to playing different kinds of parts. Whereas here they were all typed.

You said something earlier about his trouble with the Theatre Guild.

Well, he had a certain concept in that particular production in which I was involved. And they changed that concept. They said, 'We want another version. We want a different emphasis.'

Was he able to deal with them or did he have to acquiesce?

He wanted the money. He didn't give a damn about their opinion. I remember being somewhere with him and Binkie Beaumont. Tony

Right: Tyrone Guthrie at a rehearsal of *Tamburlaine the Great*, New York City, 1956.

Below: A Sadler's Wells party in 1933. Seated *L* to *R* are Flora Robson, Judith Guthrie, Charles Laughton, Lilian Baylis. Standing behind Miss Robson is James Mason, behind Miss Baylis are Elsa Lanchester and Tyrone Guthrie.

L to R: Vivien Leigh, Tyrone Guthrie, Laurence Olivier and an unidentified person sitting outside Kronborg Castle at Elsinore, Denmark 1937.

Opposite: Tyrone Guthrie discussing a point in the script of *Top of the Ladder*, St James's Theatre, London, with Toke Townley and John Mills (*L to R*), 1950.

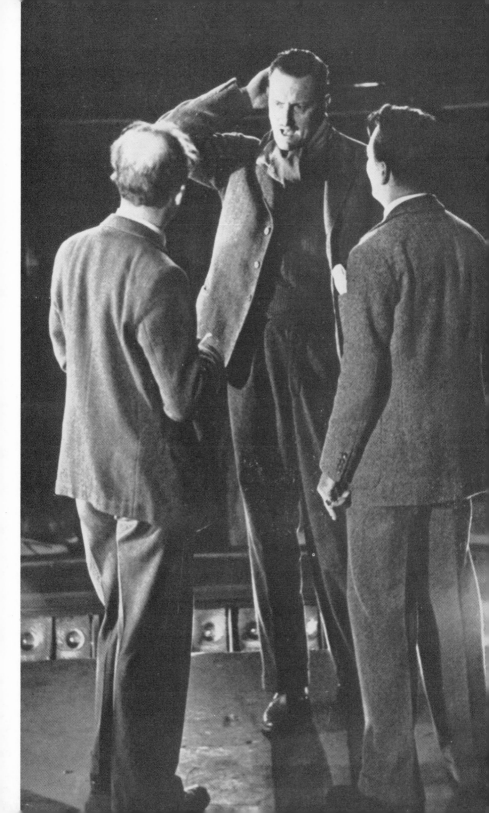

Left: Tyrone Guthrie directing a rehearsal of *The Highland Fair* on the Assembly Hall stage at the Edinburgh Festival, 1952.

Below L to R: Harry Showalter (President of the Board of Stratford Shakespeare Festival) welcomes Judith Guthrie, Tyrone Guthrie, and Tanya Moiseiwitsch to the town in 1953.

treated him like a kid. Beaumont was the big West End producer. Tony didn't care about all that. He wanted to go to Iceland and do a production, to Israel, he lectured all over. He didn't like Broadway, or middle-class successful attitudes, not from actors, not from audiences. He knew himself quite early, earlier than any other man I know of greatness. He didn't care about money, though he probably was a man of money. He told me that last time I saw him that he had this estate in Ireland and it was going to be for old actors. That's when he went on tour to get money for the jam factory in his part of Ireland.

Do you have any particular memories about off-stage experiences?

Of course you know he was very close to Lola Kipness in the end. And so was I. We spent quite a lot of time together. Kipness was dying. And Tony was nursing him. And Mitchell Wilson, to whom I was married, came with me, and we went every other weekend to Connecticut. Tony was there all the time. He left just for a while and then came back and stayed with him and nursed him day and night, right to the end. They were working on the translation of *Uncle Vanya*. They finished that while Kipness was dying, and Tony wanted to be with him. And then he did whatever was necessary.

The morning after Kipness died we spoke for a few minutes, and his attitude towards death was almost 'You damn fool, don't you know it's time to die?' Coldly saying it to me, you know, 'It's time that you die, too.' Something like that. I don't know why he said it. I was struck with it. I think he was in a mood where he was stoical and objective, towards himself, towards Lola, towards life. Also, Kipness went to see Tony a year before he died, and then Tony went and stayed the rest of the time with him. 'I want you to give me your family's picture,' Tony said, 'because I want to belong to your family.' He really wanted to be part of Lola's family. He loved them dearly.

Was he a special director for you?

He was absolutely unique as a director and as a man. He had a unique theatrical mind, and he knew a lot about music and art. I had the good fortune to have worked with some of the great ones: Stanislavski, Reinhardt, Tony Guthrie – they are the big men.

Harry Andrews

HARRY ANDREWS: My first meeting with Tony was when I was a little child, aged six or seven. His father, a well-known ENT doctor, was a friend of my father, and they used to play golf and bridge together. I was taken over there with some ear infection, and his father was terribly sweet and kind to this little child and dealt with the situation. As I was leaving, in came this extraordinary character, who impressed me enormously. Six foot six he must have been, and it was Tony Guthrie. I never forgot it, and many years later when I worked with him, I reminded him that we had met when I was a small child.

ALFRED ROSSI: *Did you note anything about him in this early part of his career that gave you any clue that this was a man who would go down in the annals of theatre history as a great director?*

I think it was unmistakable for a young actor, quite recognizable in every way. His remarkable personality and ebullience and fun and humour, *and humanity* – all these things. He was fifteen years my senior and already established as an important director with this stimulating personality and an entirely original approach to the theatre and to dealing with people. And with such, as I say, humanity and feeling for people, and sense of fun, encouraging actors to do naughty things, and being very patriarchal as well by saying, 'Naughty, naughty' and 'Mustn't.' He was a father figure. He was a mother figure. He was everything that one wanted in the theatre. To a young actor beginning his career he was a god.

Tell me about your experiences with him in Cyrano de Bergerac *at the end of the war.*

I played quite a small part, the Captain of the Cadets. I used to sit out front, because, as I say, my part was very limited. I watched every rehearsal with Tony directing. This was a great joy and experience for me, because really it was directed like a musical comedy, which is what it should be. It's such an unreal play that Tony took it by the short hairs and turned it into a sort of musical comedy. But, of course, there are some scenes which are very striking and are very moving, so that the contrast from the musical comedy to the serious moments were very effective.

At one point in the play Ralph Richardson had this long spiel about the various cadets, which is very poetic and well-translated, but with a whole list of very French-sounding names. He rehearsed it with a very Churchillian French accent, and Tony didn't approve of that and said, 'No, no, no. You must learn how to say it in proper French.' So, the next day he came back and the list was exactly the same as it had been. 'No, no, Ralph. Not good enough. You must do some more work. Can't have it like that. It's really got to be French.' Anyway, two or three days later we're coming up to a dress-rehearsal and still these beautiful French names are coming out like Churchill, and Tony has lost his patience by then. He said, 'No good. Can't do it, can you? I'll get Harry to do it. No reason why he shouldn't do it. He is the Captain of the Cadets.' So, I have to learn the whole speech and do it in front of Ralph and he has to stand there and listen to it. Well, he walked straight off the stage and into his dressing-room and didn't come back again for the whole of that day. Having been told that I had to do it I naturally was embarrassed. But there was never any ill feeling between Sir Ralph and myself. We've been together many times since. It did, I think, make its impression on Ralph, who as far as I recall, never worked with Tony again.

Tony always implied, 'This is how I want to do it. I am the director. If you'd like to come and direct it, all right, come and do it, but I'm paid to do my job and you're paid to do your job. That's it.' That was the principle of it. It's quite right, too. 'If you want to fight me, fight me now – halfway through the production.' That's what he said to me when I was playing Wolsey in his Stratford production of *Henry VIII*. I was then about forty, which was not really old enough to play Wolsey. When I got the offer to do it, I was away somewhere. I wasn't in England, so that I had to send a cable back and say 'Yes' or 'No'. I knew what the other parts in the repertoire were, but I couldn't really quite believe this one, because I thought, 'This is an extraordinary bit of casting. Let's have a look at the play, and I'll see whether I can tackle it.' But the idea of working with Tony in his production was irresistible. I knew it wasn't ideal casting, but I thought there are ways one can do it, and it was a challenge. So when it came to actually doing it, obviously there were problems for me. Tony, knowing my potential and weaknesses no doubt, got me to play it as the butcher, which, in some respects, was dead right. But I couldn't really be the *fat* butcher, more the coarse butcher, the *parvenu* with a quick, brilliant brain. This was the approach and very exciting it was to work under his direction with this idea in mind, which is rather different from the conventional approach to Wolsey.

I remember the final speech, which is a most famous one. Tony said very early on in rehearsal, 'Everybody knows this speech. It's such a bore. They'll all be following it with their books in the front row. So throw it away, dear.' Now this naturally went against one's whole instinct, because it's a great speech and probably the only important one that's really written by Shakespeare anyway. But one looked at it again and tried to think, 'Now, how can you throw it away?' One was encouraged to do so in rehearsal – just let it all go very quickly as if it were nothing. He said, 'We just get to the end, and then you can have your fit and have a nice death and that's all lovely, but let's get on with it.' And, of course, when we got to the first night I did as I was asked, and it was all thrown away. One was castigated by the critics for doing so. Guthrie himself had the sweetness and humanity to come around and say, 'I was wrong, dear. Do it your way. Just find your own way with it. But I'm coming out every night for the next seven days, so don't over-indulge.' He'd himself over-indulged in some business that he had great delight in – at the end of the play, where the Princess Elizabeth wetted her christening gown, and the Nurse had to mop it up. There were great laughs from the audience. It was all too much, and it was cut out the next night, so it only lasted one performance.

There are some descriptive accounts about your final demise in the arms of Cromwell. How did that particular bit of stage action evolve?

Eventually it did work beautifully. He was a very small actor, and I am very tall. I think Tony saw this as an interesting physical relationship. Also, there was sort of a love relationship between them. Wolsey's physical fall mirrored every other fall. He has a stroke really. This was Tony's idea, and a very good one. It was a complete physical collapse of a big man into the arms of a silly little weak man right down fore-stage. So when he said at the end, 'Take me,' we went down these steps into a sort of dungeon below. This little man supporting and collapsing under this big man. All of this is being encouraged by Tony, at least for the first night. One played it with more dignity later on, but he did encourage one to do it that way, and it got laughs, which it really shouldn't have. One quickly adjusted it, but it was a little bit naughty, I suppose. I think he did it because he thought it'd be rather fun. Send it up a bit. But, as I say, he did have the grace later on to say, 'Well, I think I was wrong.' I found the scene very moving. He didn't want to be moved, really. If only I had fought him earlier and more strongly – I remember him saying, 'Fight me now.' I said, 'Well, Tony, all my instincts are against it, but I'm in your hands. I'm just your slave.'

At this time were he and Judy living on the punt on the Avon?

Yes, indeed they were. We used to take a little time off to go way up, about three or four miles up the river. One evening we were going up there, and we saw two very remarkable figures sitting on the banks of the Avon stark naked. It was Tony and Judy. We got a little wave and 'Have a little drink', and so on. They used to punt down to rehearsal, and then he'd change into some clothes for rehearsal and back again in the evening. She'd do the shopping, and we used to have picnics with them. They'd always be naked. It didn't matter who was coming up the river. It wouldn't necessarily be actors. It could be local people. And they camped out in a field or on the punt itself. There were thunderstorms occasionally and they got drenched, but it didn't matter. It was their life, and they loved it.

Andrew Cruickshank

ANDREW CRUICKSHANK: The first time I ever worked with Tony very intensely and revealingly was in the modern-dress *Hamlet*, with Guinness as Hamlet, and I played Claudius. I don't think he was totally happy working on that, but then I don't think he was very good on great plays.

ALFRED ROSSI: *What do you mean by that?*

Well, I think there was a basic dichotomy in his mind about great plays. He *knew* that all the heroes were really thugs, and what made them great was the poetry. But he could never get past the thuggery and really appreciate the poetry for the greatness involved. Something like that was in the back of his mind, because he was always inclined to *diminish* great characters. He never did *King Lear*, for instance. I think he shied away from it, because he was really out of sympathy with that sort of thing.

However, the point I'm getting at is this particular *Hamlet* was one of the finest ones that has ever been done, because he was working with a young cast. One thing he liked doing was working with a young cast on a play like this, which he was doing in a completely novel way. He was trying something new in the modern dress, which had not been done for many years. Barry Jackson had done it lots of years before, but this was the first time it was being done rather like some contemporary pictures of the Danish court with the long naval uniforms and things like that. He wanted us to tell the story with great rapidity.

As far as my own character was concerned, he had taken a line out of Harley Granville-Barker's preface: he said that Claudius could be so attractive. And, indeed, it's just an enormous part, which, but for the gap where he's not on and the soliloquies, almost takes over the play to a certain degree. I remember it for its great pace and sensuality, because Guthrie was an enormous sensualist – I don't know if he was impotent or not – but I think he was a tremendous sensualist in the theatre, almost overtly so. There was almost a naïveté about this aspect of him. His imagination was tremendous, as you know – the sort that made an *enormous* impression on this country.

Hamlet we took abroad in the spring of 1939. And they said, 'Oh, you can't take this abroad, because this will confirm what Hitler and Mussolini have said about the English – that they are decadent, taking one of their great plays, *Hamlet*, in modern dress.' Well, of course, the reaction when we got to Italy was simply phenomenal, because they hadn't seen anything from England in a long time, and seeing a Guthrie production, with all its invention – not gimmicks. . . . For example, there was a great play scene when they took off arc lamps and shone them right round the audience, and the place went absolutely *wild*. And played with such pace and movement, that it simply took the Italians' breath away. They'd never seen anything like it. We had to cancel performances of other plays in order to do this particular one in various places. That was the sort of effect it had.

You played in one of the Henry VIII productions at Stratford.

Yes, in 1950 he asked me to go down to Stratford and play Wolsey. It's not a great play of Shakespeare, but as directed by Guthrie it almost became a great play, because of his invention. As far as the character of Wolsey was concerned he was a great churchman. And Tony didn't like that at all. I think one day he said, 'Can you play it with a stick or something, as though you had gout?' Well, of course, this was all against the view of Wolsey as a great cleric, whom people regard so much in the way of his last line, 'Had I but served my God with half the zeal with which I serve my King he would not in mine age have left me naked to mine enemies.' This redeems the whole character. Not for Guthrie. He saw the *awful* politics and chicanery behind the Catholic Church, and everything like that.

There's a line when Henry comes on, and things are very difficult between himself and Wolsey, and between himself and the Catholic Church. And he can't get away from Katherine, and he comes on the stage and says, simply, these words, 'My learned and well-beloved servant, Cranmer' and takes Cranmer off with him. Now as Guthrie produced this on the stage – there is a court in high session with Wolsey in his chair, and Tony Quayle as Henry comes on absolutely full of gout. He stands and looks and says, 'My learned and well-beloved servant . . .' And Wolsey rises to come forward to him, and takes a couple of steps. '. . . Cranmer.' And there's a great bank of English priests there. At the very back this little figure of Cranmer winds his way through all the priests, and then Henry takes him in his arms and leads him off for some sort of conference. In this one moment on the stage there is the Reformation. Everything is concentrated into this – there's the difference between the Catholic Church, the English Church, and Henry. 'My well-beloved servant . . . Cranmer!'

There was another amazing bit of production just towards the end of the play when Elizabeth is born and she is going to be baptized with priests and the whole lot. He got about sixteen soldiers from the Warwick Barracks, which were quite near, to come along. There was music written for the play by Cedric Thorpe Davie, a Scotsman. And Guthrie said, 'Now you chaps stand up on the stage. Let me see you three there and you three there and you three there and you three there, just like that. Now, I'm going to beat out thirty-two and you're going to walk round and make any pattern you like as you walk between yourselves. But by the time I've made thirty-two you will be back precisely in your same positions. Do you understand? Right. Ready . . . one, two . . . three . . . four . . .' and he counted right up to thirty-two. And these chaps began to weave about themselves, and then they got back. And after two or three rehearsals, being soldiers, they did it *jolly well* you see, and you've got a real sort of pattern. He said, 'Now I'm going to give you poles. Do exactly the same sort of thing again.' And he counted the music and these poles became, as it were, flags. During the actual production of the play the poles had flags, with emblems on them. And the effect of these chaps, just before the baptism of Elizabeth, moving round in this staging was absolutely phenomenal. You felt that the whole stage was a riot of colour. Only someone like Guthrie could really imagine this sort of thing.

Since you've also worked with Granville-Barker, could you compare him with Tony?

I think one of the things about the English theatre during that particular period of time, from say 1920 to 1940, was that there was no *great* English director. Barker *should have* been and indeed, if Shaw had had his way, Barker would have been *the* great English director, but he was half an academic, as well as a very fine actor. And he would much prefer to go away to Paris and write his books. Much to Shaw's disgust. So there was a real vacuum to fill here. It was filled to some extent by people like Komisarjevsky and Saint-Denis. But there was no real English director until John Gielgud started directing.

Tony broke new ground as far as movement and the whole elasticity of the stage was concerned. But at the same time, he didn't have the intellectual depth of a Barker. Barker talked about *King Lear* and directed it in ways in which Tony simply could not have done. Barker would analyse *Lear* to set definite patterns on the stage, so it was an absolute mosaic. He would give you very specific interpretations of the lines, because there's a tremendous amount of ambiguity in *King Lear*. Guthrie would never interpret lines. He would just say, 'This must all go very much quicker' or slower, something like that. And one would know what to do, because one is helped enormously in Shakespeare by the simple beat of the thing.

Is there a role that you wish Guthrie had directed you in?

I'd like to have been directed by him in some plays by James Bridie, the Scottish dramatist. Guthrie's first West End play was Bridie's *The Anatomist*, by the way. Some of these I would like to have done with him. Because of my being a Scotsman, you see. And, of course, he did a very famous production of a thing called *The Three Estates*. That was one of the great blobs which I made, when it was produced at the second Edinburgh Festival which was in 1948. He tossed the script to me and said, 'Read it, and play what you want.' So I read it and I simply couldn't understand it, and I said, 'Terribly sorry, Tony, I can't understand it at all.' It was written in early Scots, you see. But there, *there* I must confess, I had completely underestimated his own capacity for really making things live, whether people understood them or not. Amazing invention he had. I don't think we've got anyone now who can make the stage come alive as well as he did.

Stanley Baxter

STANLEY BAXTER: I suppose the most extraordinary thing was for somebody young to work with Tony Guthrie. It was marvellous for them, because he loved working with young people. He loved building up parts, and he was famous for taking the star part and slightly underplaying it, and that's why a lot of stars weren't so keen on working with him. But younger players who thought they were engaged to carry a spear ended up falling over them, tripping, you know, having a big comedy part, when they thought they were going to stand looking like statues while actors spoke in front of them. Tony absolutely hated that idea – of people being unimportant; no matter how small. He had a tremendous humility. I think also he was probably a great ascetic.

ALFRED ROSSI: *What do you mean by that?*

Well, I mean that when he was directing at Stratford-on-Avon, he slept on a skiff or something with his wife. He was, you know, a giant. She was a giantess.

Someone said once, and I don't think it was meant to be disrespectful, that she looked like Tony in drag.

Yeah, absolutely. But they were cousins, you see. And they were almost the same height. And with her very severe hairstyle it emphasized their similarities. And they slept, literally, on this skiff, with a tarpaulin. If you can imagine this giant and giantess, sleeping on the Avon, and when it rained pulling a *tarpaulin* over them. He almost made his life a cult of simplicity, eschewing the fleshpots, and he felt that all actors should be acolytes in a kind of religious ceremony.

I think he felt about the theatre that it was taking over from the dying churches of the world. I think he felt that after all the beginning of the theatre was liturgical, because even Dionysus, you could say, was religion. And he felt that it had lost its way and that he was, in a sense, the high priest that was bringing it back to its true roots. And the acolytes were always easier to proselytize in this kind of religion, and therefore he aimed at them as a Jesuit might. But how much more entertaining than any Jesuit I've ever met. So that he was a great entertainer. I mean he really directed through entertaining his casts.

And, although he dominated every production with which he was associated, he didn't dominate it in the way that most directors feel they have to dominate – by discipline, by talk, because I mean *his* talk was telegraphic, as you know, and where other people say, 'Let's all sit round and mull this thing over . . .' and the Method and in this country Peters Hall and Brook, you know. You hear them all sitting round and putting paper hats over their heads, instead of getting on with it. And Guthrie, I mean, would loathe that. Because his type of direction was essentially pragmatic. And although everyone thinks of him as a master showman in the sense that he could handle vast crowds and pageants with particular ease – I'm sure people thought that he did this with megaphones – the idea, when you saw a Guthrie production, was that this man must have stood on a hill, as it were, and roared instructions like Cecil B. de Mille, either personally or through an assistant. And, as you know, having worked with him, that was not how it happened. He said once that a producer should be a sort of chairman of proceedings. He was much more than that. But he never, *ever*, imposed his will on actors, in a disciplinary sense. If he were doing it, he was doing it so subtly. If immediately an actor couldn't do a direction that he gave them, he would think, 'What is wrong with that direction, that he's not getting it? Why am I not getting through?' The communication had to be very, very fast, with him. I think they're calling it lateral thinking these days, aren't they? And he had this great gift of lateral thinking. 'This person is not doing this correctly. I wonder why?' A couple of questions, a couple of gags, try to relax them, realize *why* they couldn't do it. Instead of a year's analysis, in two questions go to the very root of the matter, and a second later he was giving them the very life-line that they needed to continue with the part. This was his extraordinary thing.

There were soldiers in the castle that we used for the production of *The Three Estates*, and he got them to do fantastically difficult things, not by drilling them, and you would have thought well, that's obviously been given as drill movements and rehearsed to within an inch of its life. The assumption was that he was dealing with as intelligent men as any actors there and so the direction was minimal. But what it did do was never patronize. So that consequently he spoke to them exactly as he would to a star of the show, because God knows he hated that word; and to everyone's astonishment – not to his, because obviously he had experienced how this worked but certainly to our amazement – they all did it and they did it because he flattered them, in a sense. He implied, 'Here's something I'm just assuming that you can do, because I believe in your worthwhileness as human beings and in your intelligence.' And flags would go and create carpets and in patterns, not by saying, 'That is to go there and that is to join into that.' It was something like, 'Want you all to take the flagpoles, make a great sweep and create a great circular carpet at the feet.' The assumption was that it *would* happen – only if it failed would he say anything else. Now the times that he didn't need to go on and say anything else was a measure of the man.

Now the first time that you worked with Tony Guthrie was in The Three Estates?

Yes. And the first time that I had ever worked in the professional theatre, in fact. I didn't even have an interview with him, because he had left the engaging of the bit parts to the manager of the Citizens' Theatre of Glasgow at that time, who was an Englishman called Colin White. I went along, read the part. He didn't know what it was all about. I *barely* knew what it was all about because it was medieval Scots and very difficult, even for somebody born and brought up in Scotland as I was. And I read it with panache, if not with great understanding, and he thought I was the best of a bad bunch that he had heard and said, 'Well, you've got it. And it's going to pay you eight pounds a week, a bit more than we'd pay you for playing at the Citizens', because you're staying away from home, forty miles away in Edinburgh.' And I was delighted, 'cause it got me launched.

And I turned up on the appointed day, at the Assembly Hall in Edinburgh, the first time it had ever been used for a secular purpose as far as I know, because it was the Assembly Hall of the Kirk, the Church of Scotland, headed by this nonconformist pope called the Moderator. And so the invasion of the Assembly Hall by *actors* was, in itself, a revolutionary thing. But the fact that it was a medieval *morality* play seemed to make it all right. It had the Establishment behind it, it had the word 'morality' behind it. But if they had known what Tony was going to do with the Virtues – the Chastity and Verity and so on, they might not have given their premises so readily. But we got it.

It was the first time he had worked on an apron stage on this scale, which was especially constructed for him. It excited him incredibly because he realized from now on mainly what he was going to do was work on open stages.

Did he ever talk about his idea of the staging concept?

Yes, he did. But, again, it never became a *talk* in the sense of 'Let's all sit round'; no, it never was that. I think if I'd known him better, he might have – over enormous portions of Welsh rarebit, because he could eat three to everybody else's one, he was a very big bloke – he maybe would talk about it to actors, older Scottish actors that he knew well. But with me, no. He realized he had somebody completely raw, and he was just going to make it work.

But he did keep saying to all the cast, 'Remember, you have to keep revolving. There's no use speaking constantly to one part of the house' or 'Get anchored in your mind the pictorial stage of Inigo Jones. We've here got people on all three sides and each and every single one of them wants to hear it. And it's got to work so that you're turning really all the time through 270 degrees.' And so, consequently, he kept us moving circularly, almost right round sometimes.

And, of course, the Spiritual Estate, Spirituality, was above, rather like the Shakespearian stage in which they had the balcony above and the entrances beneath. Kind of Gothic entrances which, I think, he used later at both Stratfords. And the Spiritual Estate sat up there, so that sometimes people were on the steps of the apron way in front looking up at the Spiritual Estate and addressing them. He would say something like, 'Lechery, lean forward. Try and see down the front of her dress. You're all completely venal, completely corrupt, the medieval Catholic Church.' So the people often weren't facing the audience at all, and the voice had to project. If you were speaking to that part of the stage it bounced off the one bit of scenery you had, which was solidly constructed, backwards into the auditorium. Otherwise, the rule was simply to keep turning in circles and never to go to one part of the hall for too long.

When did you first meet Tony?

It was the very first day of rehearsal, and I was sitting alone in one of the pews and he came towards me from the other side of the hall over the apron stage and then I realized, with horror, that he was about to address me. And he said, 'Are you Stanley Baxter? My name's

Tyrone Guthrie. Very nice to have you with us. Really nothing for you to do today. Might get to you at four o'clock but certainly if you want to you could vanish till then, or at least till three-thirty, shall we say.' Nothing on earth was going to make me vanish, *ever at all*. I was going *to sit there* and watch every single bit of it. I knew quite a bit about his work, even by that time, and was very excited at the prospect of working with him. And after the first day, wild escaping horses wouldn't have dragged me away, *at any time at all*.

But there it was, the most unpromising subject in the world, a medieval morality play in unintelligible Scots playing to an international audience at the second Edinburgh Festival with bookings absolutely *minimal*. It had one of the greatest successes, if not *the* greatest success, that had happened at any Festival in the drama field and after opening night there was a rampage for tickets. It was a success such as one dreams of in our business.

And he was off that night, he didn't even wait till the next day. We were all in improvised dressing-rooms and in the corridors of the Kirk, and you know, with canvas curtains up and tin wash-basins. And he *loved* all that, he loved actors in that kind of situation, that's how it should be always – rogues and vagabonds. And they started cheering; it was a very distinguished audience, distinguished in the fact that it was a lot of people who were up from London, directors who knew his work and star performers who had misgivings about what he was doing, I'm sure, when they arranged to go and see it. By the end of the performance they were on their feet, and there was a kind of ovation such as I've very seldom heard in any building. The call, of course, was 'Producer . . . producer . . . producer', which gradually built up into a kind of chant which he might have directed *himself*. And they were stamping and stamping their feet and they wouldn't stop. And while they were doing it Guthrie was popping his head over the canvas and saying, 'Think they liked it, must rush, catching the eleven o'clock train. Don't know when I'll see you all again, do hope it'll be soon, God bless, bye-bye.' 'But, Tony, they're still calling for you.' 'Yes, smarter to leave them wanting more. Bye.'

Wonderful. You do a wonderful impersonation of him.

Well, I do mimicry a lot. But that's certainly one voice I shall never forget.

What were some of your experiences in The Three Estates?

I played very small parts in the first and second productions of the play. The first year I was the messenger of God's messenger, who had this very showy little moment, in which he heralded the arrival of God's messenger. It was only about nine or ten lines, but he built this up into an electrifying moment, theatrically. It was a fast thing, it wasn't something we talked about at all. He had already made himself known to me in the way I've described, by coming across and introducing himself. And then he came to my moment and said, 'Stanley, we've got to you now. Now, I want you to come down one of those aisles with the broadsword held high above your head. It's very heavy, so hope you're going to manage it all right, sure you will. Want you to come to the centre of the stage with great speed. Remember to keep revolving as you speak. Let's see you do it.' And I did it.

And he said, 'Fine. Don't like the way you're running up the stairs. Think it would be more interesting if you took them two at a time, broadsword or no. Also you're taking far too many breaths. I don't think you should breathe until you get to . . .' and he named the sentence. 'Take the breath to run down there. Get the breath back once the sword is planted between your feet. Then not another breath until . . .' and he mentioned the line. And I did it.

'Good. Now I want you to take those stairs three at a time, will look even more effective. And also I think we can go longer on the breath. Only take one breath in the whole speech. Keep revolving. I like the *trumpet* notes.' So, with encouragement, one did it.

And when I'd done it something like three times, four times at the very most, he then started directing what would happen when I arrived there, and I realized that this is where the juicy bit came in. That the entire cast were going to prostrate themselves at my feet, and create carpets of medieval clothes and terrible noises like 'Auaahhh', you know. So it was going to be a moment in which I'm there in medieval soldier's costume with a broadsword high above the head like a crucifix being gradually brought between the thighs, and then the revolving round using the point of the sword as a sort of compass. And after I'd done it for the fourth time he said, 'Excellent. On.' And that was it.

I mean, that's all the direction I ever got from him. He never over-directed. This was what was great about it. That's why I can't stand these chatterers, directors who want to talk about it all the time. I mean he could convey anything he wanted to convey so quickly. But then he was a great psychologist. He understood actors and he knew the ones that needed the kick up the ass, and he knew the ones that needed cuddling. He had a great sense of what an actor needed, it was quite extraordinary.

Was there any notable difference between the first and second productions of The Three Estates?

Well, I'm afraid it will sound terribly vain, but the thing about the second production was that it did involve me pretty closely. Because, at that time, God knows I wish I still had it, I had a very good memory, and when it came to having worked with Guthrie it made such a deep impression that having watched it all, there was *nobody's* part I didn't know, in the sense of where they moved, at what moment they moved, at which line they moved. And of course I'd also been with it for something like three weeks, when he had vanished right after the first night. And so the second year there was partly a new cast, which explains some of it, and a lot of the people were older than me and their memories weren't naturally as good for this reason. Even doing a second year bored him. He'd done it. So I could see now a flicker of boredom, which to me, at that age, was absolutely inexplicable. And he'd say, 'Can't remember what happened here.' And I was practically like a schoolboy, had my hand up, you see. 'Stanley, obviously you remember.' 'Yes, he rushed down the stairs, she came round to the train, he sat down, then she from that direction went from there to there,' etc. 'How extraordinary, that's exactly what to do.' And that was it. He would say, 'Did you all understand that? Well, do it.'

Then naturally I thought he was going to want to change bits, so I mustn't, you know, do the hand up too often, or he would suddenly turn round on me and say, 'May I change my own production?' So I was very timorous about doing it. But again and again it was he who would say, 'Stanley, what did we do here?' It became a kind of joke with the cast. So obviously anyone whom he'd impressed that much – it's very flattering to a director. But, as you know, if you're that age, it stamps itself on you.

What do you recall about working on the play Guthrie wrote, Top of the Ladder?

I remember weeping as he directed that. He felt it very deeply, obviously, because he had written it. His direction then changed in style. When I came to work with him on it, there was a different Guthrie, because he used the style that was needed for the play. And sometimes with clapping of hands, sometimes snapping of fingers. When he was at the very back of the stalls, you could hear that click of the fingers to mean, 'Stop, I want to say something.'

When he came to direct *Top of the Ladder* there was a scene in which the father was dying – and I was playing the son – and it was a highly stylized play: there were people in modern dress but they chanted like a Greek chorus, saying, 'He looks the image of his dad. He's damaging the look of his id.' And I remember the lady I subsequently married who was playing one of those ladies saying that at the first reading in one of the little dressing-rooms at the Citizens' Theatre where they had awful gas fires with broken clay – Guthrie loved that kind of setting because it wasn't grand, you see, it was terribly down to the kind of monastic and ascetic atmosphere that he liked – he was sitting there and she said, 'What does "id" mean?' 'Later.' So we went on with the reading.

And I remember about three days later he was directing the scene in which the father was dying and he directed that by stealthily moving like an invisible giant among the performers, whispering in their ears. Extraordinary thing. I mean, it just worked, like everything he did, you know. So magnificent. And I remember I would address the father and say, 'You never cared about me . . .' He was a semi-James Dean, a rebel. And then he realizes he's being unkind and too harsh and that the man is dying, and Guthrie would come up and touch you very lightly on the shoulder and say, 'Help him, terribly frail.' And then he'd vanish again, out to the perimeter and appear to be quite distracted. And then he'd sidle up, and you sometimes didn't even hear what he was saying to the other performer. But he'd come back again and say, 'Go and think about that. Perch on the edge of the desk. That brings memory back.' And this is another kind of direction which suited. And by the time he had finished he was really giving a performance of himself, like a kind of chorus, to the action of the play he'd written. And I ended up with tears absolutely streaming down my face. I don't think one ever played it quite as realistically as one was able to do with him going on like that.

This is a very obvious question, but do you feel that you were playing him?

Yes. Oh I don't think there's any doubt that the son was Guthrie himself.

Did he imply that in his work with you?

Well, he didn't, except in that same gas-filled reading in which he said, 'Don't know if gals feel the same about their mothers. Do they?' But that was all.

That was enough, I would say. You seem to imply that there was a difference in approach. It seemed to be gentler, less overt, less showy.

Yes, it was nudgy. The direction was given on the wing. He didn't get into any – as the kids would say – ego trips about it. I mean the whole thing couldn't have been more egotistical, in the sense that everybody was *hanging* on his every word, I mean what bigger ego trip can you get? But at the same time you didn't get a feeling that he was stopping and entertaining people because, 'Aren't I clever?' But it really was *for* something, it was about helping the next development of the piece or the character of the person he was directing.

It was often done very quietly by sidling past and saying, 'Do you think you have a stutter maybe?' or something as simple as that. Or at the back saying, 'I want all the flags to be made into a great circular carpet', and getting non-actors to *do* it. Without saying any more. Because the charisma is such that, if he says 'Do it' I can do it. And so people were working at the *zenith* of their confidence. And what people can do when they are working at the zenith of their confidence is extraordinary to behold. Because bad directors *sap* belief or the suspension of disbelief. And Tony constantly made you feel that with this leader it cannot not happen. It was like the disciples I'm sure must have felt when Jesus chatted them up. You cannot believe it's not true because the charisma is so great. I don't know if he was as entertaining as Tony.

It would seem almost as though the audience is frosting on the cake. I mean, 'We've had a lot of fun and hopefully they'll enjoy it but if they don't . . .'

'If they don't, tough titty.' Absolutely. And he understood, as very few directors did, how it can be a kind of nightly crucifixion for an actor working along all the wrong lines with the wrong direction and a wrong part, miscast perhaps. And so he knew that what he was asking us to do wasn't an easy thing. I think that's why he could never bear to watch them do it for even a second time. He was notorious for *refusing* to go back and ever tidy up, and distraught stage directors and company managers would phone up and say, 'Tony, you've got to come back.' 'No, that's your job, do what you can. I'm off to Israel tomorrow.' And that was it, they never got him back again.

Why do you think he didn't want to go back?

I think he thought if he saw it again that there might be a call on him to stop being Father Christmas. And he enjoyed being loved, very, very much. If you go from entertaining a cast to actually having to give notes and say, 'Now at that point you were too loud', and 'Why are you doing this?' well, that was a *chore* and at that point it was boring to have to do it and not very creative, because it was going over ground that we'd all covered. And it would also be 'Smart to leave them wanting more', I mean, applying to the actors as well as to the audience. So there was very real ego at work there. But the ego was the ego of St Augustine. It was an ego of fantastic personal humility.

But stars didn't like working with him so much. And that's the significant thing because I think the thing that annoyed him about stars is that they were stars. I mean the very fact that they were stars and maybe had homes in Sunningdale was enough to make him froth at the mouth. I wouldn't be at all surprised if he's sitting on Olympus today saying, 'There's the Burtons on their jewelled way to an outdoor location. Let's piss down.' I mean, it wasn't quite Christian, his view of stars. It was unreasonable. But it was there. It was very much a puritanical view of people that were earning far too much money.

There was one very distinguished knight that I worked with once. And he took me to lunch at his club, and I liked him very, very much, and I said, 'You've worked a lot with Tony Guthrie. Lovely, we'll be able to reminisce about him. Wasn't he wonderful?' 'Well, certainly most people thought so. I couldn't myself relate to him well. It was terrible.' And one couldn't believe one's ears, you know. It was like being told there's no Santa Claus, over lunch. I sort of choked on the broccoli, and said, 'What on earth do you mean?' And he said, 'Well, Tony sent for my wife once and said, "I can't do anything with him, undirectable." No,' he said, 'I couldn't please Tony.' And I just sat there miserably unhappy.

I said, 'Well, do you think that's what he thought you needed? That's terribly unlike him to obtain any results through pain, it was almost always through joy.'

And he said, 'Well, he was better with younger people, I think,

131

really. After all, the Old Vic had been established for so long by then, and we were all somewhat famous, and I don't think he liked that so much. Maybe he wanted to make us suffer a little for this reason. It didn't seem a good enough reason, because you know I've suffered as much as any other actor.'

I said, 'Well, you gave a marvellous performance in the end, although I know that the end doesn't really justify the means. And his means were usually a joy.' 'Yes, everybody says that, I couldn't get on with him.' So that's the other side of the coin. And I was always very grateful that I had worked with him early and not when I became pretty well known.

I know there was one girl, an awfully nice girl who came up to do a part in *The Queen's Comedy*, had made some movies. She hadn't become any great star, but she had been earning a living in British films. And this alone seemed to upset him, and a couple of times I thought he was terribly harsh with her, which was so untypical. And I was equally convinced that this was the reason why. He became almost pompous. She was playing the part of a flibbertigibbet, as indeed everybody in Heaven was meant to be totally decadent and uncaring about the mortals that prayed to them every night in their slit trenches. And she was playing this decadent sophisticate, and she had a posy of flowers on a kind of silver loop and started swinging them idly at her side – seemed like business that would seem reasonable, for somebody as uncaring as that, and Guthrie suddenly snapped, 'Don't do that with those flowers. They're God's.' And it was all of a sudden a terribly kind of John Knox thing to say and awfully untypical of him. So, again, I think she'd made a few quid in movies and wasn't going to come up here and queen it over the company. She was going to be quickly chastened and put in her place. But the girl was shitting herself, I mean she was just terrified, you know. It wasn't fair. And you can't present a rounded picture of Guthrie without including that type of thing, because unless one does, one really paints the portrait of someone completely superhuman, which in 'most every way he was. But things like that proved even Tony Guthrie was a human being and not a god. But, thank Christ, he did have weaknesses of *some* sort.

The Messianic quality that he had. One reads about men like this in history whom, simply, people followed. Like Alexander the Great and so on. They had this thing. And Tony had it. It was wonderful, it was thrilling. Because you felt you were on the winning side.

Another thing he did: he would sometimes say, 'It's become very static, nothing very much has been happening for three minutes. Would like all the soldiers to lift their halberds, walk right round the stage, go back to exactly the same positions as you were in the first place – great sillies will never notice.' He had this thing about audiences being 'great sillies'. Nobody was fooled by it because, of course, audiences are made up of individuals. But an audience is a corporate body and less intelligent than the parts of the whole, that is true. But nevertheless it wasn't said with any of that meaning.

It was just, 'Don't let the bastards frighten you before you've even met them.' And that 'We have the tricks; we have Pandora's Box here, and we are going to keep them blinded with magic, because no matter whether it's "Clive Thing" or "Ten Kynan" or whoever's sitting out there, we are on top of them, because they don't know what we are going to do from minute to minute, and they must *never* be able to anticipate accurately and for sure, or we're boring them. So that if we keep a few jumps ahead, we are the bosses, we're calling the tunes, we are the people that have been revealed when the curtain drew back, and it's a box of tricks. Follow me like the Pied Piper.' He didn't even have to say that. We just did it. 'And we'll keep ahead of those great sillies. We'll just keep astonishing them.' Which was another one of his great phrases when someone would say, 'How should I do this?' Sometimes he used to say it like a comic. He kept using the same gags in different parts of the globe, and it's only when you meet up finally that you realized that he had a sort of repertoire which made actors laugh. And why not? You're dealing with Israelis one minute and Scots the next and with people in Canada or America the next. And *that* phrase I've heard quoted more than once from many different sources. If ever he was asked, 'What should I do with this scene, it's an awfully difficult thing and I . . . any ideas, Tony? What can I . . .? Tell me something.' And he often said, 'Absolutely no idea. Go home, think about it, come back and astonish us in the morning.'

John Mills

ROBERT HARDY: *Mr Mills, the first question I want to ask you is when did you first come across Tony Guthrie, and what effect did that first meeting have on you?*

JOHN MILLS: Well, I first came across Tony when I was going through a very bad time myself. I'd stayed out of work for about nine months, trying to get out of musical comedies and wanting to get back into the straight theatre again, and I was at the Oliviers', having a drink, and Tony Guthrie blew in and said that he was doing a season at the Vic, and he was doing *A Midsummer Night's Dream* and *She Stoops To Conquer*, and Larry said, 'Johnny wants to get back on to the straight stage again; there's the man to play Puck.' And Tony said, 'I couldn't possibly afford him.' It was £15 a week. I convinced him that it was on the level, that I wanted to do it, and that's how I got into that season in 1938 and that was a marvellous experience for me, because I had never worked with Tony before.

What method did you see Guthrie using, not only with you, but with other people, in any part?

I don't think he had a method. I think that he was totally anti-method, as far as I'm concerned, and the extraordinary thing about Tony was that he treated everybody differently. He would handle Teddy Chapman quite differently. He would handle Ursula Jeans differently, Bobby Helpmann differently, Dottie Hyson differently, and he had this gift of making light of something, but making it terribly important at the same time. He would laugh at himself all the time, if he thought he was getting highfalutin'.

Do you think that Tony would laugh a great deal at this solemn collection of people's recollections which is going on now?

I think he would, yes. I think he'd have a ball.

But do you think he would also enjoy it? Do you think he would rather approve?

I think he would. He was a great theatre man, wasn't he? I'd love to think somebody was doing all this about me.

Can we go on to Top of the Ladder, *his own play? Can you tell us something about how that started, how you first came to read the script?*

Yes. I was acting in Mary, my wife's, play, up in Glasgow, and she came tearing along to the matinée in a great state of excitement and said she'd seen a fantastic play, which was *Top of the Ladder*, which was done at the Citizens', and I could only see about ten minutes of it, because I was playing at the same time. She was absolutely mad about it, and then she got the script for me and I read it, and I fell for it completely. I thought it was way ahead of its time, and of course it was, because it was a commercial flop. Then we got it laid on and Larry Olivier said he would do it, and we did it at the St James's. Then I saw – fault is probably the wrong word – I saw a weakness of Tony's, in that I don't think he should ever have done his own writing, his own piece. I think that he was blinded in a way by it. He didn't think it was great, he took the mick out of it, but he couldn't see length or cuts, he couldn't tackle that.

It must be incredibly difficult for anybody.

Frightfully difficult. Some, of course, are ruthless. Willie Douglas-Home will cut an act if you suggest cutting a line, but Tony – it was very difficult to get Tony to cut, and some of the rather extraordinary, advanced, almost double-talk in it which we should have taken out, he insisted on keeping. I thought it was a staggering play, and brilliantly written, and of course we made the cuts – I'd cut thirty-one minutes and he put the cuts in after the horrible notices, and of course it made all the difference to the play.

That was a play that was so right for Tony. I mean it was a kind of madhouse in a way, wasn't it? It was such an extraordinary play. Very weird. It was most odd, it jumped backwards and forwards in time. At one moment in any given act I would be four years old, drawing with chalks on the floor, and then turn round and be a man of sixty-five, the same man grown up. I think he wrote very obscurely and I think that if you tried to ask him what it meant, he said he didn't know. I mean, I often asked him in *Top of the Ladder*, 'What did that mean?' He said, 'I don't know, my dear, it's just a lot of nonsense, it's a lot of poetry. Just say it.' There was some hidden meaning about the

Freudian father and son, but you never could pin him down to explain really what was at the back of his mind.

Did you get to know him well personally?

No, not really. I mean I didn't go and spend weekends with them. I got to know him quite well because we often used to go back home and have dinners together, with Judy, and kick things around. We became very good friends and he was wonderful to Mary about her writing, and terribly helpful about a most difficult play she wrote. She really thinks he's the greatest. She wrote a play in New York – it took her a year to write it – while I was doing *Ross*, and another marvellous thing about Tony is that he wrote fourteen pages from Ireland about the play. He'd obviously taken a day to sit down and analyse it and write to say what he thought about it.

Robert Hardy

ALFRED ROSSI: *When did you meet Tony Guthrie?*

ROBERT HARDY: It was just at the end of the war, after I'd come back from the States where I was being taught to fly. I was having my voice trained by an extraordinary Irishman called Bertie Scott, who betted on my future possibilities, and said that I must meet Tony Guthrie, who was his friend. So I went to meet Tony at Lincoln's Inn at, as far as I remember, nine o'clock in the morning.

I got there and was ushered up, thinking, 'What a strange man this must be who's a theatrical director and lives in a lawyer's chambers.' I got in and the washing was hanging all across the room, and I was sat in the one corner of a sofa which wasn't occupied by cats. I was immediately offered very hot and spicy mulled claret. Guthrie was courteous and kind, not in the least dismissive. But he wanted to know why I thought it would be a good thing to be an actor. Wasn't I the kind of person who would do something else, perhaps do better in the Navy, be a good farmer, or whatever? I tried to explain why I felt I should be an actor, and he understood that there was no alternative for me, so he said, 'We'll see if we can't do something about your getting to Stratford, at least for an audition. You'll have to say, "My lord, the carriage waits" probably for three seasons in a row, but that won't do you any harm, you'll have a chance to watch other people and learn what to do.' And that's what I remember of that meeting: Giant Tony, Giant Judy, a mixture of cigarette smoke, mulled claret, washing and cats.

I was engaged for the 1949 season by Anthony Quayle. Guthrie was directing *Henry VIII*, one of the six productions of the season. We were all assembled, and he said, 'Are there any Welshmen here?' I immediately spoke up – I am part Welsh – and he said, 'Right. Would you read Griffith?' Which is a most lovely part, the aged gentleman-usher to Katherine of Aragon. Having lots of elderly relations and also having heard Welsh speech sufficiently from childhood, I was able to read like an old Welshman. Guthrie called for me afterwards and said, 'I know we've met. You didn't strike me as Welsh. You made a very convincing display. I think perhaps it would be nice if you played it. Would you like to?' It was my first sizeable part, in anything. He took a risk, which was typical. It was a very important production, in every way. It was important to me, obviously, but it was also important in the English theatre, I think. It resuscitated *Henry VIII* and showed what a marvellous play it is. And Guthrie made it a thoroughly political piece. He had an extraordinary comprehension of power politics, in any country. He was fascinated by the politicking, chasing power, the weaknesses and strengths of people. He made all the political scenes, which read dully on the page, absolutely electric. He worked and worked with the actors in those scenes, until they became politicians.

As a young actor given that kind of opportunity by someone who really had been already recognized as a great director, do you recall the initial work that he did with you?

I think that one of the reasons I was really blessed enough, more than lucky enough, to get on well with Tony in the work that we did together was probably because he rather enjoyed my contributions to his plans, his tapestries. In those days, as a young actor, I saw no danger in anything. I went too far. And he used to enjoy it. I would catch him grinning sometimes, and then he would stop me, usually if I had been too slow and was enjoying myself too much.

When *Henry VIII* had been on for some months during the season, alternating with the other plays, he came back, and we all had a session after the performance, in the rehearsal room at Stratford. He gave notes to the great ones and the lesser ones. There was no note for me, and I felt rather hipped. I thought, 'Oh God, he's bored with my performance.' So I waited behind afterwards and said, 'My performance, was it all right?' As an excuse to talk about it, I said, 'I wondered if it was getting too slow, do you think it was too slow?' He said, 'Did you think so?' And I said, 'Well, no, I just wondered if *you* thought it was too slow?' He said, 'If you think it was slow, why not try it quicker?'

I remember another part that I played in a production, not by him, two seasons later in the famous 1951 history season, another old man, an English archbishop who shouted and ranted all over the place. I met Guthrie on the stairs after the first night and he said, 'Loved it,

thoroughly enjoyed it. Thought it about the best thing you've done.'
And I said, 'Oh no, oh no, I don't think it was.' Because I wasn't
happy with it. He didn't like that. He said rather coldly, 'I thought it
was very good. I shall see you. Goodbye.' Something which comes
into my mind – a differentiation which he used to make – one particular thing he used to do to put us, the lower echelon, at our ease, was to
call us 'Robert' or 'Jack' or 'Johnny' – as you know he used to know
everybody's name from the top to the bottom in no time flat – but if
he thought the stars were getting 'starry' he would use their surnames.

Guthrie was giving us notes one day after a dress-rehearsal of that
first production of *Henry VIII*. He said to Diana Wynyard, who
played Queen Katherine, 'Must ask you to get the line right. It's not
so-and-so, as you've been saying, but so-and-so.' Diana bridled, and
said nothing. The next set of notes, next day, he said the same thing.
'Forgotten what I told you to do. Simply must go back to the text.'
The third time he said, 'Boring, I know, but I simply must ask you to
go back to your book and try to remember what the author wrote.
You've said it for the third rehearsal running, wrong. Naughty
Wynyard. Please get it right.' And went on to somebody else. Diana,
with a rustle of papers, got to her feet and said, 'Tony, I have looked
it up. I am right, and you are wrong.' There was a fraction of a pause
and Tony said, 'In that case I apologize and have a very red face.'

*Do you think he gave you that direction about going a bit faster because
he knew, like all actors, you wanted a bit of attention, whether or not your
performance required it?*

Yes, of course, and I *demanded* attention from him. If I'd said to
him, 'Is it not Welsh enough or has it got too Welsh?' he'd have said,
'Do you think so? Try it a little bit less. Try it a little bit more.'

I remember he said to me one day after rehearsal, 'Come and have
a drink. Do you like Irish whiskey?' 'I don't think I know it.' 'Then
it's a challenging experience.' We walked to a pub and in the conversation, on the way, he was talking about casting in Shakespeare, all those
nobles, dukes and earls and so forth, and he said – this is the gist of
the thing – 'Do you think it will be possible to do these plays about
aristocrats in the future when there won't be any aristocrats left or
any people who remember the aristocratic tone?' And I said, 'Well, I
suppose it'll be difficult, but aristocracy is in constant revolution,
particularly in the British Isles, isn't it?' (I mean, in the past, each
century, almost each decade, has thrown up its own particular kind.

'Aristocracy' simply means the power of the best, or of the ones who get there.)

'Isn't it going to be more difficult,' I remember him saying, 'as the population increases and people live more and more in enormous groups and cities and are less and less aware of space, of countryside, of big rooms and grand occasions, of the unquestioned arrogance of command, of the assumption of service, of the steps on the ladder of command and power – isn't it going to be more difficult for actors to have recourse to that kind of experience in the future to play the grand parts of classical drama?' And, as I tried my Irish whiskey and found it perfectly drinkable, I agreed with him.

Curious, when you think of Guthrie as somebody who *continually* dashed off, away from England, away from Ireland, to Israel, Holland, Denmark, Canada, America, all over the world, opening up new theatres. He was constantly coming to terms with the New World, in every sense of the phrase. It's always seemed to me that there was a kind of dichotomy in Tony Guthrie which is a not unusual dichotomy in the British Isles. That there lies side by side a desire to make the great look absurd, make great traditions look desiccated and worn out and yet as you pan back, so to say, you'll find that the joker is kneeling on one knee. I think that Tony was in many ways a great traditionalist.

Kneeling on one knee, not two.

Oh, never two, no. When I say that he enjoyed some of the trappings of the autocracies and the panoplies of the past, while digging at them, I'm reminded of the film that was made about him in the BBC series *One Pair of Eyes*. He was then Vice-Chancellor of Belfast University and he had a very grand, a sort of ambassadorial gown, an Elizabethan affair with gold lace frogging all over it; it was an absolutely enchanting scene. He came from behind the camera and rotated quite consciously and enjoyingly in his gown, so that everybody could see the gold lace – rather like one of his characters in *Henry VIII*. I could hear him saying at the same time to himself, 'Quite good. Think we'll try it again. Cut out one or two of the turns.' But he *enjoyed* doing it. He was quite properly made Vice-Chancellor. And quite properly wore the clothes, and quite properly was going to show them off.

It's probably the reason he approached some of those great traditional plays with . . .

An enormous elbow in the ribs? In those great ritualistic plays, those grand pieces about people of power, he nearly always, at some point, went too far. The critics used to censure it in those days, perhaps they wouldn't now. I often wonder what they'd say about him now, if a new Guthrie production went on in England. I think that they might suddenly say 'The greatest!' because they never did, you know, none of the critics ever said, 'This is the greatest man who has ever directed theatre', which made me rage, because it was so apparent to me that nobody else held a candle to him.

You know when *Henry VIII* was redone for the coronation production at the Old Vic, and Queen Elizabeth and Prince Philip came and sat up in the circle, Tony came round to the dressing-rooms before the curtain; we were all ready ages early – it was a grand occasion, nobody knew when the curtain was going up. I remember saying to Tony, 'Have you been given the Garter or anything yet?' And he said, 'Oh no, no, no, no, they haven't the faintest idea who I am.' He was lighthearted about it, but I think he was a little bit sad. It took a long time, but don't forget he ended up with a series of titles: Dr Sir Tyrone Guthrie.

You did all three of the productions of Henry VIII *he directed?*

Henry VIII went on forever, because we did it two years running at Stratford, 1949 and 50. I was in both, played the same part. Then, when it was redone at the Old Vic for the Coronation, I played a different part.

And there happened an interesting thing. Tony gave me the Lord Chamberlain, lots of comedy, another old man, a controlling role in the mechanics of the play. In an early rehearsal, Tony said to me, 'Going to change what we did before. Going to give you the Prologue and the Epilogue.' They had been done at Stratford by a very good elderly actress who was also 'inside' the play. And she came again to the Vic. He said, 'It would be much better if the Chamberlain had all that, and controlled the whole entertainment "inside" and "outside" the play at the same time. Can't think why I didn't do it before.' I said to him, 'She's not going to like that.' He said, 'No, no, no, we'll do it, there we are.' So the news was given to her, and she was terribly upset. And after a few rehearsals she really was extremely unhappy. And I went to Tony and I said, 'You know this is marvellous for me, and I'm enjoying it, but it's not going to work. She's miserable.' He said, 'It's my decision, we stick to it.' The poor woman was in tears at one time. I went to him again and said, 'Please, give it back to her.' And he said, 'Yes, I think I'll have to. Think it's a pity. But till the end of this week you will do it. Question of discipline.'

I was absolutely fascinated by that. He'd agreed that he was going to give it back, the *status quo* of the previous production was going to be restored, *but* somebody had gone against his artistic decision; punishment must be administered. And, you see, without that kind of hard spine of discipline I don't see how you can run a company. I mean even with all the extravagant things that he did, all the glorious stories about him, and all the fun we've all had with him – except a few people who couldn't bear it – I don't see how that kind of morning excitement and newness and dawn thrill can work unless there is a hard core to the central man, the director. And certainly Tony had that. And when he was crossed, he would yield where it was necessary to yield, but a kind of autocracy would be in evidence at the same time.

Why do you think he found a need to do that disciplinary action?

Because I think he believed in discipline. We were talking about Robert Morley earlier, and I just remembered that both he and Tony Guthrie had been to a famous public school in England named Wellington, an authoritarian school, for the production of the élite soldiery of the future, parents who would like their sons to be generals, that kind of thing. Both of them, in some degree, I find similar. Because they were both witty, each unique in his own fashion, both rebelled against authority as they met it. Robert totally rebelled against it, and has continued his rebellion vociferously ever since, while perhaps not altogether implementing in his life-style the derived philosophy of such rebellion. Although he is now a fully paid-up member of the Labour Party, a socialist. Tony Guthrie rebelled against authority, and spent his life theatrically making fun of tradition and authority, while revering those elements in them which are strong and good. His and Judy's life-style was a splendid example of not caring a button about convention, smartness, luxury. Perhaps you could call Tony a sort of grand and humorous Puritan.

After Henry VIII *when was the next time you worked with him?*

He asked me to be in a production of Thornton Wilder's *Life In The Sun* at the Edinburgh Festival. Originally Montgomery Clift was going to play the King, Irene Worth the Queen, and I was to play the Prince, the son. Montgomery Clift at the last moment wasn't going to come over, and an English actor, whose name I shall keep dark – he still exists and is an extremely good actor – was engaged to do it. We'd been in a successful play in the West End and we discovered in the last fortnight of our playing together that we were going to be in this new Guthrie production. I asked if he had worked with Guthrie before. 'No? How marvellous! You'll love it . . . this is going to be exciting!' I couldn't have been more wrong about that.

We met on a Monday for the read-through and the first rehearsal and at the end of the day already there were signs of division between my friend and Tony. He was one of those – and I've seen a few – actors and actresses who found his satirical, rather grand telegraphese simply wasn't their spiel, they just hated it. Then we were dismissed. By that time I'd rehearsed my three scenes. Two days later somebody came and said, 'It's Tyrone Guthrie on the telephone for you.' And I said, 'I know what it is, I've got the sack.' I thought I'd got the sack because it was the first *young* part I'd played for him. 'Very good as an old man. Going to have to tell him. Terribly sad. Hope he won't be upset.' I could hear it all happening as I went to the phone, picked it up and said, 'Hello.' He said, 'Tony Guthrie here. As you may have been aware on Monday there was a little rift developing between Mr X and me.' And I said, guardedly, 'Yes.' And he said, 'Perhaps it'll not surprise you to learn that now the rift has become a gulf. And we've agreed, quite amicably of course, to part company; which leaves, as you'll understand, the role of the King vacant.' Tiny pause. 'Would you like to play it?' I said, 'But, Tony, I'm too young . . . and too short . . . and the wrong kind of actor.' He said without the slightest pause, 'Quite concur with all your strictures. Might it not be fun to try?'

When you were working with him, did you feel his help was more as a general guideline, signposts along the river of creation as it were, or was it specific?

Oh, along the river of creation. I see him standing on the banks of the river of creation, while I am hopelessly lost in a canoe, in a whirlpool of fear. He would shout some absolutely cogent phrase, not 'Do be careful, don't do this, or do that' – no! 'Thrilling, isn't it? The fell insensate pass of mighty opposites.' Yes, that's how I see him, cliff-high, shouting encouragement, trumpeting his delight in danger. Small fears could not survive that onslaught.

John Gibson

ALFRED ROSSI: *What was your first acquaintance with Tyrone Guthrie?*

JOHN GIBSON: I first met him just after the war. I was working in Glasgow in the Iona Community which you may have heard of. It is a Christian organization which was then run by a rather remarkable man called George MacLeod. I worked in the Community theatre company. The job involved doing plays with alcoholics and in mental hospitals, and all that kind of thing. I rather suspect that the Old Man had seen one of these plays, because he wrote me and said, 'I want to meet you.'

I was a bit awed at the thought of meeting this great big man, who was at that time in Glasgow doing his own play *Top of the Ladder* at the Citizens' Theatre. Anyway, I went across to see him at the theatre and we had a very brief interview in a paint dock. He was up the top of the paint dock and I was at the bottom. He looked so huge and I thought 'God!' He was such a big fellow you know. Well, we chatted a bit and then I went away thinking, 'that's the end of that'. About two weeks later, I got a cable from him saying, 'Come to London'. So I got on a train and went to London. He met me at the station and the first thing he said was, 'We're going to Brighton to see a play.' So we went to another station, caught another train and saw this play. We went round afterwards to see the author who wanted Tony's opinion. Well, the Old Man told him what he thought of the play and then he suddenly turned to me and said, 'What do you think?' Christ, you know I was terrified! I was only about twenty-four and there I was with all these grand people being asked for my opinion. 'Come on, speak up,' he said. So I told him that I thought the play was pretty dreadful and that was that. We went back to London where I stayed with him in his flat. The next day, he said, 'We're going to the Arts Council.' So we went to see the Arts Council and we met various people and talked, and afterwards he said, 'Well, we've sown the seeds, we'll see what happens.'

I went back to Scotland thinking, 'That *is* the end of that.' Not at all. Another cable arrived from him, this time saying 'Come to Ireland'. So I went to Ireland. 'Now,' he said, 'you've been offered a position in charge of a rep, or you can come and work with me.' And of course I said, 'I'll come and work with you.' They were going to start the Irish Festival Theatre.

Do you remember Tony's basic approach to directing in those days?

Well I think the important thing to remember about the Old Man is that he didn't like working with stars. He was essentially a man who was much happier with amateur actors. He was very keen on the amateur theatre. And of course this stemmed from the fact that almost all Irish actors inevitably came from the amateur theatre. He was a great discoverer of people. He liked building up people, he liked exploring latent talent. He loved going into country districts to see what the amateur dramatic societies were doing. He might see a performance that impressed him and say, 'That's a splendid actor – we'll build him into an extraordinary one.' He liked giving people chances.

Did he like the freshness of their response, as opposed to a more jaded, although more experienced, sophisticated response?

I think so. This all goes back to the fact that the Old Man was really a countryman. He loved the land and the people on the land. And he loved anything new, that was beginning. That's why he went to North America and built all those theatres. And then he would get bored, and he would move on. He was an explorer. He was a creative man, a creative genius. The Old Man hated any kind of Establishment. It was much more fun for him to go and find an actor and make him into a star than to have handed to him half a dozen stars who knew all the tricks. Because out of these amateurs he would get all kinds of unexpected things. They would do things by accident and he would say, 'Splendid. Keep it in. Keep it in.'

Did he provide an atmosphere that would allow these young people to blossom?

Oh yes. The great thing about him was that he loved people. And I think he felt with amateur actors that they were bringing a kind of freshness and an originality of invention. I mean, if a man had been a grocer, like a great many Irish actors had been, or a jeweller for example, this man had met so many people and had so many anecdotes about the people he had met, that some of that was going to come into the theatre. He knew that out of *his* experience he could use *their* experiences.

People often think of him as a man who could only do big crowd scenes but that's rubbish. Of course he could do crowds, but he could do two-handed scenes, three-handed scenes like an angel. You know, there were two of that man – there was also a joker in him. For example, he would make a lovely love scene and then he would say, 'Well now, you'd better eat sweets during that.' This was a curious quirk in his nature.

I remember a marvellous moment he created in a production of the *Passing Day*, which very briefly is a play about a man who has a store in a little provincial Irish town. He has lived all his life for money. Everything he has done, he has done for money. One day his wife goes away and he goes mad – he falls in love with a nurse, he drinks, he does everything. This is his one day of freedom and the day is passing. He gets drunk and he knocks over a bottle of whisky. He's pissed, he falls on his knees and so on. Now Tony had asked me to do that scene, and I did it all with the actor Joe Tomelty and it was great. Then the Old Man came in and said, 'Yes, very good, very good, yes. The bottle, the glugging, that's life going away.' Then he said to Joe, 'Open the drawer, Joe. There's the money. Pray over it – like a Rosary. Pray.' This was the magic. This was the genius of the man. So that it was never just another rehearsal. He made people flower.

You mentioned that sometimes he would create a love scene and then undercut it with a joke that would be in contrast to it. A number of people have mentioned it, and I'd like to get your opinion about it as you knew him so well, that he was not comfortable with any sentimental scene, particularly male–female relationships.

I can only speak for myself, but I think there's a good answer for that. The Old Man was a profoundly emotional man. He was a good man and a most loving man. The important thing to understand about him is that he was a man who felt deeply about everything but who spent his life hiding things that affected him personally. I think his public school background, and his Presbyterian upbringing were largely responsible for this. The reason why he loved the big crowd scenes was because they were impersonal. And when it came to the personal things, if he found them difficult, it was not because he couldn't do them – no one could do them better than he could – it was just that he didn't want to get too involved. He didn't want to get hurt. Now people don't understand this about him.

The Old Man would cry very easily you know. We used to read together in the old days when they had the oil lamps at Annagh-ma-Kerrig. Often a poem or a piece of prose would move him intensely, and he would be overcome with tears.

I'll tell you a story about him. We went one night to the playwright John Stewart's house. And there was a young man there who attacked him because he thought he was square, an Establishment figure, all that kind of stuff. Of course you know, I could have killed the bastard. Afterwards, we had to drive all the way from Belfast to Annagh-ma-Kerrig. It was a long way. And he said to me, 'Shouldn't have got like that with the young man.' 'I don't like to hear people saying that about you,' I said. 'I love you and I don't want to hear that.' 'Shouldn't go as far as that,' he said.

But I knew that he was very moved. He was moved that I did it. He understood why I did it.

I know that for him I was a kind of son. But he missed the fact that he didn't have children very much.

I adored him, and I think he loved me In the film we made for the BBC there is a sequence where he goes to the railway station. He said, 'Can't do this, John I cannot talk about when I was a little boy.' I said, 'This'll be the best part in the film ' 'Do it for you,' he said And he did it. Remembering when he was a little lad and worrying about his ticket. The little cart coming to take him to the station to go back to school, leaving everything that was valuable to him – going back to Wellington. He was very moved by it And at the end he said, 'Not a bad performance '

Can you pick up with what happened after the experience in the Irish Festival season?

Yes, after that all kinds of things happened. A job came up in the BBC in Northern Ireland. They were looking for someone to be head of Drama there. In those days it was a big thing to get a job in the BBC. Anyway, the Old Man said, 'You must go in for this. I'll back you and MacLeod will back you.' I got the job.

He believed profoundly in the artistic possibilities of the radio play, and obviously I got him in to do things. We did his plays *The Squirrel's Cage* and *The Flowers Are Not For You To Pick*. And now and again he would ask me to go and work with him. 'Come and help me with *The Three Estates.*' We did the last production of that play at the Edinburgh Festival together. And that was great excitement. I did one part and he did the other half.

I remember a very funny incident in that production. We were doing one of the big crowd scenes. The Old Man rehearsed part of it, but then he had to go off somewhere for a couple of days, leaving me to do all the ensemble work on the scene while he was away.

One of the crowd artists was an amateur actress, who was quite well known in Scotland. She had been in all Tony's earlier productions of *The Three Estates*, and it was obvious that she didn't much like having to take direction from me. Anyway, Tony came back and we had a run through, and we were right in the middle of it all, when suddenly this actress called out from the stage, 'Dr Guthrie, Mr Gibson has told us to moan here. Now do you think we are moaning enough, Dr Guthrie?'

Well, you could have heard a pin drop. The Old Man just looked at her, then he asked, 'How long have you been in the theatre, dear?'

She replied, 'Twenty-five years, Dr Guthrie.'

'Fun, isn't it?' he said.

During that production I discovered that he was very meticulous in his planning. The impression he gave, of course, was that he hadn't planned anything he was going to do. But that was erroneous. What he did, you see, was to have a series of climaxes in his head, and then he worked to achieve those climaxes on the stage.

I've been told that you went with him when he was knighted, is that true?

No, but I did drive him to the Palace to have lunch with the Queen once. He was staying with me at the time. 'Better get my suit pressed,' he said, 'got to have lunch with HM the Queen.'

So we got his suit pressed and dressed him up with his cuff links and all that. He looked absolutely great. We were about to leave when he said, 'Feeling a bit cold. Better put my cardie on.' I said, 'Come on, Tony, you can't do that!' 'Not at all,' he said, 'I'm feeling cold.' Well, he put on this blue cardigan that covered his lovely cuff links and hung down underneath his jacket – and we got him into my little Ford car and drove him off to see the Queen. God, what a drive! We went out over the Chiswick flyover, and there was a car crash, so we had to come all the way back. All the traffic lights were against us.

Every L driver in London was out – they were even driving milk
floats. Well we were cutting things a bit fine by now, and I didn't
want him to be late, and he'd got this great big invitation card with
him. 'If we get stopped,' I said, 'wave it in the air,' and I went screech-
ing along breaking all the laws. When we got to the Royal Court
Theatre, he said, 'I know a way. If we can turn left we're saved. If we
have to turn right we're fucked.' Well, we couldn't turn left, but I
dodged round the one-way streets and finally, driving past a startled
sentry, I did get him to the Palace on time.

When he came home I asked, 'How did it go?' 'Bottled beer on the
table for the actors.' 'What was the food like?' I said. 'Rather stodgy.
Difficult to enjoy when you're being savaged by corgis under the table.'

Did he ever talk about his work in opera with you?

No, not really. But I do remember once I met him at the airport,
when he returned from America, where he directed some big opera or
other. He'd worked his bloody guts out, and it was a disaster. But I
didn't know that, so when he got off the plane I raised my thumb up
and said, 'Yes?' And he put his thumb down and grunted in an un-
mistakeably negative way. He never said another word about it, but
of course he was hurt by it.

He had brought a record of Verdi's *Requiem*, which someone had
given him. He very much admired Verdi, and this was a marvellous
Russian recording. He would put it on at Annagh-ma-Kerrig, sing
aloud and shout out, 'Yes, yes!' And Judy would say, 'Tony, can we
just listen to it?' And he'd shout, 'No, get involved.'

*Did you know much about his aspirations for the jam factory in County
Monaghan?*

One of the great heartbreaks of his life was when the jam
factory failed. He was robbed. His idea had been to create employment for the people in the area. There was so little work in Co.
Monaghan and most of the local people had to go away to get jobs.
His plan was that they should grow fruit on the land and work in the
factory. The failure broke his heart much more than any failure in the
theatre. The jam factory, he said himself, was the most important
production of his life. He had an extraordinary sense of values. He
knew that the real importance was not the theatre but what was going
on all round you every day. He could make jokes about the theatre
because he knew that what happened in the world was what really

mattered and not what happened on a little platform. He knew that the theatre was only a reflection of what is real. And what is real is the world and people in the world, and relationships, and politics – these are the real things. Many people can speak about him as a director but they didn't know the man. And the man is infinitely more important than anything he did on the stage.

Would you say that was one of the qualities about Tony Guthrie that made him great?

Yes. I think what was great about Tony is what the Scots say, 'He loved the brethren.' I mean he truly did love the brethren. He was the most unselfish man I've ever known in my life. Do you know, every once in a while he'd say to me, 'Come, let's go and visit the poor.' And we'd go around to different places, and he'd give money to a number of old actors and actresses who couldn't work any more. Not many people know this. And he didn't want anyone to know about it.

He could also be a cruel man, and he could be a hard man, but he was a totally just man. I don't ever think about him in the end, as a theatrical man. I mean he was a theatrical man; he loved all the fun and work of the theatre, the quips and all that business. But at the end of the day, I think what was important about Tony was that he was a giant in every sense of the word. I cannot think of any other comparable person who is as great as Tony. He loved human beings and he knew how to get the best out of people. The actors will tell you that. He did not go to Israel just to make plays with the Israelis. He went to Israel because he was fascinated by Israel. 'How am I going to change these people?' Same with Canada, same with Minneapolis, same with Ireland. He was more worried about a man emigrating from his own country than he was about any bloody play. And it's not without importance that he always wrote plays about failures. So I think you will get many people to talk about how he was as a director and the brilliance of his productions, but what is important is the way he saw his work in the theatre in a much greater context. I don't think he deliberately saw it that way. It just was. He was like a rock standing out in a great sea.

You know, he was obsessed by trees. He always talked about the great tree in the forest as the father and the little flowers that grow around as the sons. And when I went to his memorial service at St Paul's, Covent Garden, a tree had fallen down the night before in the courtyard. When I spoke to his steward, he said to me, 'A great tree has fallen out the sky.'

All I know is that I've never met a man that I loved or respected as much as Tony. If he walked through that doorway, I wouldn't be at all surprised – bending his head to get underneath it.

Constance Tomkinson

CONSTANCE TOMKINSON: I was at the Vic from 1949 to 1952. We had one year when Tony was the Director and I was his secretary, assistant, general dogsbody. I think he had a great instinct for people and a real talent for spotting *his* kind of a person. He was frightfully loyal to people who worked with him. He never forgot. He was an incredible encyclopedia of good performances, and I daresay he never forgot a bad one. He would know about actors all over Great Britain. He remembered them from the Glasgow Citizens' Theatre or heaven knows where. He often got with him actors whom he had worked with in the past because for one thing they could take his direction. He wanted people around him that he liked, and he wasn't like some other directors I know who were just employing people as favours. I mean, for instance, Coward was terribly kind about employing people that he thought nobody else would employ when perhaps they were going off. All the ones Guthrie backed were good actors.

ALFRED ROSSI: *During the time that you were Tony's personal secretary, did Judy Guthrie attend many rehearsals?*

Oh yes, indeed. I think she was the only person whose opinion he really valued. She always came in at the tail end of every production. She would arrive with a thermos flask of hot tea and tasty little sandwiches, and he would prowl around like a lovely leopard all up and down the aisles and be totally unaware of food; but it must have been tiring. It was then that she would nip in with the sandwiches or a cup of tea. She didn't say anything. She just put the cup of tea in his hand and he would eat the sandwiches without ever even knowing what he was doing. He really valued her opinion, and when the rehearsal was over he would always go right up to her and listen intently to what she had to say.

Were you ever privy to any of those conversations?

Oh I was always there too, sometimes running around the stalls with him. In rehearsals I would take notes, and eventually I found myself writing in the dark. He talked as he wrote. I mean when he wrote you a letter it was marvellously brief and staccato, you know, about three words to a line. When he was under pressure in rehearsals he would assume that you knew the other half of the sentence. He would just give you the key words, and you put it together. I can remember getting some little flashlight and trying to get it all on the page. But the notes weren't extensive, just key things. He wasn't like some producers I've worked with where you took endless notes and chewed over them afterwards. It was all in his head really. And then lighting notes would go to whoever was in charge of the lighting. He didn't go through me; he went directly, and he was very tactful.

How did Guthrie get along with Wolfit in that 1951–2 season at the Old Vic?

As a personality Wolfit had been an actor-manager too long. As is often said, any actor who ever worked with Wolfit always spent his whole life behind a pillar. Everybody knew all about this. And that Guthrie could handle him at all for the first time outside of being an actor-manager was great. Of course, he had great admiration for Guthrie. Otherwise I don't think Guthrie could have handled him at all. Wolfit was a strange character and really behaved very badly during that season.

How?

He had been asked to do a special performance, in the Lincoln's Inn Fields I believe it was, which the Queen Mother was to attend. So he said he would not be able to appear at Malvern, and we'd sold all the tickets and Guthrie said, 'Well, you've got to do this. You've simply got to do this. We can't simply say you're missing for one performance.' Eventually Wolfit pulled out, and that was very difficult because the whole season had been built around him as an actor. This was in the middle of the season and it was really nightmarish, as I recall, to move in people to take over the roles he had been contracted for. By this time of course all the leading actors were committed.

Did he leave the company as a result of that particular incident?

That's true, yes. That sounds incredibly childish, and I think it was probably something more than that. I think that he simply couldn't take the strain of not being an actor-manager. When they were staging their calls I can remember Wolfit saying, 'I don't think it's necessary for us all to come down to the curtain to take the call, because the audience really comes to see me, and I think if I take the call that's quite enough.' He actually said that and Cecil Clarke said, 'Now look, Mr Wolfit, it is the policy of this theatre that we take our calls as a group. This is not the star system.' And, of course, this he'd never experienced before.

I think he simply was too old. I don't mean in years, but too old, like a leopard, to change his spots, and he found it an awful shock to his system. He couldn't stand not being the actor-manager. As a matter of fact he was so silly, because he was a great actor, and it was an opportunity for him to hit heights that he never could have done before with a company that wasn't in a class with the Vic. He was backed with a fabulous cast which would have made him shine like a marvellous lamp, as indeed he did in *Tamburlaine*, but he just simply was incapable of seeing this. So it was a tragedy for him as well – most of all for him.

What was Guthrie's reaction to Wolfit's leaving?

He was very upset on behalf of the company. It shook them, a thing like this happening. *That* I think he was more hurt about.

But dear Guthrie was a lesson to me which has always stuck in my life ever since. He was always at his best when things were at their worst – *absolutely* at his best. And his marvellous line, which I'm sure you have heard time and again: 'Rise above,' he would say. And you rose. If you were on your last legs, you rose.

One of the surprises to me in his personality was that Guthrie was deeply religious, but he never mentioned it, never tried to argue anybody else into being religious. I don't know that it's very common among actors, except often Catholic or Jewish actors absorb religion as part of their background, and just don't question it or anything. They just are. But I think with Protestants it's sort of a conscious thing – they are or they aren't or they continue to be. I don't remember, honestly, many actors being very much interested in religion or politics. I mean, they've got their hands full as it is, thank you very much. But Guthrie really believed in God, and every now and then it would emerge in some odd way. God existed for him, and he didn't have any doubt at all. This might have been his upbringing, but, you see, he was somebody who would have questioned anything along the line. Look at all the things he *did* question. He no doubt questioned it, and for him God really *is*. He was very quiet about it. I'd known him for some time, before I realized that he was very religious.

Why did Guthrie return to the Vic?

I think it was just put to Guthrie that only *he* could save the Vic. And as he made the Vic, so to speak, the big thing – all right, dear Lilian Baylis laid the basis but he made the Vic what it is today – it was his own work that would have gone down the drain, if he didn't come back and save it. But he didn't really want to come back, because after all he was going to do an exciting production of so-and-so in Tel Aviv and then he was flashing off to Stockholm and doing so-and-so, going over to the Met to do *Carmen* and this, that and the other. He didn't have to carry all the worries about keeping a theatre going. It's a tremendous strain. He was so much in demand that he could go anywhere, and it was stimulating for him to go to various places. He didn't want to do this, I'm absolutely sure.

Is that why he left after a year?

I think once he'd saved it he wanted to go off and do exciting productions here, there and everywhere, and who could blame him? He phoned me up on a Sunday morning. We were reading the papers in bed and my husband Hugh answered the phone, and he said, 'It's Tony.' I said, 'Something's wrong. Nine in the morning on a Sunday?' He said, 'Could you possibly meet me at the Vic?' So Hugh drove me to the Vic, and I was there by half-past nine. We walked round and round the Vic outside, and we discussed the situation.

You see, I didn't want him to go because we all loved the Vic very much, and he was the right man in the right place. But on the other hand I did see his point, absolutely. Financial considerations never meant anything at all to Tony so you couldn't say, 'Look, here you're absolutely certain of finances.' As a matter of fact, I think he was very comfortably off. Anyway he could pull large sums of money from anywhere he was going. Of course, every now and then he'd go somewhere where they could only afford fifty pounds, because that was all they had in the kitty. And he'd say, 'All right, that sounds very interesting. I'll do it.' As he did time and time again.

Do you know whether the Stratford, Ontario, venture helped influence his decision to leave?

I think it probably did influence his leaving, because it was all so close. It was within days. You see, I'm a Canadian and I remember when the letter came in. I was thinking, 'Now really, if he is going to leave the Vic I would like to plead with him to go to Canada. Only he could do it.' Then one day he said, 'I've decided to do Stratford.'

Also, I think one of the things that bored Guthrie very much at the Vic was some of the governors that he had to deal with. Sir Bronson Albery knew a great deal about theatre, but some of the rest of them, distinguished as they were in their fields, knew very little about theatre. Here was poor Guthrie, this giant, trying to explain to these characters! As I would sit through these governors' meetings, I really could have hit some of them over the head with the minute book. It made me so angry that anybody could have wasted this man's time. I could have killed them, you know. And if I felt that way I'm damn sure Guthrie did. In fact, he always called them the 'Govs'. There we'd be at these long mahogany tables, with Guthrie the only one in scale, so to speak. I would be at his right arm, taking these notes, and every now and then he would be looking at you and just looking a little longer than was absolutely necessary to look at somebody, and then you knew that he was trying to give you some message like 'How much longer is this going to go on?' Or, 'There goes that nit again.'

I've been told that you had a party here in your house to celebrate his knighthood. How did that come about?

Well, after he was knighted I called him because he was so busy, and I was busy by this time batting away on books, and the only way ever to see Tony was to work with him, or else pick him up off a bus and walk with him from there to where he was going. But we always started with each other as if we'd left each other half an hour before. If it had been a couple of years we were back absolutely where we were.

So I called up, and I said, 'Now, Tony, we want to give you a party to celebrate your K in this house.' And he said, 'Well, what do you want to have a party for that for?' And I said, 'Well, darling, if we don't celebrate this, what do we celebrate? And as far as I'm concerned it's long overdue. Now would you please give us a guest list? What would you like? A dinner party for about twelve? Or would you like a cocktail party for forty, fifty, sixty?' He said, 'Well, I think it had better be a cocktail party, dear, because otherwise somebody's feelings would be hurt.' So I said, 'Right. Now you give us the guest list. I'll phone them all and we'll get it all organized.'

We were given the guest list. I knew a lot of them, of course, but we had everyone from very big names to unknowns. There was one pair, a husband and wife, that I simply couldn't place at all. The address was Lincoln's Inn Fields. They accepted and arrived, and he was one of the caretakers at Lincoln's Inn Fields who had been very kind to Myrtle, the Guthrie's cat whom they absolutely adored. Myrtle, I might say, was the size of a cheetah. I remember going into this tiny flat in Lincoln's Inn which was so sweet and so cosy and there in the very best chair was Myrtle. Myrtle was a very grand cat who just ruled that roost. But this couple had been very kind to Myrtle because often the Guthries had to be away or something. So they were here. Olivier couldn't come, but his first wife, Jill Esmond, came. Now, you see, Guthrie kept friends going way, way back in time, and they'd go marry somebody else and then he'd been friends with this husband or that wife. I mean he just rose above all that kind of thing.

It was a lovely party, and I can see him standing right there. I said, 'Well, Tony, we've got to place you. Do you mind if I do the production this time?' We had about forty here, and it was not summer so we weren't out in the garden, we were all inside. So I said, 'Now if they're going to see you, Tony, we'll put you right in the corner there, and then they can come in and move around.' It was a very happy party, and I think he really enjoyed it. As a matter of fact I think he did greatly enjoy his knighthood.

Did he ever talk to you about it?

No, I think one wouldn't talk about it. I *know* he was very pleased. And when my husband was knighted, Tony sent the most marvellous note. Nothing more than, 'Dear Hugh, Welcome to the Company of the Horsed.'

You know, I remember that even in the midst of that party, which was after all for Tony, he found time to be kind to various people. An actor, who was a very good character man (and who shall be nameless), was going through a rather bad patch at that time, and he wrote a note to me afterwards thanking me for the party and saying, 'I was so heartened. I had a word with Guthrie. I was beginning to lose hope and to think that perhaps my career was finished. After I talked with Guthrie I took on a new zing, and I feel all right again. If Guthrie told me I wasn't finished I knew I wasn't.' And shortly after that he was hired. He had this kind of kindness.

I was writing plays when I was working with him. I had written a lot of them, and none of them had ever been produced, but they were getting to be very near misses. I didn't like to take advantage of Guthrie and ask him to read a script, but I finally mustered up my nerve and asked him if he would read one script. He read it and said, 'You must leave the theatre right away and write. You're just wasting your time here. Now you get out and write.' And I said, 'Tony, I'm not going as long as you're here.' Anyway, when he saw this script he said, 'Now you've got to rework the last act. It goes downhill. It's got to go uphill.' I rewrote it, and it didn't make it, but that wasn't his fault.

Judy, when she read the script – because she read every script that Tony was ever given – said, 'You're going to make a fortune out of this.' And in a way I did, because I turned it into book form, and it was *Les Girls*. But it was so typical of him to come and say, 'Now look, you've just got to leave me, you've got to leave the theatre. That's all there is to it. You're a writer now.' I was beginning to get a little down-hearted, rather like the actor, you know, because if you get enough rejection slips you think, 'Well now, look, I must be out of my mind. It isn't going to work. I really must be. This just isn't going to work.' And he would never tell you it was a good script, if he thought it was a bad one. He always took great pleasure in other people's successes. He was always pleased if any of his friends had any success. He'd say, 'How lovely for so-and-so.'

How would you characterize the relationship between him and Judy?

They were almost one. They had a telepathic thing so that speech was hardly necessary, and just absolutely were on the same wavelength. Judy was, of course, a very clever woman herself and really, in a way, sacrificed her own career to support Tony. It was their joint career, because Tony couldn't have done all that he did without Judy.

How did she help him?

She helped him by believing in him nonstop and being absolutely behind him to the last ditch. If Tony had been up for embezzlement, Judy would have been out raising money to get him out. So would I, I daresay, and so would a lot of other people, but she certainly would. Her judgment was very sound. I've never known her to be wrong about actors or scripts or things. Also her knowledge of the theatre was long and vast, you see. She was almost Tony's age. She'd sat in on productions with Tony since the thirties. She may not have known anything when she started, but she was certainly exceedingly knowledgeable when she got through. He trusted her judgment more than anybody else's. If Judy said something was good he'd listen to her regardless of what anybody else said, I am sure.

They were so at one that I thought when Tony died it would kill her. She died a year after, and though she died of cancer, I think she just lost the will to live. I kept in touch with her right through, until I realized that she couldn't write at all. Her letters were not making any sense. She kept saying things like, 'I don't know why Tony just doesn't send me a p.c.? I haven't heard a word from him. If I'd just had a postcard.' In a way she just couldn't stand it, I suppose, and she escaped by going out of her mind.

Kenneth Griffith

ALFRED ROSSI: *Can you tell me about your experiences in that renowned production of* Tamburlaine?

KENNETH GRIFFITH: *Tamburlaine* opened the season with Wolfit. And this was a most interesting experience with Guthrie. Because for the second time in my life – I'm a very opinionated actor – I did not know what to do with a character. I was playing the King of the Persians. And the only two occasions when I hadn't known what to do were both Marlowe, and that's because Marlowe would go on a blinder obviously, and then come back and write something marvellous, but very often they were contradictory.

So Guthrie and I had lunch in a pub and I said, 'Tony, I'm so worried. Maybe it's because I've been in the film industry for four years. I just don't know what to do with this character.' Now every other director under the sun would say, 'Right, my cue', and talk for two hours. 'That's what you should do with it.' That's what they dream of. Guthrie replied, 'Much rather leave it your donation.' Then I went on, and he saw my misery and he did this smothered laugh that you would hear from the stalls and he said, 'Well . . .' This was his reply. He didn't tell me how to play the part but he told me in detail how he prepared my entrance. And I think this is so valuable for other directors to consider. He said, 'When the audience come into the Vic and sit in their seats when the lights are up, the curtain will be up. And they will see in the foreground an enormous Perseean tent of war' – he didn't say Persian – 'and behind that, other Perseean tents of war. And indeed,' he said, 'these Perseean tents of war seem to stretch away into the far distances of Aseea,' is what he said, not Asia. He said, 'Through these tents coming down to the hole we have where the orchestra used to be, and the steps, going down to the orchestra pit that was, will be a path of light. The first thing that the audience will . . .' It didn't actually quite happen like this but very near, and this is what he said long before rehearsal started. 'Down this path of light will come the young man, the young actor who speaks the Chorus', which was about fourteen or fifteen lines, about war and about this great beast coming out of Asia. And he said, 'I think as he walks on the stage he will be finishing his make-up, and he will have on his dressing-gown over his costume. And as he speaks these lines he walks through and down the steps and out of sight. The lights go down and then into the darkness comes a spot on to an empty isolated golden throne.' Obviously the tents had been withdrawn, you know. 'Then from the OP side, from the *prompt* side, you begin to see in a little light enormous figures of generals and court officials emerging. Enormous figures in golden armour, glorious costume, the Court, heads of state. And then they all turn ceremoniously to the OP side,' he said. 'Then, Kenneth, it'll be quite clear to the audience that the King is expected. They all turn ceremoniously to the OP side. At that moment from the prompt side comes the little rat-like figure of the King and sits on the throne.' I said, 'Thank you. All is clear.' That's all he said. And all my problems were solved.

What was your impression of Donald Wolfit working with him in Tamburlaine?

Wolfit was guilty of gross vulgarity, but, my God, he could be a big actor. And in that there were wonderful things from him, from Marlowe, and from Guthrie. That was the miracle of that production. Magnificent. I thought that now the theatre had reached its zenith, and I was right. (I mean, I did see Guthrie do it again in *Henry VIII* – not a very good play, by Shakespeare standards.) It was so magnificent. The theatrical achievement of having a big actor, Wolfit, and a play with on-and-off magnificent content, you know, and what Guthrie did with that! That is the great lesson to learn, I think, for every bloody director that I can think of – to honour your playwright and your actors. Use them and honour them, because we're all vulnerable.

Are there some things relating to the rehearsal work, particularly about Wolfit, you might want to share?

Yes, there was one thing that amused Guthrie enormously. I admired Donald Wolfit's performance very much, but I do think that it is possible that the moment of most pleasure for Guthrie was a line I had to say as King of the Persians when he was defeated by Tamburlaine and he runs out on the great open stage, clutching his crown which was really the desert. A very naïve character, as Guthrie had communicated to me in that very indirect way, and he – to paraphrase whatever it was he said – said that if he didn't have his crown nobody would know who he was. So he looks round the bare desert, and what Marlowe gave him to say was, 'Ah, here will I hide it in this simple hole.' And I remember each time I had to say it there were giggles of joy from Guthrie. And this somehow was an image that I caught from him, the idea of a hole being simple.

I remember before rehearsals started Guthrie talking to me about Donald Wolfit coming into the company. I remember him saying to me, 'Kenneth, you know Canada' – I was attached to the Canadian Air Force during the war – 'the size of the place.' He said, 'There are many reasons why we must respect this man.' Donald Wolfit, at that time, had got a reputation of being the last of the actor-managers and sometimes, without justification, of not employing very good actors, of not really caring very much who he employed, as long as they did the job, and that really people only came to see him and the productions were thrown on, and that he was totally convinced that all that really mattered was himself. Though he certainly was always well worth watching and was one of the great actors of my time, nevertheless he suffered very seriously from not having the very best round him. And Guthrie's argument was that we must remember that Donald Wolfit actually took, personally, his company right across Canada and would supervise the box office takings in Saskatchewan – Guthrie loved these names – and *personally* stuck on the labels of the theatrical baskets in Moosejaw. And he said, 'It's a size that we must appreciate apart from being a great actor. And I'm sure that now when he's surrounded by a talented young company he's going to appreciate this, and we're going to *see* things that we haven't seen from him before.'

Well, to underline the fact that about Guthrie I'm not blindly sycophantic, and I'm not blinded because I love him so much, during those rehearsals I was disappointed by Guthrie for the first and last time.

I'd like to digress here for a moment. At the end of the war, having had a bad time, I did have recurring nightmares, and the very last recurring nightmare I had was about Tyrone Guthrie. And I don't exaggerate. I was sitting up in bed sweating with fear. I suppose this is the most telling thing I can communicate to you about Tyrone Guthrie – what he was and what he meant to people like myself. I would sit up in bed, sweating, because I had dreamt that Tyrone

Guthrie had stolen something, or that Tyrone Guthrie had told a lie. Because I had learned to place so much trust in him, since I had seen how shallow the British theatre was, not only today but yesterday and the day before, when I first started. I mean, I've seen it change from a sort of entertainment for the people in the south of England to the intellectual arrogance of second-rate intellects running our institutional theatres. And then suddenly to have this very human giant and intellectual artist in every respect – I mean if I hadn't seen him for four years he would say, 'How is your Auntie Polly?' And I would think, 'God almighty, Auntie Polly?' And I'd say, 'Well, she's very old now.' And he'd ask questions about things that you'd said to him eight or nine years before and he really – this was the quality of him – he really was deeply, humanly concerned. There's not a shadow of doubt. But on top of that, a brilliant intellect, and a strong man, and a good man. If there *is* such a thing as a saint, in my opinion, it was Guthrie. An unpretentious, humble saint.

But there was Wolfit, suddenly, in the Vic, playing Tamburlaine, with this company of fifty actors around him. Guthrie didn't stay in the stalls. Initially, he put his chair where the footlights used to be and sat on it – this tall figure on the chair, quite close. And Wolfit did his piece, and everyone else was in awed silence. And I saw him doing things and getting away with things that he shouldn't have been allowed to get away with. I was not a fool, and I thought, 'Well, Guthrie has taken on a tremendous gamble, you know, and he doesn't want to see this thing blow up in his face.'

Wolfit, by reputation, was a formidable man. I loved Wolfit, not as I loved Guthrie, but I admired things about him. And he was a romantic figure, and he had a direct hand out to Macready and Kean. And he *believed* it. I mean as the last curtain came down on *Tamburlaine* – many of the company heard it – he prayed, 'Kit Marlowe, we've done you proud.' And, you know, it was not a joke. It was a direct appeal to the past in the theatre. And his performance established this.

But I used to sit there and think, 'Well, yes, I can see, but when are you going to draw the line?' In actual fact – and there were fifty witnesses to it – I was responsible for the first line to be drawn. Because, in playing the King, there is this scene in the end where he is defeated and runs out into the desert and looks round for the simple hole, but before he can put the crown in the hole, suddenly this monster appears, which is Tamburlaine. I don't remember the text, but

Tamburlaine says something to the effect, 'What have you there?' He says he has his crown, you see. And Tamburlaine says something complimentary, as far as I remember, to which the King replies, 'Aye, did'st thou ever see a fairer?' Crown, you see. Now there are no stage directions as to what happens to that crown, but Tamburlaine certainly takes it because Tamburlaine refuses to hand it back to the King. And the King says, 'But I gave it thee.' Now, as I remember it, Tamburlaine tosses it back to him and says, 'I'll take it the hard way. You know who I am. I'm Tamburlaine.' And the poor little King shits himself. And suddenly Wolfit said, 'Tony, I have a very good idea. My boy,' turning to me, 'very good for you. Tony, instead of Kenneth giving me the crown, I will take it on the point of my sword.' Well, the first thing I thought was, 'How's that good for me?' you know. I couldn't quite see *that*. But then what I really saw was that this absolutely destroyed the innocence of the King. You know, he says, 'I *gave* it thee', and the implication is that 'because I gave it thee you must give it to me back', you see. So we did it. And Wolfit was delighted. So we did it again. And Guthrie said nothing. And finally I said, 'Mr Wolfit' – he wasn't Sir then – 'I must say that I think from my character's point of view this is most unfortunate and totally wrong for the following reasons . . ' Well, Wolfit froze into position, which was always highly dramatic, and he changed colour like a chameleon. There was a long silence, then Guthrie said: 'Must say, Donald, I think Kenneth's right.' But Wolfit was like a bulldog, although he finally suggested that perhaps it was possible to do, if *I* put the crown on his sword. So it was a compromise.

But the interesting thing about Wolfit is that from that day onward he took a very special and affectionate interest in me. And indeed he wanted to propose me for something called A Society of Individualists. When he first said it I thought he was being facetious or ironical or something. But in actual fact it was a Fascist organization which he belonged to. And from then on I was treated, as near as Donald could, as an equal, and I was very proud of that. And when he hailed me once in the Haymarket across the road, 'My boy', in a black cloak and a great black hat, it was one of the great memories of my life.

It was a great production and a tremendous theatrical achievement. I wasn't on the stage at the time, but every night I went to watch an extraordinary scene where Tamburlaine, towards the end of the play, is dying. The great beast, who's conquered the known world, is dying. He'd just discovered that his sons are effete, weak, useless. And, as I remember it, the great stage was empty except his generals now were sort of half-naked savages – these great, enormous actors – and they were crouching over what would be a fire in the desert and suddenly on staggers Tamburlaine who was wearing a great shaggy bearskin. And all his generals and followers shrank away into the perimeters of the darkness because the beast, this great terrifying figure that ruled the world, was dying and had staggered on to the stage. And he barks, 'Fetch me a map.' And forty men go off, and forty men stagger back with a great map and they roll it out, and it covers the stage and down into the orchestra pit. And Tamburlaine staggers across it saying, 'Here did I the Persians vanquish and here the Egyptians' and here this and here that. The stage is empty, just in the perimeter the people watching. I paraphrase, of course, and he said, 'Here the Mediterranean Sea and here the Red, and I did mean to cut a channel through so that I might quickly sail to India.' Jesus Christ! I mean the frustration of this, that he couldn't do the fucking Suez Canal, you see. It was a meeting of Wolfit's ability to do it and of Guthrie setting it and bringing it to maximum effect, and, of course, Marlowe writing it. Oh, it was fantastic. But the whole thing was bloody marvellous.

Why did Wolfit leave the Old Vic that season?

As I recall, he was going to play King Lear at the Old Vic for Guthrie. Then we went on a tour and we played Stratford-on-Avon. And there Wolfit was ill, so he was off. Then, he had been invited to a luncheon in London at which the Queen was going to be present. And this was on a Saturday afternoon. And he announced that he was going. And, as I understand it, because I wasn't present, Tyrone Guthrie said, 'No, Donald. Your first duty is to your audience.' And Wolfit said, 'I have been invited to have lunch with my Queen.' And Guthrie said, 'No, you will come to the matinée.' And Wolfit said, 'No, I will have lunch with my Queen.' He had lunch with his Queen, and I can only assume that he was *sacked*. Because, the next time I met Wolfit it was in the Waterloo Road, and he was in black and he met me outside the Vic, approaching the stage door, and I said, 'I'm terribly sorry, Mr Wolfit, that you're leaving.' And he said, 'My boy . . . I have done it for *you*!' With tremendous dramatic pauses, you see. 'My boy . . . I have done it for *you*! Someone,' he said, 'has to make a stand against *them*', pointing up to the Old Vic offices, you see. 'Do they think that I do not want to play Lear? But I have done it for you, my boy.' By this time it was such a performance that passers-by must stop. Anyway, he left, so I presume that over this issue Guthrie finally drew the line.

Why was Guthrie so special?

I think to be a truly great man, whatever you do, whether it's a soldier or a theatre director or a prime minister, you cannot be great unless you have the capacity for great human concern, which is a way, I suppose, of saying a capacity for loving. And that Guthrie had. It would be a very insensitive person who didn't love him. You see he had this capacity for caring for human beings, and it wasn't who they were. He just cared for people to an abnormal degree. You see this reflected in the jam factory. And he didn't make a great deal of money.

I once talked to him about that. I remember he asked me to go and see his production of *The Pirates of Penzance* in the Haymarket. And he said something about finances, and I said, 'But I've always presumed, Tony, that you had a private income, and that you didn't have to worry.' And he spoke about Lady Guthrie, and he said, 'No, we've always been rather short. We've always managed, but now that I've got this production and one in New York which have been successful, for the first time we've got a bit of money to spare.'

Then there was his concern for my Auntie Polly, you know, especially in a world which is so shoddy. Even if you can become a millionaire out of it. I mean, O'Toole once said to me, when he was rejected and unemployed before *Lawrence*, 'Our profession is a monumental shithouse. And I'm going to be the biggest shithouse keeper of the lot.' Of course, having become the biggest shithouse keeper of the lot he behaves professionally. In this world, suddenly to come across Guthrie, the whole potential of what the theatre could be was personified by him.

That's why I used to pursue him. If he lectured I pursued him, and stood up and asked questions. And I'd be as impertinent as I could. I remember saying at one of these meetings, 'Why don't you stay and make a National Theatre in this country?' And he said, 'I'm much too old.' That was twenty years before he died.

You see, the only actors who couldn't bear him were those who were very proud. I do remember him telling me – and it was rather indiscreet of him, I suppose – that Sir Laurence came to see him in Burnley, with Vivien Leigh, Lady Olivier, to ask him if she could join the company. And he described it to me in great detail how this was an extremely difficult time, because, he said, 'Kenneth, after all, she's not a very good actress, is she?' And he explained how Laurence Olivier never actually said it, but in this oblique way, that's what they were up for, but he never said, 'Look, I want Viv to have a job.' And how Tony pretended, he told me, that he didn't know what they had come up for. That's how he got out of it. He entertained them and sent them off. He said, 'After all, I don't think she'd fit. You know, she's rather a grand lady now, and I don't think coming here would be the best idea.' And at the same time he can pick up Joe Snooks or Kenneth Griffith and treat him with honour as an artist. If there's ever been anyone like him in the history of the theatre from the word dot, I'd be very curious to know who it was.

Paul Rogers

ALFRED ROSSI: *You played Bottom in* A Midsummer Night's Dream *the second time Guthrie directed the play. He had directed the gorgeously romantic production in the late thirties at the Vic.*

PAUL ROGERS: Yes, that's right. Of which he was deeply ashamed.

Did he tell you that?

Yes. He made it quite clear, just in conversation, not having said, 'I did such-and-such and it was terrible,' because it wasn't – it was absolutely wonderful – but, in fact, he was rather ashamed of that huge success, because it was all wrong. And he was aiming really to discover what the play was about.

He genuinely tried to really put the play on its three levels – fairies, lovers, mechanicals. Fairies and lovers got the most work out of him, because they stylistically were a greater challenge than the mechanicals. He had cast in the mechanicals a collection of favourite sons. Which doesn't mean to say that the others weren't, but it would often happen with his favourite sons particularly, often to the detriment of the production, that he would not only give us our heads but would, as you know very well, encourage us to go sometimes too far, and it was all 'lovely and delightful and most enjoyable'.

He shocked people by his fairies – little boys, in the main: scrubby little boys, who looked as though they'd crawled out from under stones.

The lovers – this is where I came across Tony the great teacher of verse speaking, because he wanted to achieve – and did achieve, my God, because it was a superb quartet when he finally got it going – a matching of movement and speech and the wonderful high comedy. And this was achieved by the use of the text, the wonderful *use* of the text. And he could be merciless, as you know, particularly with actresses, on verse speaking. He could be brutal. Well, no, it was merely a matter of that marvellous tall, tall gentleman saying, 'Now little Miss So-and-So, don't be so silly.' That sort of lark, you know. And his old thing that any actor worth his salt should be able to do five sentences on a breath.

Do you recall some of the work he did with the mechanicals?

Tony had this gift for bringing things out, and then he allowed us to make a marvellous big mistake. And what was hysterical was that that mistake was perpetuated later by an admirer of the mistake, namely Peter Hall. Tony and I were talking about the ass's head, and I said, 'Wouldn't it be fun if the head was actually open – ears and sides, so that what was actually happening to the poor devil inside could be seen?' It *was* marvellous, at Cambridge, with all those undergraduates. And that was where Peter Hall, as a student, saw it. And later on at Stratford-on-Avon Peter perpetuated it.

And Guthrie obviously liked it and allowed you to do it.

Oh he loved it of course, absolutely loved it. He encouraged me, and we had the head made so that this was the case. But seeing it, in the way that actors instinctively know, one discovered it was wrong.

Why?

The essential thing was that indeed Bottom should seem to be *completely* transported. That there was no virtue in seeing the 'Bottom' inside the head. I forget at what moment it was that we decided, but we came to that conclusion very strongly, and I said to Tony, 'We were wrong.' And interestingly enough, later on, with Peter Hall directing, when I was to do the Bottom for him for the television movie with the Stratford company, Peter wanted me to wear a head like that, and I said, 'No, my darling, I know where you got *that* idea. It was my idea. Tony allowed me to do it and it was wrong, utterly wrong, and we're going to have a real ass's head. He must be turned into an ass.' This is just illustrative of Tony taking an idea from an actor, with pleasure, and encouraging him to do it in order to see what did happen.

Another example of this attitude was in *Troilus and Cressida.* You know the famous speech – Pandarus' last soliloquy to the audience when he gives them their diseases. The style in which this thing was done – and Tony did explain this to us – was that he put *Troilus and Cressida* into about 1912. He said it was the last moment in history when war was considered as glorious by the young men, when it was as much a sport as grouse shooting, among the better-bred young men

– which is why he had the Trojans dressed very much like an Austrian court, with silver cuirasses and lemon yellow uniforms like peacocks, and loving the whole thing. And it wasn't until the scene with the Myrmidons that the whole thing turns filthy and the brutal modern aspect of war suddenly raises its dreadful head when Achilles murders Hector. The thing suddenly turned over and went sour, horrible, disgusting. Until then the chivalry of war was demonstrated, and the Greeks were Prussians in their dress and in their attitude. When it came to that last speech, I had been thinking about it and I said, 'Tony, I think I ought to sing that.' He said, 'Dear boy, I've never thought of it done in any other way.' And, in point of fact, I did. It was a kind of unaccompanied blues thing, which I composed myself. That was, again, another thing that he allowed me to do.

He quite obviously had a plan for that production; then when it came to individual interpretation of character, how did he lead you towards that?

A general suggestion as to what kind of person Pandarus might be. But it was very gently given, sort of tossed to one. That's quite a good word. Tony never drove. He would 'toss' you things. And being what we were, at that time literally – like a lot of seals – we were ready to snatch at any of these lovely fish that were coming, you know.

For instance, because of Pandarus perhaps being connected with the royal house of Troy in a remote way, and being this old voyeuristic character, the first scene, which was the return of the troops from the day's battle, was done like a sort of Ascot, with Cressida and the servant and myself waving to these characters coming in, high camp in a sense.

And the detail work he did, for example in the morning after Troilus and Cressida, as it were, had been to bed together. And this was an enchanting little sort of house, Cressida's house, with an upstairs and a downstairs and the whole thing – and Tony said, 'And you come in with a tray of tea, you see, for the lovers.' And I said, 'Oh no, Tony, not on the morning after – champagne!' 'Of course, dear boy.' You see, it's give and take. His notion, which was gloriously outrageous and yet utterly right, of this terrible old thing coming in to see just how they were . . .

And maybe taking a peek.

Oh, several. But that little detail – and of course it led to a further touch, because, of course, the champagne cork gave a noise, which was right, also.

Did you ever disagree with him?

No, not really. Certainly there I had said, 'Oh no!' But that wasn't disagreeing with him. He'd said something that had made my imagination bounce, so that indeed I didn't do what he wanted, but it all sprung from what he wanted, it was just an elaboration of his wishes. He would never make you do something you didn't want to do.

The naughty side of Tony was that he could be very wicked. With people who imagined themselves, or perhaps *were* established actors and actresses, he could be brutal. The size of the man – I don't mean in terms of height – so that a particular sentence, the way it was used, was enough to reduce somebody who'd inflated themselves. In joke, I often used to say in those earlier days, 'Well I'll know when I'm *there*, because Tony will tell me.' And in fact, it happened – and of course it's terrible, because one loves the man so much and still I don't even like to speak about it: it was an extraordinary moment.

I hadn't gone to Canada with him, which he would have liked me to have done. There were emotional reasons behind that, and all sorts of other things. But I think that in the back of his mind, somewhere, he thought, 'This is the character who didn't come. He's taken the bowl, or whatever it is, sold his soul for . . .' You know? Inside somewhere. And this incident happened when we were having a celebration at the house of a very old friend of his, Constance Tomkinson, for his knighthood. This springs from the seals and the fish image. Tony did that to people. I'm sure he did it to the very end as far as the young were concerned. Less now but certainly, because this was several years ago, I was inclined to sort of leap in like a great fluffy dog, an overly affectionate fluffy dog. And I bounced into the room full of love and effusion and thrilled, and it was quite extraordinary. His reception was not only cool, but he actually put me right down. And I sort of staggered away from that party thinking, 'Christ, what did I do? What happened?' And I was living here at the time, and I suddenly said, 'Roz, I'm there. He's done it!'

And after that story, there's another side of this amazing, beautiful man. I was rehearsing *Troilus and Cressida*, and Roz was expecting Lucy, who's been quietly getting cups and things there, who's now seventeen years old. Roz was actually in hospital waiting for the baby, and we were rehearsing. And a message came to the stage door saying that Lucy was born. And I said, 'Tony, Roz has had the baby.' And he said, 'Oh, my dear boy, get up there as quickly as possible.' And I did – I exited into a cupboard! I literally went off the wrong side of the stage! And this was the other aspect of him.

I know you played the title role in Henry VIII *the last time Guthrie directed it. Do you recall the well-reported scene at the end of the play where Elizabeth, the baby, is brought in?*

Yes. It had to do with a good Shakespearian theme, hope for the future, and because of that, in collaboration with Tanya, of course, who was his favourite designer, that scene suddenly burst on the eye in pure gold, yellow and white. That was the message of the last scene. There were all these ramifications from the beginning of the play, through the whole Katherine relationship and the Anne Boleyn episode and so on, and the play exploded at the end with the hope of this tiny thing that this gross man held in his arms. Actually, you see, there isn't much in that last scene. Therefore he had to demonstrate his ultimate idea, which is probably the best way of phrasing it as far as Tony was concerned, in a visual thing. Again, the actual placing on the stage was very interesting. You know, in a picture, there are one, two, three, four points of interest that can geometrically be worked out. Well, in point of fact, Tanya had done it. The stage was filled with people and banners, all in this wonderful blaze of colour. And it did have a wonderful contrast.

The court scene was magnificent, but it was very heavy. And there was one bishop that was *so* old that it took about thirty seconds or more to get across the stage and he was more or less carried by two people. But it was not self-indulgent. Tony could be sometimes, but this was not. This was a case of building up in front of the audience's eyes what the fabric was, and at the end of the scene he was going to destroy this great assembly of all these powers, some very sturdy, some very strong. And, as I say, this one stands out in my mind, a clear old favourite actor who wasn't very good, but Tony loved him, and whenever he could employ him he employed him, because he was that kind of man.

Some people have told me that there were some funny things that came into that last scene.

Oh yes, oh rather. It gave it all the more point. It was a very human thing, indeed. And he encouraged, quite rightly, an almost idiotic pride and delight in Henry with this tiny creature, which again made it a very human thing in this magnificent setting.

A lot of critics censured that invention as a Guthrie trick, and now talking with you I realize that it literally was a way in which he humanized these incredibly magnificent scenes that could undoubtedly be very beautiful but with no humanity in them. Maybe that was the secret of all those great crowd scenes in so many productions – they were so human. Most critics looked at that and thought, 'Oh well, he was bored with the scene.' Or 'It was his prankish nature, he could never take anything too seriously.'

There were certain naughty things that he *would* do. I mean, for instance, the imaginary dog turd in *Henry*. That, frankly, was just Tony being naughty. He had a prankish thing. He was part Irish, you know.

Sort of a giant leprechaun.

Yes.

How did Guthrie help you develop your talent?

He never worked that way, at least not to one's knowledge. What he did do was set one on fire. This is quite an achievement, because it demonstrates to an actor what he can do, given certain sets of circumstances. Tony was always wanting more. He opened doors in you, for the sheer joy of seeing what came out. And being a young actor at the time that was precisely what I wanted to do. So what he did was give me a knowledge of the huge excitement there is to be had in the process of creating. That's it! What was the best part of a Tony Guthrie production? Playing it, yes. But the great part was the *rehearsals*. I've used the word 'teacher'. It's the only word that can be used, but it was nothing to do with a school, nothing to do with that at all. It was *educo*, a leading forth. This was why he loved the young actors, and a few of the older ones. But as soon as you got any notion in your head that you knew even a fraction of it, Tony began to lose interest in you, and quite rightly.

Did you ever seek his advice about choices in your career?

Yes, I did. I recall a time when Hugh Hunt had asked me to go to Australia, to the Elizabethan Theatre Trust, to play in *Macbeth* and to direct it. And I sent back a letter saying I'd had it. As far as I could make out, I'd played the part possibly more than anybody else in history, but certainly in modern times, and I'd had it, really right up to there. I was to play it again later on, but for that moment, no. Then came a cable, 'Think it's time you cracked Hamlet.' Well now, this is the kind of suggestion which, in England, is utterly out of the question: I was forty then, and you certainly don't cast a man of my build, my shape, my qualities, as Hamlet, ever. Until *now* when they even cast Nicol Williamson to play it. The thing has changed. I remember saying to Roz, 'Hugh's gone out of his mind.' I said, 'I think I'll do it, I will.' But I did want to talk to somebody about it. We were in New York, and I asked Tony if I could take him out to lunch or something. And there was this marvellous moment when he said, 'Take me to Lindy's. We'll have cheese blintzes. Have you ever had cheese blintzes?' I said, 'No.' 'They are the greatest in the world,' he said. 'We'll have cheese blintzes and coffee, and we can talk about it.' And, as always with Tony, if you were ever given the opportunity to go somewhere and do something, his advice was to go. It all links in, I suppose, with what I'm saying he gave me, which was a sense of adventure in the job. I mean we've all got it, but it was never quite as explicit as it was in the company of Tony Guthrie.

A further complication of the man was that he was perfectly capable, when he saw a talent that he thought ought to go, of being able to kick the fledgling out of the nest. But similarly there are people who come to my mind who *should* have been kicked out of the nest. But he held on to them with a sort of octopus-like grip, which was mainly just his personality. And *those* he did not let go, those he kept with him through years and years. Sometimes not always to the benefit of their development because Tony was a very powerful, terribly attractive influence – that was the problem.

How do you compare him with the other directors with whom you have worked?

There are two people who have touched my life and really changed it. One is Tony Guthrie and the other is Peter Hall. Talking about this, this would appear to be ungrateful to Hugh Hunt, who certainly gave me my first opportunity, and then many, many opportunities afterwards. And he's a man I loved working with, tremendously, because he gave me a great freedom. Michael Benthall, similarly. Without Michael I don't know where I would be today. But we're talking about something different now. We're talking about people that meant you would never have been the same had you not worked with them. And Tony and Hall are two such people. Tony, as it were, put me in contact with an explosion of enthusiasm and excitement and fun. Hall suddenly dragged me from having spread about a bit, as an actor – I'd become a bit untidy – and it was he who, through *The Homecoming*, almost imprisoned me for a while, and then gave me a new kind of freedom. He really dragged me back by the hair to the text. In point of fact, I'd been there with Tony, but I'd got sort of untidy, particularly working in modern plays, when literally one rewrote the entire play. I mean literally *that* kind of attitude towards the text. With Pinter, you know, it's merciless, and Tony with Shakespeare could be quite merciless in the demands of the text.

So discipline, in a way, you got from both Guthrie and Hall?

Yes, but a completely different kind of discipline. But those are the two men that I would say have a parallel, in my mind. Utterly different, excepting that Peter also has got a marvellous quality of never letting the situation override him. In the same way as Tony was never overridden by any considerations at all. To start off with, the basic one of money. It was to be *found*, and it was not necessarily *his* business to do it. Hall is the same in that area. They both have a wonderful artistic arrogance, which in their cases is utterly and completely justified. And *astonishing* to me with my rather Church of England, bit parsimonious background.

Was Hall influenced by Guthrie?

I don't think, you see, Hall ever entered the stable, as it were. But without a question he must have been influenced. I mean, after all, the *Midsummer Night's Dream* Bottom story. I know where that one came from, because nobody had done it before. But then they were all influenced to some extent by Tony. It was impossible not to be.

Leo McKern

ALFRED ROSSI: *You were telling me about a letter you had from Tony Guthrie.*

LEO MCKERN: I was over in Ireland, doing *Ryan's Daughter*, that monstrous film. He happened to be at his own house, a great Jacobean thing with an impossible name. He wrote to me about this project in Australia, to do *Oedipus* and another play, and he asked me to come up for a weekend, so I drove all the way up. I went into this strange house, which was the most extraordinary jumble of things – furniture, bric-à-brac, antiques – a real Irish house with all sorts of souvenirs. I was surprised to learn that he had been ill. He said, 'Oh, yes. I've been told to sit in this chair and stay here. I can't live like that. I couldn't bear it.' Then he said, 'I'm going to do this Australian work. Well, I'm thinking about it. I don't know whether I should do it or whether I shouldn't. It would be very embarrassing to say the least if I started on it and dropped dead.' Anyway he decided to do it because, of course, he wasn't the sort of person to be able to sit down even if it meant a couple of extra years. So he did go to Australia. Of course, during the production he was terribly ill and probably that tour finished him off; nevertheless, he got through it.

Did you play in the company that year?

No. I couldn't. He wanted me, as I was an Australian actor.

He was very keen on that; in Canada he tried to get Canadians, and in America, when he started the Guthrie Theater, he wanted American actors as much as possible. What was your first experience with him?

The Arts Council of Great Britain run tours in this country. Not so many now, but they used to run tours on one-night stands to places like mining villages in Wales and in the North Country and in the Black Country – that sort of thing. A winter tour like that can be absolutely a horrible experience. You play in these extraordinary places – village halls, people's houses, old decayed cinemas that have closed twenty years before and are freezing, of course. But occasionally they had some extremely good actors and directors. Being in the Arts Council thing is like being admitted to a public hospital in this country, if you wait long enough for an appointment. You go free to any hospital and you'll see the biggest and the best ear surgeon in the world, because he has got to give a certain amount of time. This seemed to be the sort of set-up of the Arts Council, which could command all sorts of big names for these tours. Guthrie directed Miles Malleson's new translation of *The Miser*, and I went on that tour and played a small part and did stage managing at the same time. The play was taken into the Old Vic, Guthrie produced the play, and I had the same part.

What was your initial impression of him as a leader of rehearsals in those days?

I knew about him, of course. His name in the theatrical world was perfectly established from years before. Being a young man and getting into the Old Vic and getting into any company that Guthrie was directing was the height of one's ambition at that time. One was very impressed. I remember we were rehearsing with Miles on the stage during *The Miser*, and there was something to do with the walking stick. It wasn't working. I was sitting in the stalls as I often did, and I was watching every minute of rehearsal. Guthrie leant over to me and said, 'It's not working, is it?' And I said, 'Uhhhhhhhh.' And he said, 'What's the matter? What's wrong with it? Why isn't it working?' And I gave him what was in my head at the time. But to be asked like that from this sort of demi-god really took the wind out of me sails. I was a very young and inexperienced man. That was the sort of bloke he was. He did the same thing from time to time, without being, as some directors are, a brain-picker. There are directors I know (and very famous ones) who in fact construct the whole bloody production on the ideas of the actors.

After that season at the Vic, which was 1949, I didn't work with him again until the opening of the new Nottingham Playhouse, where he came up to produce *Coriolanus*, which he put into the Empire period. It was a marvellous experience – the opening play of a new theatre. He had a streak of boyish, peculiar, prefect-like irresponsibility. He's told me, watching a scene, 'Look at so-and-so. Isn't he *terrible*?' And he's bursting with laughter. This I found absolutely captivating. It was really Tony.

Did you find rehearsals particularly interesting with Tony? More fun than performances?

Well, I enjoy rehearsal so much and when you have to perform, it becomes a repetitive thing so that you have to bring technique to bear to keep it fresh all the time. I can't bear to do a play for more than three months, because after that I've exhausted the part. It's like eating the inside of a coconut, and you're left with the shell. After that it's like going to the office from nine to five, and that's not why we're in the business. But with Guthrie rehearsals were always exciting, marvellous and funny. Comedy rehearsals were hysterical, and he did the most outrageous things. In *The Alchemist* the play opens with a screaming argument between the three leading characters – the girl and the two men. He had us coming out of an upstairs room in a terribly decayed Victorian terraced house, and the Alchemist, me, chasing the others downstairs carrying a chamberpot full of piss and splashing it all over the place. There's a terrible row off-stage and suddenly these three figures emerge. Once the audience sees what is happening, shocked or not – you don't have time to be shocked – you spill over with laughter: instant, visual, explosive.

Is that typical? Would you say that he would normally give a physical guide as opposed to a psychological one?

He would use every aspect. He would use the approach to an actor that he knew that the actor could understand. In *The Alchemist*, for example, he had the idea of having me play this character pretending to be a seer and a sage (it's not in the script), and it is a marvellous stroke of imagination. Now once you've decided that he's going to be a *swami*, how do you bring him on to the stage? Now he can't walk on, because he needs to be three inches above the ground. So you can have him carried on, but again, somehow the character would be dependent on the people that were carrying him. So you have him *glide* on, and you have him three feet off the floor. How can we have him three feet off the floor? We'll put him in some sort of wheelbarrow. A tea-trolley, that's it! So he accomplishes a whole presentation of the character before the character opens his mouth. The fact that it's a tea-trolley, well, it was the only thing they had in the bloody house. This sort of imagination is so bizarre that you gasp at his suggestions.

How would you describe Guthrie's notes?

Always direct, revealing in three words what possibly another director would take twenty to express. They were always succinct, and terribly economic. Sometimes in a short sentence he could give you the whole. You'd be kicking yourself, because you'd say, 'Oh Christ, why didn't I think of that? What a bloody idiot.' He was able to put his finger on something so simply. Sometimes he would work with an actor, and he couldn't get what he wanted from him. Now realizing that he couldn't get it in the way that he wanted it, he would change his approach radically by, for example, concentrating on the voice. He would say, 'Right. Now I want you to play the whole thing in a *basso profundo*.' Or 'Let's try you with a walking stick and with a slipped disc.' In other words something terribly simple that would help to get across to the actor what Guthrie wanted out of that particular performance. If that didn't work, he would do something again quite different.

What was unique about Tony Guthrie?

There are two things which were most remarkable about him. The first was that he had what I call – and it is an extremely rare thing – a universal manner. He would speak to me, to the lowest man of the company, to the highest man of the company, to Prince Philip, to the Prime Minister in exactly the same manner. Also, he had an enormous consideration for people. For example, you got into a discussion or an argument with him – he had such a quick mind – and you would start to say something and look at him and realize that he knew exactly what you were going to say, either as an answer to a question or to explain something. And in an argument, instead of breaking in and saying, 'Yes, I know what you're going to say', he would wait until you'd finished. This is a courtesy and a consideration that is very rare, and it's an intellectual thing. Probably realizing that he was way ahead of you, he at least paid you the courtesy of listening to what you had to say. Those were the two most memorable things about him – his universal manner and that courtesy.

William Hutt

ALFRED ROSSI: *I know that you were in the original company at Stratford, Ontario, and have played many seasons there. What productions did you do under Tony Guthrie's direction?*

WILLIAM HUTT: When Tony was in charge of the company the first three seasons he directed *Richard III*, *All's Well That Ends Well*, *The Taming of the Shrew*, *The Merchant of Venice*, and *Oedipus Rex*, which was done in both the second and third seasons. He later came back to direct *Twelfth Night* in 1957.

How much freedom did Guthrie give you in a part? How much did he suggest or was it, as is usual with most fine directors, a blending of the two?

Well, I suppose basically it was a blending of the two, but, at the same time, singularly enough, I found that Tony was a director who would follow rather than lead: in this respect, that he, of course, early in rehearsals would know the play better than the actors would know it. But as the rehearsals went on the actors would seem to take over and he followed them. In other words he set up a scene that he knew roughly how he wanted to go, the direction that he wanted that scene to take. But then along would come an actor who might do something that Guthrie didn't think about, perhaps, and Guthrie would then elaborate on it, encourage it, make it grow, and possibly even change the direction of the scene to suit what this actor had done.

I noticed this specifically in his production of *Taming of the Shrew* back in 1954. Guthrie had a rather outlandish and perhaps even outrageous interpretation of the piece. But the comic talent which suddenly burst forth was staggering to behold. I remember one day just watching Guthrie sit there absolutely bemused – he didn't know what to do. In fact, the production I *think* went farther than he ever intended it to.

Guthrie wrote in his autobiography that the coaching aspect of direction is a relative thing and in working with professionals of the calibre that you have at the Stratford, Ontario, festival, there is very little teaching. In other words the equipment already has to be there or you probably wouldn't even be in the company. Is that correct?

Well, as far as the company is concerned I think you are right. You have to have the equipment. But as far as Guthrie is concerned I know that he was one of the few directors in the world who could take absolutely rank amateurs and make them look all but totally professional. Because he had so many tricks, particularly with crowd scenes. He could take a bunch of amateurs and make them look magnificent in a crowd scene, because he just knew how to move people on stage.

Is there any specific way he did this? Did he break it down into certain sections and take it piece by piece, or did he take areas of the stage?

He didn't take individuals. He didn't give twenty individual directions when he'd direct a crowd scene. More than likely he'd just say, 'You twenty over there.' But what he gave them was an object against which their mass emotion must react. And the object that he gave them was very clear. For example, in *The Merchant of Venice* I remember at the end of the trial scene, the exit of Shylock, he just said to the entire assembly, 'Now, what we want here is just absolute Jew-baiting. When this man makes his exit from the court do anything you want – spit, yell, scream, anything, all of you.' Which they did, you see, and they had this marvellous object in Freddie Valk (Shylock).

I know that you were the Chorus Leader in Oedipus *which of course is one of Guthrie's most famous productions, and as Guthrie's only film has a certain significance. How did he handle the Chorus?*

Well, to describe how he used the Chorus one has to describe very briefly how he saw *Oedipus Rex*. He saw the play as a symphony of symbol. I mean both those words. A symbolic symphony. The man who played Oedipus was not a human being but a symbol. That's why he put everybody in masks. The Chorus, therefore, was simply an anonymous symbol of humanity. And he used the Chorus, really as, I suppose, the brass in an orchestra. He used the voices to create sound rather than to create personalities. He wanted a sound from the masks. It was a mass reaction to what was going on in the life of Oedipus. And choreographically the way we stood, the stances we took up, would indicate what we were feeling.

What do you think Guthrie contributed most to an actor's performance?

Freedom is the best word I can think of at the moment. It's not licence however. There is quite a difference. It is *freedom*. One felt when working with Tony that he would accept anything you did, however outrageous it might be if it was done with courage and conviction. And if it came from inside you. He might refine it, hone it, or perhaps tone it down, but he would accept it. And he made this willingness to accept quite clear in his attitude towards the actor in rehearsals, so that you had unlimited confidence in yourself, working under Guthrie. And if you'd gone too far he would say you went too far, but you'd never take offence at it, since his willingness to accept bred infinite trust, and you'd know, in fact, that you *had* gone too far.

In the planning stage of a production, let's say Oedipus, *did he include the chief characters in the play in the preliminary discussion?*

Yes. Although, singularly, *Oedipus*, to the best of my memory, is the only production where Tony called the whole company together at the first rehearsal and had a long chat about the play. Usually he would make a little five-minute dissertation at the first rehearsal – just what he thought about the play and what he wanted to do with it – but I remember the first rehearsal of *Oedipus* it was quite a long chat he gave to the whole company about why he wanted to do this play, and why he wanted to do it the way he was going to do it, saying that he fully realized himself that it might be classed as a magnificent failure. He said, 'We're all sticking our necks way out, but let's do it with courage and conviction.'

Why do you think he did that?

Well, I think first of all he wanted to get the company on his side. He wanted them to understand exactly what he was going to do, what his ideas were. And particularly in a production like *Oedipus Rex* it was essential that everybody agreed on the concept he proposed, since nobody, as I say, was really being a personality. It wasn't Douglas Campbell or James Mason that he wanted. He wanted a symbolic *Oedipus*.

Can you talk about the unusual interpretation of The Taming of the Shrew *that Guthrie did? Did he have to convince the company as he did in* Oedipus?

No, I don't think he had to convince the company because in those days Stratford was in its infancy and professional theatre in Canada was more or less in its infancy as well. And all the actors were so bloody glad to be at Stratford and certainly delighted to be working under somebody like Tony, that we just submitted like sheep. I feel that Tony thought less of the play than he actually should have. Tony sometimes tended to be slightly frivolous if he thought a play was not as good as it should be. He had a tendency to try to send the play up in his approach to it. And his whole idea was to reverse the traditional interpretation. Instead of having Petruchio the broad, *bravura* personality who would take the stage and sweep Katherine off her feet and instead of having Katherine a sort of female counterpart to this, he simply turned the coin right over and saw Petruchio as just really a stubborn country bumpkin, insisting, 'I want that girl and I'm going to get her. And you nor nobody else is gonna tell me any different.' And Katherine was just the spoiled daughter of a very rich man, that's all. So that was the way he saw the play. With a certain stubborn shyness in it.

Does this affect the verse any when you take an interpretation like that?

Yes, it does. I think it keeps the verse closer to the ground than it should be, instead of letting the verse soar. It keeps the verse on a tunnelled stubborn level.

If you could tell me one thing that was the secret of Guthrie's success, what do you think it might be?

Well, I think it was Guthrie's approach to life, really, perhaps even to the universe. He saw the whole world in sharp contrast. In observing the world, he saw that there can be no darkness unless there is light. There can be no white unless there is black, there can be no good unless there is evil. And in all of his productions, when he wished to create an effect, he would lead the audience the other way first and then bring in the effect that he wanted to create. To give you a specific example of this I hark back to *The Merchant of Venice* and the trial scene. As I said before, when Shylock made his exit the entire court booed and hissed and in fact some of them literally spit on Shylock. Now it was a Christian court that was trying this man. And after Shylock had made his exit, and everybody booed and roared and spit and baited this Jew, there was a sudden hush, and *one* person on stage started to cry. Which meant, of course, that there was a sudden shame from the Christian element, and a realization of how they had treated this man. And this was the effect he wanted, this in fact made Shylock's exit for him, in spite of the fact that by this time Shylock was off stage and back in his dressing-room. That was Shylock's exit, that man crying. And this in fact was what he wanted his audience to do.

Do you think that this is the type of thing that was repeated in his direction in a number of plays?

Yes, I do. As another example, I remember in *Taming of the Shrew* at the moment when Petruchio returns home and food is served to him and he looks at this horrible piece of meat and says something like, 'Who cooked this?' and at that particular moment all the servants in Petruchio's house were lined across the stage and up the stairs on to the balcony. And Petruchio turned to the first one, who was a very tall man, and said. 'Who cooked this?' And the first man looked at the second and the third and the fourth and finally got up to the man at the top of the balcony, who was the tiny Eric House. So that just *physically* the thing was made, you see. Finally the little man was left holding the bag.

Arthur Hill

ALFRED ROSSI: *When you played Cornelius in* The Matchmaker *did Tony Guthrie treat you in any different way from Ruth Gordon?*

ARTHUR HILL: Well, we were all in the same beneficent atmosphere, the feeling that a big, glowing personality was there. But there was no doubt that he would seem to spot – in ways that I was astonished at – differences in people. If he thought somebody was lagging, and just not trying, believe me he could let loose very neatly. Suddenly the atmosphere became very electric indeed. For example, an actor was standing there in the middle of the stage one day with the script still in his hands and saying, with his eyes rolling around, 'Now, shall I move down here, or shall I move over there?' And Guthrie said, 'Whatever you like.' It was a Mexican standoff because he'd keep saying, 'Well, I don't know whether I should or . . . ' And finally Guthrie said, 'Oh come on, just do it!' And what he really meant was, 'Now you do your part and we'll see what happens. And if it's good, it may be so good that no matter what I say you'll say, "Go to hell." ' He gave you that freedom. He knew the actor's province and whenever he invaded it it was for a very good reason. I don't know how he sensed that. I've met people who thought he was unkind and tough on them. Well, maybe he misread them. Maybe the relationship just wasn't the same. It may have been their sensibilities. Also, sometimes it was the piece, as he would call it, the work they were on. I suppose if it didn't jell and go together properly, then everybody's in trouble all the way around.

Since he has been recognized as one of the great comedy directors, are there any particular techniques that you remember Guthrie using? For example, in that hilarious hat shop scene?

Well, it came from all of us. That's really what I'm trying to convey about him. I think we all invented things. He didn't insist on doing it all himself. Often he'd let you go too far, to see how it worked out. And then say, 'No, that doesn't work, does it?' Or 'That's boring, I think, don't you?' Always seemed to be consulting you while giving you his opinion at the same time. For instance, I remember inventing a piece of business that I didn't even do, which is just an example of the kind of thing that he would just lap up, and say, 'Yes, good, go.' There we were in the hat shop and, of course, we took off our hats and put them down on the table and I said, 'Wouldn't it be funny if we left them there when we crawled into the cupboard under the table? And now Eileen Herlie is left having to do something with these two men's hats.' And he said, 'Yes. Good idea. Right, right. Get a bit of veil, Eileen, wrap it around and put them in the window.' I never saw the piece of business being done, because I was in the cupboard.

Did Guthrie ever demonstrate anything for you?

Oh, very badly, yes. I think he did it deliberately. He told me he was a bloody awful actor himself. I remember he said he was in two or three films, one with Charles Laughton called *The Beachcomber*, and I remember now that great big tall man who played the Dutch resident general in Java or wherever the film was supposed to have taken place. He said, 'Oh, I was awful, I was just dreadful.' But yes, he'd come up on to the stage sometimes and start moving around like a great big camel or something and moving this there and doing this and saying, 'Try something like this,' and he'd do it deliberately badly, so that you hadn't any sense of trying to imitate. Because if you imitated it was just going to be absurd. But it was just laying it out: 'Something like that and see what happens.' Always 'See what happens.' Not 'This is the way to do it.'

Did Guthrie approach the American production of The Matchmaker *any differently?*

He found the producing of the thing all over again, directing it for America, extremely boring. The man was easily bored and as far as he was concerned he'd done what had to be done, and I think the fact that he gave it any time at all was a tribute to his regard for Ruth Gordon. He found it very hard because of the management. He was not used to having this kind of manager, David Merrick, who would insist on travelling here and there out of town nursing this thing along. As far as he was concerned he'd done everything there was to be done. There were two or three cast changes, but he'd settled all that in Philadelphia and gone back to Ireland or wherever the devil he was going to go. And he got severe summonses to come back immediately – or else. I didn't learn about this until later, but I could see that he was most unhappy.

It was just a simple difference of attitude towards what a director's work is in the two countries. I think that directors don't *nurse* plays in England the way directors are expected to nurse them here, and David Merrick was going to have none of it. He wanted the same kind of treatment that all directors would give a play. I suspect there was justice on both sides. But knowing the kind of man that Guthrie was I could see that he was now scouring around the bottom of a dingy barrel and there was nothing there and what was he doing, except going through the motions? And he disliked the opening night enormously, because he felt there were claques in the audience who had been paid to laugh. I remember at the party afterwards he would keep going, 'Ha, ha, ha, ha, ha', and not a smile, nothing – like a death mask. That was his comment on the evening.

Do you think Merrick did hire some claques for the audience?

I have no idea. You know how frozen you are on opening night, you're so busy doing what you're doing. I don't remember the evening that well. All I know is that in the previews that we did during the week I had the impression that the theatre was bought and sold under us two or three times. They were sure it was going to be a terrible flop. Our first rehearsal in America was made a grand occasion. The Theater Guild was there, with Armina Marshall and her husband Lawrence Langer sitting out in the front of the house, because the Theater Guild had some hold on this play. I remember Guthrie leaning over and saying, 'Who are they? What are they doing here?' – he knew of course, who they were – to the stage manager. And the stage manager saying, 'Well, I guess they're here for the first reading . . . etc.' 'Well, okay, what's first?' And the stage managers, you know, in American productions, in those days had to get up and read the Equity rules. The first day of rehearsal you have to read all those rules. This went on for quite some time. Guthrie was sitting there opening his mail and reading it and one thing and another, waiting. Finally, Biff Liff finished reading the Equity rules and sat down. Then Guthrie said, 'Well, all done with that then? Now we're going to start.' And he went over to the footlights and he said, 'Distinguished guests, we are now going to get to work, so will you kindly fuck off.' Where do you go when somebody says something like that? I mean, there's nowhere to go with it, he just splattered things all over the place. So they just got up and walked foolishly away. And yet he did it in such a way that you couldn't really be offended because he smiled, that wonderful little beam on his face. All done with great humour.

I get the impression from this story and the from the difference of opinion with Merrick about babysitting the production that he may not have been happy with the way the American theatre was approached commercially.

Or just not used to it, I would have guessed, because after that he did several American productions and I presume he fell into whatever the pattern was. You know, no dummy he. When in Rome you finally do it that way, I guess. I think it was just such a surprise to him. He didn't know what on earth was to be expected of him. But he would learn, I presume, to play the game in some way or other, you know, more acceptably than that time. That time was unhappy and unfortunate.

Did you find that when you came to America with the play – and of course you eventually played a thousand performances – did you find that there was any change because you were playing to American audiences?

Yes. I think things which had seemed amusing to English audiences were not necessarily so to American audiences. Americans are not particularly amused, for instance, by the idea of men being dressed up as women, which is part of the action of the play. It's a tradition as old as pantomime in England, where they think it's screamingly funny. So as soon as Barnaby would show up with his lady's hat and gown and everything, right away you're going to get a laugh the like of which you can't imagine. And with Americans just no amusement. So right away you've got to start altering your timing and your attitude. I think there were lines which to Americans . . . Yonkers is a funny idea, right? I can remember Gar Kanin saying, 'Nobody ever came from Yonkers.' Right away it's funny. It's like saying 'Hoboken'. But to an Englishman it has no meaning. It's not funny whatsoever, it's just a place over there on the other side of the water. As an illustration of the difference of things there's a line in the Harmonia Gardens where Eileen Herlie says to me, 'Come on, dance.' And I say, 'I can't dance, the Hackles are Presbyterian.' Well, I can tell you when you play that line in Edinburgh it's the funniest line in the whole play. They just stop right there, because it was the heart of Presbyterianism of a kind that this country knows nothing about, that's Scots Presbyterianism. A very rigid form of that particular faith. It got a laugh, sure, but not that show stopper that nobody was ready for at all.

Just to add to what you were asking about observations that I made, I remember that in *The Matchmaker* there were several of us that came out and gave little talks to the audience, a kind of sharing where the action stops. What Guthrie said was, 'In the theatre, if you want to concentrate your power, the less of your body you use the more concentrated it will be.' And he was right. If you really want to say something dead serious, don't move one limb, move only your jaw. And suddenly everything stops dead and everybody says, 'This is serious, this is important.' And I remember going home and thinking about that and watching the touring Billy Graham doing his 'act' on the BBC. A perfect demonstration of a guy who didn't know how to do it. There he was pounding the pulpit and waving his arms all over the place and creating the impression that he didn't believe what he was saying, didn't have that real conviction.

Do you have any observations about Guthrie's personality?

He had a lot of wonderful contradictions about himself. I think that's, again, what made him so human. And that's why I discount his books more than I do the actual experience of being with him. Odd little vanities.

He had a great sense of occasion sometimes and then sometimes none whatever. He told a wonderful story on himself. He was invited to go up to Vancouver. And he knew that I'd been in Vancouver, and he said, 'Do you know Mrs Clegg?' I said, 'Oh yeah, I know Mrs Clegg.' She was a famous old eccentric, a great old lady who in her late sixties canoed across Canada with an Indian guide. She was a woman of some distinction. Anyway, Guthrie had been invited out to Vancouver, I suppose as a result of the success at Stratford, to talk to Vancouver movers and shakers to see whether they could do something of the same. And he said, 'I remember arriving bombed out of my mind, because I'd been flying on that damn plane all the way across Canada, and I hadn't really thought about what I was going to say, and I went to this small gathering of people who thought they were going to be able to do something, and gave them a short and not very well organized address.' Then he said, 'I just sort of fumbled off at the end and went over and started shoving ham sandwiches into my mouth and drinking cups of coffee and this lady, Mrs Clegg, came over and introduced herself and said, "I've been sitting here listening to you for the last forty-five minutes and you haven't said anything. I paid a dollar and a half, and I want my dollar and a half back." ' He said, 'I had to fish around. I had nothing but pounds, shillings and pence. I had to borrow the dollar and a half and give it to her.'

Alec McCowen

ALFRED ROSSI: *How were you engaged for* The Matchmaker?

ALEC McCOWEN: Well, I had just finished a year's run in a play called *Escapade* playing a sixteen-year-old schoolboy. I was in my middle twenties then, and I was known as the oldest juvenile in the business. They were auditioning for *The Matchmaker*, and I was asked to read for the part of Barnaby Tucker, partly on the strength of having played this schoolboy for a year. I was very thrilled that it was going to be a Guthrie production with the great Ruth Gordon and Sam Levene. I went along to the Globe Theater for the audition, and there was a crowd of young actors of my own type. Anyway, I went down and read with the stage manager. I only read a short amount and Tony Guthrie said, 'All right. Thank you,' and came up on the stage. He said simply, 'Well, if we *don't* work together in this play, I hope we will in something else.' It was a clever remark to make because I thought: 'Right, I *haven't* got this play, but he seemed to like me.' I went away with my self-respect, at least, and very often you leave auditions with the feeling that 'I'm going to give up the business.' Also, I didn't fret. I thought, 'Right. I haven't got that part. That's that.' And I didn't do that terrible thing that young actors do after giving an audition, sitting by the telephone for days and days waiting for their agent or the management to ring. But, in fact, it was about a week later when Binkie Beaumont, who was the management, rang me up and said, 'Tyrone Guthrie would very much like you to play Barnaby Tucker in *The Matchmaker*.' So, I was absolutely delighted.

Do you recall the very early rehearsals?

Yes. I don't remember if we read through the play, but I do remember the completely original way, as far as I was concerned, of Guthrie starting off rehearsals, by saying, 'We will start off by doing the simple scenes.' Maybe he always did this; I don't know. He said, 'We'll start off with the duologues and then scenes with perhaps three people on the stage, and we'll leave the complicated stuff, the ensemble stuff, the crowd work till later.' And so rehearsal started with us just working on the simplest scenes and then stopping when he decided, 'I don't want to work on this yet.' It was a very clever way of working because actors got confidence in the personality of the parts they were playing without being terribly fussed with enormous technical problems in the early stage. There were a lot of chases and dances, and that sort of thing, and he left those until much later on in rehearsals; until he was happy with the acting scenes.

How did he guide you in that early work?

I think it was in a very loose method. He would say, 'Try it this way; let's try these positions.' He would make many suggestions, though one of the leading actors argued with him one day. Tony said, 'All right. If you think you know better do it yourself.' And he didn't speak to him for a week, by which time the actor was *pleading* for direction. After we'd been working for a week or ten days, Tony hadn't given me any real notes of any sort at all. I think it was a weekend and I went home and did a lot of work on my own, which I thought was very good. I came in Monday morning and started to put this work I'd done into practice and quite soon he stopped me. He said, 'I don't know what you're doing. I wanted you to do Barnaby Tucker, because you read it for me so beautifully at that audition. That's what I want. Don't do anything more.' This, in one way, was a disappointment to me because I didn't actually have very much acting direction from Guthrie. He thought, obviously, that I was a natural for the part. And all I had to do was do it naturally. The minute I tried to get clever with it he would stop me.

Was this characteristic of the way he cast the other roles too?

I think he was very good at casting. Although I wouldn't say it was true of the entire cast. I was very much the type. Of course, I remember particularly, and you yourself must remember, that he was apt not only to direct the small parts with the same importance as the star parts, but perversely very often with a little more importance, so that he would spend more time directing the waiters or people playing tiny parts rather than stars.

How did this wash with the people in the major roles?

I remember at one rehearsal Eileen Herlie, who gave a delicious performance as Mrs Malloy, was doing a speech and suddenly Tony Guthrie shouted out at me, 'Stand in front of Eileen when she's saying that line. I don't want to hear it.' Which, for somebody playing a relatively small part, I found a bit embarrassing. But he did do those unpredictable things from time to time, which kept everybody, particularly the leading players, in their place.

Do you recall any of the work he did in putting together that hilarious scene in the millinery shop where everybody's in the closets and under the tables?

From what I remember, it was like a child making a castle out of bricks. It would start very simply, and he would add and add and add, until quite often the actors would think, 'No. You can't, you can't, you can't do anything more.' I think it was a *slow* process. I don't think, I may be wrong, but I don't think he was what you'd call a blue-print director, that he came to rehearsals with everything mapped out on paper. I think he, in the type of scene you're talking about, choreographed it on the spot. He said, 'You try coming from the left. You come in from the right. You collide, and the time you collide, somebody comes in from centre. As you break this time we want to hear a voice down on the left, and the focus will go down there.' That sort of thing.

Was there a lot of give and take with him?

Oh, I think mostly taking, because of the enormous respect everybody had for him. I think the behaviour of a company is very often influenced by the behaviour of the star, and Ruth Gordon had *enormous* respect for Guthrie. Apart from only one instance at the very end of rehearsals she was a completely obedient actress, did everything she was told, never argued about anything, so that if your leading player is behaving this way certainly the company is obedient also. She set a fantastic example. Working with her was one of the greatest experiences in my professional life. We opened the play in Newcastle, and I remember when Ruth Gordon got to her soliloquy, she not only got a laugh a line, but I think she got three or four rounds of applause. It was fascinating during the run of the play. She would *change* things, not to throw anybody else, but that soliloquy eventually became, during the London run, a very sad soliloquy with perhaps one laugh at the end and then she could switch back and play it again for comedy. It was equally effective either way.

How did Tony and Thornton Wilder work together?

I recall very amicable relations between Guthrie and Wilder. Thornton was a sweet, sweet man of the theatre and was apt to sometimes drop a hint of direction in an actor's ear. He couldn't resist. I remember *vividly* on the Sunday morning we set off for Newcastle he arrived at the railway station with the last speech of the play, which was the speech for Barnaby Tucker about adventure, written on a sheet of schoolboy paper. I still have it in my desk. It's a very treasured possession.

Actually my favourite story about Guthrie is what happened towards the end of rehearsals when the play was completely plotted, everybody knew their lines, and we had a run-through. At the end of the run-through Guthrie said, 'Well, that was perfect. Everybody knows what they're doing. Everybody's doing it very well. *Now we're going to mess it up a little.*' And he proceeded then to stop it looking like a smart, technical, beautifully rehearsed comedy, and somehow breathed *natural* life into it, and he did mess it up a little. It had the impression of spontaneity and exuberance and wasn't neat in the sense that I think that French farce is, sometimes so boringly neat, *so* choreographed, *so* perfect, that you don't really believe it's happening.

During the first weeks of the tour, I think he felt his work was done. I admired greatly the way he was then ready to take *advice* from the producer, Binky Beaumont, who was a brilliant man of the theatre and could be a creative man as well. I remember Binky making many suggestions such as the explosion at the end of Act I. Binky said, 'Why does it have to be such a small explosion? It should be five times that big.' So this was changed. And Binky made suggestions about the make-up, about the set, and sometimes even about business in the play. Tony was *happy* about this and would tell us, which he had no need to do at all, 'This is Binky's idea, and I think it's a very good one. That's Binky's idea. Binky thinks this.' It's generous, and it's very sensible. It's a sign of a really big person that he would take advice at a time when he was tired, and he'd given the play everything that he thought he could give it. I remember Tony on the first night. He came around every dressing-room with a bottle of whisky and a tooth mug. He gave us a drink out of this dreadful tooth mug, you know, a mug you have in the bathroom to keep your toothbrush in. 'Yes,' he said. 'Very, very good. Have a drink.' He had a few himself.

Very often he didn't watch the production on opening night.

Well, maybe he hadn't. Maybe he'd been at the hotel, drinking whisky out of the tooth mug. I don't know. That was in Newcastle. In Edinburgh after the first night, they needed to take some press photographs after the performance and there were a lot of photographers there and the cast was asked to stay on the stage. And, of course, a lot of notables, friends, and management came back after the performance, so the stage was crowded with people, and it was rather chaotic. Suddenly, Tony's voice rang out. 'Now there's a photograph call for the cast. Anyone not involved – piss off.' All these people in evening dress were somewhat startled.

Now, you didn't play in the American production, did you?

I had a very unhappy experience with *The Matchmaker* to do with the New York production. I was asked to go to New York, and I didn't want to. I was bored with the part, and I had an offer of a new play in London, but the play I did was not a success. While *Matchmaker* was on tour in America, the management decided to replace the boy playing Barnaby Tucker and asked me to come over and play for the opening for four weeks, and I agreed to do this. When I got there I discovered Guthrie had not been told. It was a terrible position for me to be in. He didn't agree the thing should be done anyway. I saw the show in Boston the Saturday night, and I thought the boy playing my part was better than I'd been in it, so I was doubly embarrassed. Indeed, I think he had improved very much since the time they were worried about him. The whole situation was appalling. I'm only telling this story to illustrate Guthrie's character, presented with a situation like this. The company had been called together on the Monday in New York, and he made a speech telling us what had happened, saying that he had been perfectly happy with Robert Morse playing my part. And, of course, he had always been perfectly happy with me playing the part in London. He said however, 'This is what the management wants, and we have to do it, and I don't approve, but would everybody be as nice as possible to Robert Morse and Alec McCowen, because this is a hideous situation for them.' So I rehearsed with the company, and played two previews and then American Equity forbade my appearance in the play. I think there is evidently a rule that an alien cannot take over once an American has played the part. So Bobby went back into the play. He had an enormous success in it and was the only member in the company who was in the film.

Guthrie was understandably upset with the whole thing, particularly with the management. I stood with him in the back of the audience on the first night for about ten minutes. Then he said, 'Oh, come on. Let's go have a drink.' So we went across the road to the theatre bar where most of the stage crew were, and also Mrs Guthrie came with us. Guthrie – I don't know if it was characteristic of him – had no money on him at all. I remember he borrowed from his wife, then he borrowed from me, and he was buying drinks for the entire bar. We had a wonderful evening with the stagehands of our theatre and all the theatres around. I think we just went back for the curtain call. It was quite a typical evening.

Kurt Kasznar

ALFRED ROSSI: *You worked with Tony Guthrie only once, and that was in the famous production of* Six Characters in Search of an Author, *playing the Director.*

KURT KASZNAR: Yes. At the Phoenix Theater in New York in 1956. To meet him was quite an extraordinary thing. He liked me – I knew that in a way – or he wouldn't have cast me. I have a very strange acting temperament. If somebody lets me do what I want to do, I go terribly far. But strangely enough he never said much to me. Finally, one evening he said after rehearsal, 'Would you have a little nip in the bar next door?' You know the Second Avenue bars there? You get doubles for sixty-nine cents. I was nervous, and I thought he was going to say, 'Listen, I'll find somebody else.' He ordered a double bourbon. I ordered my scotch. I hemmed and hawed for a long while and finally said, 'Dr Guthrie, don't you think I'm doing too much?' He said, 'Of course, duckie, but I love it.'

After that he did something which is interesting. I've learnt that when an actor reads from the script the first three or four days, you're very inventive, much more inventive than when you know all the lines and when you're all glib. In those four or five days you want to prove that you're the only person to really play that part in the whole world, to prove it to yourself and to your colleagues. This, of course, happens in all new shows, but Dr Guthrie returned all these things to you after three weeks in tiny gift packages: he gave you back what you have lost now with your glibness! I found him telling me things that I did before but, now that I knew all the lines and knew exactly where to go, I thought were unnecessary.

Did Guthrie talk about his conception for the production of Six Characters?

There were all kinds of ideas, because we were doing it on Second Avenue in an old Jewish theatre, and he thought in discussions maybe it would be interesting to have an old Jewish New York troupe be the actors and the characters that were coming in very British or something like that. And Mendy Wager was very involved in the adaptation of the script. He also played the son. I'll never forget how Mendy, who always wanted to be a romantic juvenile, looked forward to playing the Italian son. When we actually read it through Tony said, 'Mendy, you forget this is a very myopic man with glasses and you're not going to be pretty in this. You can't see at all. You're ugly.' Mendy said, 'For that I'm playing a romantic Italian lead?'

Anyway, what I think is so funny, for instance, is that the English have a marvellous way of saying four-letter words *without* being insulting. Tony would say, 'Come on, you little twat, why don't we do this?' Natalie Schafer's glasses fell off. They couldn't understand it. They were called these names, and they were really endearments.

Of course his wife Judith was always around. They looked so much alike to me. They were like brother and sister. It was extraordinary: it looked like incest. But she was like a gazelle. She used to run all over the theatre and say, 'Tony, he's being *masked* by someone.' Right up in the balcony. They were extraordinary people. They asked me once to their room, and I thought they would have the penthouse in the St Regis. They were in a tiny hotel in the Village, in the crummiest room I'd ever seen. There was a curtain division with the beds and sort of a burner and things. They asked if I wanted a drink and I said, 'Yes.' She said, 'But we have no glasses. Could you have it out of an egg cup?' So I had the thing out of a dirty egg cup; it was literally incredible. She had just made a big buy of those felt cats that you get for fifty cents on Houston Street, cats playing with spools. 'They make lovely presents in Ireland, you see.' I expected the great Tony Guthrie to be living in luxury, but they were living in squalor, *absolute squalor.*

When he started working on his conception of the play, did it at all match with what you had seen in the play? Certainly, he did things with it that really no one else had ever done or has since.

It got so that, for instance, my wife, Leora Dana, was in a play with Tyrone Power on the road, *The Quiet Place.* Tony had to go to Canada to finish *Tamburlaine* and left us before the opening. And I said, 'Oh, my God. The cast is doing fifty per cent more than they used to do.' And I said to Tyrone Power and my wife, who were coming through town, 'Why don't you watch this show because I'm in the middle of it, like the inside of a washing machine!' And they said, 'Don't you ever worry what they do. Where Dr Guthrie wants you to look, you look.' Everybody was so *stunned*. Madame Pace's entrance, for instance. She *appears*. People said, 'How is that done?' You know how it was done? The actors were all waiting for their thing to do, and Natalie Schafer, at the very end, dropped her handbag and there were forty curtain rings in it. It made quite a tremendous noise. Everybody looked there. Madame Pace steps out, a little puff of smoke, and there she is. They started with an empty stage. The whole thing is an empty stage. The stagehands were going back and forth with ladders and flats and suddenly one flat goes by and there are six characters standing there. The flat went on, and they had come in behind it. It was very inventive and exciting, and it was done out of *nothing*.

How did he help you most?

He simplified everything. I'm prone to do a great many things. He said, 'Why don't you find a simpler way?' Or when something went a little bit out of focus for me I would say, 'I think I feel a little strange. I think I'm over-emphasizing this.' He said, 'Why don't you go back to nothingness and start from nothingness?' I said, 'What is nothingness?' He said, 'Just do the line and think what the line *really* means. Forget all the other effects – your eyes, your mouth, your head, whatever.' It does work, and I still apply that at times when I get overburdened with a situation or a speech or something. I think of 'Go back to what it is.' Then, of course, all the accoutrements will come again.

Did you ever find yourself disagreeing with him in that production?

No. It was hard to disagree with him because, obviously, he was right. This strange situation happened, though. I decided to give a closing-night party for *Six Characters*. So correspondence went on between my wife and Mrs Guthrie about the party. Three or four days later comes a list of people that Guthrie wanted to see. It was not just a party for the cast, but it included Leonard Bernstein, Geoffrey Holder, Alan Schneider – all the short directors; directors he picked to be there were all from five feet nine to less than six feet. And so I had to invite all these people. I had to get a caterer. It really became quite a thing in a small apartment, for about sixty people. Judith wore the same velvet dress (with shoes that matched) she had worn for her aunt's funeral – I think she only had one dress. And he was very tall. Talked to all the little directors, and that's it. They left the next day, and I never heard from them. They never thanked us or said anything. But I said, 'Why not?'

Do you feel that the response to the production was something that you, as actors, expected?

It was exciting. There was another production by Bill Ball, which I saw much later. It was a marvellous production, but I felt it absolutely had no guts. Somehow Tony, in his haphazard way, made it spectacular. I would say, for instance, that he left things undone in the production, which was always to me very exciting in some ways – if the play is really organized *and* if you leave certain things undone, *and* if you're a genius. I think that is a little secret that he might have had. He left things undone so that something else could happen. There was room. You could circle a table this way, or he didn't mind if you did it the other way, as long as it happened, whatever the reason. In contrast, for example, with Mike Nichols directing *Barefoot in the Park*, we were like a Swiss clock. I think these tidy, dictatorial directors sometimes defeat their purpose. I stop at improvisations. I think it's ridiculous. Improvisations, to me, are the biggest fake things.

Tony didn't believe in them either.

No. no. There was a little left to chance in *Six Characters*.

Why do you think he was so special?

He had a good track record to begin with, but I think he was a very dear man. I don't think he *was* that dear, really, underneath it all, but he *seemed* so. He mothered a company. He made you part of his family. You'd do anything. You'd do things that you really thought you can't do, like jump off five feet or something. You do it anyway. You do it for Guthrie.

And you don't question it.

And you don't hurt yourself.

Norman Ginsbury

ALFRED ROSSI: *How did Tony become acquainted with your play,* The First Gentleman?

NORMAN GINSBURY: Tony had been asked by the sponsors to direct my first play, *Viceroy Sarah,* and I was to meet him in the lounge of the Arts Theatre Club. I had never seen him before and I was looking around hopefully when a voice which seemed to float down from the ceiling said, 'Congratulations.' That was in 1934. I wrote *The First Gentleman* the year afterwards and Tony was the first person to read it. It was a smash-hit here, running for 654 performances in an excellent Norman Marshall production with great performances by Robert Morley and Wendy Hiller.

We opened in Manchester and Tony went there to see it. When I heard he wanted to do it in New York I was thrilled. The result was disastrous. I think it was about the worst production he ever did. When he first read the play he said, 'This is for Charles Laughton.' I sent it to Laughton. He phoned me and said, 'I'd like to discuss this play with you.' I went to see him and he bought an option and renewed it until he left for Hollywood before the war. Charles was a great man. I asked the management to try to get him for the New York production but he wasn't available so, at Tony's suggestion, Walter Slezak was cast. Walter looked exactly right. I had heard wonderful things about him in *Fanny* which I had not seen. But I had seen him in films and he is certainly an extremely fine actor.

The play had been rehearsing for a week or more before I reached New York. I soon realized that Walter was not right for the part except in looks. I told the management. They said, 'Look, encourage Walter, we know he can do it.' So I went around saying, 'Walter's doing fine, Walter's doing fine.' But never believing it. At the very first rehearsal I attended I took Tony aside and said, 'Tony, Walter is wrong for the part.' He bent down like a hairpin and whispered in my ear, 'I know it now but I didn't when I cast it.'

But was there no way that he felt he could make a change then?

At that stage, no – although there was a time when I think Walter felt it, too. The play went well in Boston and everybody's spirits rose. I must say I thought for a little while, 'Well, you never know.' But then further alterations went in. An important character was cut right out. I didn't know what to say to the young man playing it because he was playing it very well.

At another time I had to go to the management and complain, 'The actress who is playing Caroline of Brunswick – the lines she is saying started off by being my lines but they're not mine any longer.' By the time Tony had finished writing up her part (because he thought she was so good) I hardly understood a line she was saying, especially with her accent which was much too foreign. Another actress played the part in New York.

Then there was this mad Irish servant Tony had introduced. He had nothing at all to do with the play. I pointed out to him and the management that this was not the play I had written and they had acquired. Tony replied, 'This is the way I see it and I must direct it as I see it.' I had reached the point where I did not want to stay for the Broadway opening but my wife was halfway across the Atlantic making for New York so I just had to stay.

How did he work with Sleẓak who was not getting what he was after?

Well, for a time, Walter seemed to be very impressed by him. Whether he remained impressed I don't know. Walter was a delightful chap. I liked him enormously and the thing that worried me was how it would affect his career. As for Tony, everything about him was gigantic. Some of his productions were gigantic miracles like *Peer Gynt*. He had asked me to do a new version and had directed it for the Old Vic in 1944. Earlier on, in 1939, I had given him a new version of *An Enemy of the People*. It was another of his gigantic miracles. But *The First Gentleman*, despite his frequently expressed admiration for the play, was one of his gigantic flops. One thing I *do* want to point out – I never, never had words with him. I loathed what he was doing but I used to comfort myself with the feeling that 'Well, he thinks it's good for the play. Perhaps he's right and I'm wrong.'

It sounds as though there were key decisions that Tony pretty much made on his own.

Well, there was some of my play left, obviously, but there was so much I didn't recognize. I am convinced it was the rewriting and the production that caused the play to fail. I know that where we were getting great gales of laughter in London there was just nothing at all in New York. It was an ice-cold atmosphere.

Did Tony do the rewriting himself?

Most of it. But other writers were brought in, too. There wasn't much of mine. And Tony, in his book *A Life in the Theatre*, said that 'the unfortunate author was persuaded to cut and rewrite and really to harm the style of a stylish comedy'. Fourteen years later, I was staying with him in Ireland. It must have been about eighteen months before he died. He turned to me and suddenly out of the blue he said, 'Norman, it was my fault.' I knew what he was referring to and he knew I knew. *The First Gentleman* was never mentioned.

But that's typical of him in a way, isn't it?

Absolutely. Basically, he was a very humble person. But he did have a fine brain. Intellectually I used to think he was much above most of the actors he was directing. Politically he was leftish. He discussed Freud and his theories like a psychoanalyst. And he was a wit. When we were casting *The First Gentleman*, a young actress was mentioned as a possibility for the Princess Charlotte. Her husband was having a big success in New York and a nice time with another woman. I said, 'I think so-and-so will be delighted to go to New York because her husband has a hit there.' Tony replied, 'She'll be delighted to go to New York because her husband has a Miss there.'

Tony was a great personality. I think the word *simpatico* applied to him more than to any man I know. If he walked into this room now I would feel more thankful and delighted to see him than nearly anybody I know.

Walter Slezak

ALFRED ROSSI: *Tony Guthrie directed you in* The First Gentleman *by Norman Ginsbury: correct?*

WALTER SLEZAK: Yes, in 1957, and the whole thing started when Tony sent me this play from London. I'd never met him. And I wrote him that it was a very interesting part but not for me, because you have to be English for it. Not so much the accent, but the flow of the language. And he wrote me a very sweet letter that he completely disagreed with me, and he persuaded me. He came from New York, and we had a long talk and finally I said, 'Well, who am *I* to contradict Tony Guthrie!'

How did he convince you?

He was a very convincing guy. Of course, we had a producer who also wanted me very much, Alexander Cohen who, besides, was a friend of mine. And so we started rehearsing, and I got more desperate all the time, and at one of the rehearsals I stopped and went to the footlights, and Tony was in the audience, and I said, 'Tony, it's no good.' And he said, 'No, it isn't. It's terrible.' And that's all I needed. I said, 'Well, what are we going to do, do I bow out?' He said, 'No, you're not going to bow out, you're going to work.' So he was wonderful really. We worked. And I've never had such reviews in my life.

But I was right. I wasn't good in the part. You know there's a certain classical flow of language for which you need breath and for which you actually need a more classical actor than I am. I could do it in German *easily*, but in English I just didn't have the training. And Tony saw it, but he was wonderful. All during the rehearsals he kept his cool. He was never hysterical, and during the tryout they all started blaming everybody from the usher to the electrician for why it wasn't good. At dress-rehearsal we had a full house, and Tony provided the biggest laugh I've ever heard in the theatre. Alex Cohen had a chauffeur, John Wiley, and he put him on the payroll, and let him play one of the gentlemen-in-waiting. And just before the entrance of the Prince Regent – me – John Wiley had one line: 'He's coming down the long corridor.' He felt the audience and suddenly he shielded his eyes like a sailor and yelled, 'He's coming down the long corridor', and from the back of the house – the house was full – rose Tony's voice. 'John Wiley, what the fuck *are* you doing?' The emphasis was on *are*. And the people *howled*.

There were funny little things in the company. One of the old ladies objected to one of the gentlemen-in-waiting wearing a padded jock-strap.

During the tryout in Philadelphia we had a few meetings, thinking what we could do, because the play was not getting off the ground, you see. And Tony one day said, 'Come over for breakfast.' So, the taxi couldn't find the hotel, it was so unknown. Tony was terribly thrifty, he *and* Judy. And finally we found the hotel and I went up to the fourth floor. In the room, there were two couches put together and on a chair there was a plate and a couple of forks. Then Judy opened the door to the toilet and on the toilet seat was a bowl with cold potato salad. She brought it in and said, 'Have some.' That was breakfast.

Incidentally, Alex Cohen and his wife saw Tony and Judy at Stratford once, living on a houseboat. And the river was dirty, had swans crapping in it, and everybody throwing papers in it. Judy was on the boat with a big pitcher, which she dipped in the water and said, 'Anyone for tea?'

We had a very lovely house, a house that was built in 1751 in Larchmont on Long Island Sound. Tony was there, and he said, 'It's disgusting the way you live, you rich millionaires!' Very disapproving.

And, of course, people always talked about how much money would be lost when the show closed and all this. Tony always said, 'Walter, why are you worried? So it isn't a success. We'll go down with flying colours, and the investors will lose their money.' I saw his point of view. It was very sensible and the night we closed I sent him a wire, 'Just went down with flying colours. Investors lost all their money. Love, Walter.'

It sounds like while you were working on the production you sensed that it was not something the public was really going to support.

Oh no, I had a feeling long before dress that this was not *Victoria*

Regina, which was more or less an equivalent, anyway in the hopes of the author. And Tony was wonderful. He worked and worked and worked with actors. We always kept a wonderful spirit. Nobody made any star pretences. He was doing *La Traviata* over at the Met with Tebaldi and he was at our house and he said, 'The most amazing thing happened to me today. I said to Madame Tebaldi at a certain scene she should jump on the table and sing from there, and she looked at me and said, "No." I repeated the request and she said, "No." Well, you can't hit Madame Tebaldi, so I said, "All right then, don't do it."' Then he was doing another opera with Zinka Milanov, one of the prima donnas. Tony said, 'You come in from the left.' She said, 'No, I come in from the right.' He said, 'No, I want you to come in from the left.' 'No, I come in from the right.' He said, 'Why?' 'Because my dressing-room is on the right,' she answered. Enough to blow your top at – such idiocy, such *silly* stuff.

Not too many people did that with Tony in the theatre. But in opera he appeared to have allowed some of these things to go on.

Oh yes. There is a German expression called *narrenfreiheit,* which means 'the freedom of the fools'. If somebody came with such idiotic things he didn't really change his whole conception. She came in from the left later on. He talked to Rudolph Bing, and Bing laughed about it and said to her, 'Come on, dear, you're not that old, you can walk around.'

Did you see much of Tony socially?

Naturally, during rehearsal we couldn't spend so much time to-gether. We went to exhibits of paintings and stuff like that. And he had a very peculiar taste. We went to some opening of a gallery on Madison Avenue, and there was a picture of women being cut up and hung on hooks in a butcher's shop – one of these wild things – and he stood there for half an hour, transfixed. And I thought, 'What makes him tick?' I said, 'Tony, what do you like about it?' He said, 'Oh, that's fascinating, that's fascinating.'

When Tony was working with you, you'd been established as a star for a number of years in various media, so what did he think you needed?

Well, there are so few really good directors, when you suddenly smell that there's a great director with you, you get very small and humble and you say, 'Thank God, I don't have to use all my old tricks.

I can depend on this man.' And I tried to play it as honestly as I possibly could, and at the same time still get comedy in it. And he helped me in something that I always had difficulty with; getting comedy in it. I was kind of overawed by the regal attitude of the play and so forth. I thought it was a piece of art.

So you became a little self-important, or somehow displayed these attitudes?

Yes. And he got rid of that so beautifully. Then he had a German actress, Maria Fein, who always played – she's dead now – a madwoman. She played the second act Queen. One big scene. The wife of the Prince Regent, who was half-mad and then went back to Germany and lived in a tower room and died there. He let her go *wild*. And finally the whole play fell apart, because she played in an entirely different style. And that's why they had to change her. And they got Isabel Elsom, who is a nice pleasant American, round smooth actress. There was so much pressure put on him by the producer to get rid of Maria Fine. But she really chewed the scenery, and he couldn't have been happier. He loved real theatre and flamboyance in actors. And he instilled a lot of that flamboyance in *me*.

Do you recall any specifics of direction in his work with you or people in scenes with you?

Well, there was an old Jewish actor, Clarence Derwent, who was quite wealthy – he gave an award for the best supporting actor. He played the Bishop. He was very old and he took a breath every second word, and one day Tony said, 'Clarence,' he said, 'fill those dear old lungs of yours and do say the whole line in one breath.'

I read one review, I think, that said something to the effect that the play was overproduced. Now what was the motive for that?

I think it was just kind of sprung on Tony. He didn't expect it to be that big. Of course, they tried to get this room in Brighton, this Chinese monster, where the Prince Regent has his chariot, you know. They did a very clever decoration of this thing, but it was all overloaded. And the costumes, my God! The Prince Regent was a peacock, and he dressed up, but everybody walked around in gold braids and on and on and on. And then nothing comes out. Marlene Dietrich once said to me – somebody wanted her to do this musical about Queen Catherine of Russia – 'These costumes and that voice?' And

Above L to R: Thornton Wilder and Tyrone Guthrie, Stratford, Ontario, 1955.

Right: Tyrone Guthrie directing a rehearsal of Sean O'Casey's *The Bishop's Bonfire* at the Gaiety Theatre, Dublin, 1955.

Personnel of the Tyrone Guthrie Theater, Minneapolis, 1963.
Tyrone Guthrie seated on balcony.

Opposite: Tyrone Guthrie and George Grizzard in rehearsal for
Hamlet, Minneapolis, 1963.

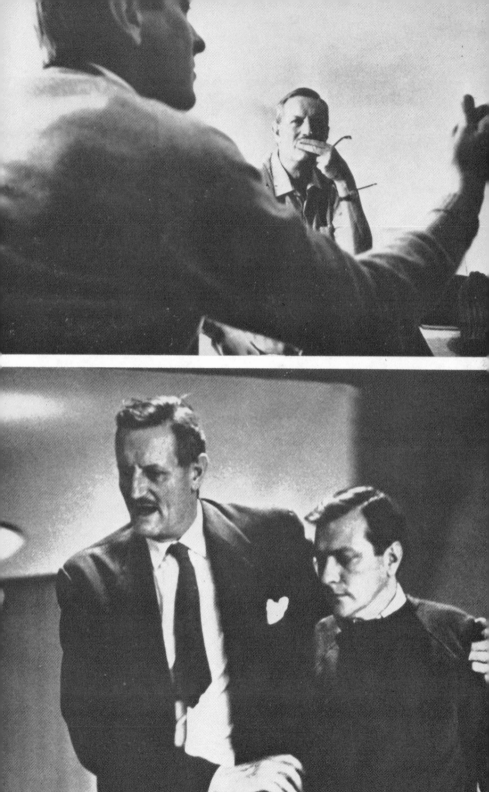

Hume Cronyn and Tyrone Guthrie, Minneapolis, 1965.

in this case it was these costumes and that text? The whole thing was out of proportion. The costumes cost a fortune. Eaves Brothers really got rich on that. I remember I had a big coat for the crowning, for the christening of Queen Victoria which ends the play. A coat that cost, I think, three or four thousand dollars. One coat – I mean, you wear it for an exit.

As an actor did you learn anything from him?

Yes. I learned something very important – on which I have to put a reservation, that it only applies to somebody who is financially secure – that the European way is a much better way of play-acting. That is, 'All right, it's another show, who cares, we did our best, so it closed.' But if you are dependent for your rent and your family's life and whether or not you are going to be eating on the opening of a show, and if it closes it's six or eight months until you get another job, then you can't have this attitude. Thank God, I made my money in Hollywood, and made so much more than I ever did on stage. So I could afford to take this attitude. Not that I adored anything that came afterwards, but it's such a wonderful knowledge that 'All right, so let's have *fun*. If it doesn't work, it doesn't work.' I remember Leo McCarey, a Hollywood director who was a friend of mine, once said to me about how quickly *bad* things are forgotten. He said, 'Nobody points at John Ford and says, "He made a picture, *She Wore a Yellow Ribbon*." ' That is the main lesson I learned from Tony.

Peter Donat

ALFRED ROSSI: *How were you engaged for your role in* The First Gentleman?

PETER DONAT: I didn't have an agent's connection in New York at that time. I was just 'making the rounds', as they say. I heard that Guthrie was casting *The First Gentleman*, and I knew that he had known my uncle, the late Robert Donat. So I made contact with him and used Robert Donat's name, knowing that would create some attention. I think it was by letter. And indeed I did get a reading, and of course he did remember Robert, reminisced a bit about how he (Guthrie) also wanted to be an actor in their early days, but that he was 'so bad and turned to directing'.

I did the reading for Guthrie and Alex Cohen. Guthrie made you feel like an actor, that you belonged there, and 'Let's go to work'. I did the reading and they thanked me and left. Then I heard nothing about it. So I figured, well, I'm not right for it, or they didn't like me. Weeks later, I got a call to go back and read, and both Alex Cohen and Tony Guthrie said, 'Why haven't you been in before?' Neither of them remembered that I *had* been in before, and I was exactly what they were looking for. I suppose they see so many people, and they change their minds and the idea of the part gets changed and suddenly one afternoon you just look like it, and you didn't on Monday three weeks ago. I don't know what the hell happens. But anyway I was delighted because we were just in New York and my then wife, Michael Learned, was pregnant with our first baby at the time, and it was such a great breakthrough for me to get a job in a show on Broadway and with Guthrie. It was really exciting.

Can you illustrate the way he worked on the show?

Well, the first day of rehearsal he said, 'Of course, we've all read the play. Let's get on our feet.' Most directors sit around and read but he said, 'We've all done this, why should we sit around the table and read it again?' And he started from page one, scene one and he began to block it, very, very quickly. He would let things go for a while, watch actors feel around a bit, and then you'd hear a snapping of the fingers, a clapping of the hands, and he'd immediately give some direction.

I remember there was one guy, I can't remember his name, and it was his first acting job. He was an assistant stage manager and was playing one of the butlers in a huge entrance with Slezak and Helen Burns coming into the ballroom. It was late in rehearsals and he was supposed to open the door and bring on the whole regal retinue. The entrance was organized carefully by Guthrie, then snapping of fingers, clapping of hands and we were running it. In the middle of all the movement, this guy said, 'Sorry, Dr Guthrie. I goofed. Okay, everybody, let's run it again.' Everybody thought Guthrie was going to clobber him, but Guthrie loved it. He said, 'Right. Right! On! On! Run it again.' He loved it. That guy putting himself on a limb like that. I found he liked people to take personal chances – on and off the stage. He wanted you to try stuff. You'd come on with something and, by God, if it was in any way valid he'd begin to build on it so you could *really* make it work. He seemed to be gratified by that, by an actor who just went out on a limb. Anything rather than be safe. I don't think he could stand that very much. Or someone who was waiting to be told what a thing meant or what a role is about. He was not very patient with great justifications; he felt that's an actor's homework.

He was also wonderful, I think, in giving emotionally right stage directions which need no more explanation. Like Guy Spaull in that play, who played a doctor delivering my baby, Victoria. He kept coming downstairs saying that everything was going to be all right, but she was dying, and he didn't know how to handle the situation. And Guy had a lot of trouble. I mean coming in with such a thing to play, with no lines that deal with it. Guthrie finally had him come in eating a heaping plate of sandwiches. That's all. And you just knew by the way that doctor was eating those sandwiches that something was wrong. It was quick as lightning. And if it didn't work Tony would have him try something else there. But his mind seemed to be very quick and would jump instinctively, without question, to certain conclusions.

Now this was a play that had been done in London with Robert Morley and had been quite a success. Were there many changes for the New York production?

My memory of it is that there weren't many changes. I have a feeling that it was not one of his passions to do the play, that he had said he would do it and was committed to do it. His health was not always on top. He did it respectfully and well, and then that was it. But he wasn't deeply involved in rewriting or developing particular scenes or restructuring the play in any way. I don't think that he was on fire about it like some of his Shakespeare productions.

Did the rehearsals have a sense of fun?

Yes, quite a bit. There was an interesting orchestration between Walter Slezak and Tony Guthrie because Tony's pulse beat was so mercurial, whereas Slezak is more Germanic and more slow. Guthrie's verbal attack was just bristling with speed and energy, and I think Slezak's German accent puzzled him or got in the way. The rhythms were quite different between the two.

I think that one could feel a little ill-at-ease with him, that you couldn't keep him entertained or occupied. He'd be bored and go on to something else. Sometimes he could become irritable and you would feel it. He was such a powerful man that it always influenced you slightly. I asked some question about blocking in a scene with my wife, played by Inga Swenson, in *The First Gentleman* – something about getting close to the fireplace, and it irritated him. I think he made some slightly angry remark, 'English winter. Draughty rooms. Don't ask a stupid question.'

Tony's wife Judith was there some of the time, and I remember it always seemed to be nice for him when she joined the company, joined the train ride or came to Philadelphia or whatever. He was getting off to go somewhere and they had to separate for a while. I remember seeing her crying as he was leaving the train, crying quietly, no great fuss, since it was probably an event that occurred many times in their lives. I had the feeling that she just endorsed and helped his career in any way she could and that she loved him.

Another thing that really impressed me about him was that over the years, on a number of occasions, I requested a letter from him, either for something I was looking for from the Canada Council, a scholarship to write something or a recommendation to a producer. Sometimes, my God, it would be a letter that would catch him somewhere in Israel working on some project. And it never failed that I would get a handwritten postcard from wherever he was, anywhere in the world, dealing with whatever I had requested, briskly, quickly, same telegraphic approach. I've observed that a lot of busy people don't do that. Or they may have a secretary eventually do it. It's impressive to me that he somehow found time to keep it in a briefcase or whatever. And he must have received mail from all over the world.

He had a wonderful sense of the grotesque. I remember him describing something he was reading in the paper in New York about a fire in a nunnery. And he said, 'It must be wonderful to see those nuns jumping out the windows like great black bats.' It was incredible. On the other hand he seemed very touched describing how he once saw a dying man sucking eagerly at a damp cloth that had been put to his lips to relieve fever, as if it were going to make him live. Guthrie made some comment about the wonderful persistence in life and how strange we are to think it will go on forever.

Once Guthrie spent some time giving a series of lectures or talks at the University of Detroit. They gave him an apartment there and at some point he was carrying some books in from a car wearing only some floppy slippers and old pyjamas. One of the professors was helping him carry stuff, and he said Guthrie's pyjama bottoms fell clear to the ground. And Guthrie said, 'Jim . . . ' He nodded for help but didn't put his books down and couldn't care less. Jim said it felt so funny to be pulling up the great Tyrone Guthrie's pyjamas and tying them. But still it was hard to have access to a man like that on a psychological level. It was the same problem I had with someone like Robert Donat. These men, to me, were so great that I didn't know how to really see them as guys who eat a fried egg in the morning – the ordinary humdrum of human life. I'm sure Guthrie was not really as immediately bored as I thought he was. I think he was most interested in people being themselves – real, not phoney.

George Grizzard

ALFRED ROSSI: *Ten years ago you played Hamlet. As you think back on that, do you remember any comments that Tony Guthrie made to you about both your performance as Hamlet and the production as a whole?*

GEORGE GRIZZARD: I remember the next day the reviews came out and the Minneapolis paper printed about fifteen reviews from all over the world side by side. Some of them were disappointing, some of them were good, some of them were stupid, and some of them were helpful. I was reading them and he came into the theatre (we were opening *The Miser* that night), and he said, 'And did you read the reviews?' I said, 'Yes.' He said, 'Were you disappointed?' And I said, 'A little bit,' and he said, 'Don't be. I did the same production thirty years ago and got the same reviews.' Reading them all together made me realize that it really is one man's opinion. I was disappointed. I think that opening night I held on to the form that Tony and I had planned. That was my big achievement: I held on vocally and physically and emotionally to the form we set up, except that I was nervous and hollow and there was nobody inside.

That, eventually, is what I found marvellous about rep, because I got to play it six months, whether they liked it or not, and I got to be much more satisfied with the performance. He asked my parents, for instance, 'What do you think of the *Hamlet*?' My father said, 'More importantly, what do *you* think of it?' Tony said, 'I think it's a very intelligent Hamlet. I wish he had more *vocal* range.' Because I'd had no vocal training at that time. That improved a good deal. It was just exercising those muscles. I think because he was such a musical man, and was so interested in the sounds in the theatre, that was his big disappointment in me. I couldn't give the vocal colours that he wanted. But I think he was pleased with the production.

We were great friends, I believe, and admired each other. He was marvellous about listening when we did later productions, like *Henry V*, *Volpone* and things. He always listened when I had something to say. He would say either yes or no, but he paid us all the great respect of listening to us.

How did you get cast as Hamlet? Did you read for it?

Well, I was contacted by Peter Zeisler. He was the business manager of the theatre. Peter and I had worked together as stage manager and assistant stage manager on a play by Bob Anderson, so I had known Peter for several years. I came in to meet with Guthrie, because he was setting up a rep company. I didn't know what they were doing. I came and I read a poem by Robert Frost. When I got through I said, 'You're disappointed, aren't you?' He said, 'Well, yes, a little. I wanted something more rhetorical.' And I said, 'I don't know what rhetorical means.' He said, 'Well, it means you talk loud and then you talk soft.' I said, 'Oh well, I can't do that because Ellis Rabb is out of the country, and I've only done Shakespeare with Ellis.' He said, 'Could you do it with me?' I said, 'I don't know.' He said, 'I'm looking for a Hamlet.' That shocked me, because I had no idea that was in his mind in regard to me. Then he said, 'Would you come back next week and read me something from *Hamlet*.'

So I went and read the play several times, and went back and Doug Campbell was there. He said, 'Dougie's going to play the Ghost, and I want you to do that scene.' That's one of the most difficult scenes in the play and that's what we started with. Dougie has this magnificent voice, and I sounded like the mayor of Boys' Town. When I was reading he would say, 'No, no, no. You're breaking the rhythm.' And I said, 'I don't know the song. When I know the song, I'll know the rhythm.' He said, 'Oh, yes, you're damn right, of course.' So we both flared up at each other; not in a mean way, but more like 'I don't know what I'm doing, and you're not helping by interrupting me.' When we got through he said, 'You're a damn good actor, but you don't know *anything* about this, do you?' And I said, 'Not much, but we have a year, and I'll work on it every day of that year until we do it.' He said, 'Yes, I think I want you to play Hamlet, but I can't say. I have to talk to some people.' Then he started to show costume designs. Three days later Peter called and said, 'He wants you to play Hamlet.' So it was the most exciting thing that ever happened to me, I suppose.

If you could articulate the thing about Tony Guthrie's direction of you in Hamlet *that you feel helped you realize the role most, what would you say it was?*

That's not an easy one. I know that the rehearsals were joyous. I think that was one of the things that helped everybody in the company the most. Whenever he would correct or stop someone from doing something, he did it with great love and great wit, so that you never felt put down by him. For instance, after the play scene he wanted me to sing something in a very loud, exuberant way. And I said, 'I don't sing, and I can't do it that way.' He said, 'Try.' I tried. He said, 'You're dead right. Let's do it another way. Let's whisper it.'

And he constantly found another way just as theatrical to do it. In *Henry V*, for instance, he wanted me to climb up a ladder in armour with a sword. I tried it, and it was difficult. So he said, 'Oh well then, don't. We'll have someone carry you up.' So two soldiers carried me off on their shoulders. It was the same effect. He was never stymied by your inability, so he was always able to come up with something else that you *could* do.

Do you remember any of the specific work that Guthrie did in Henry V?

Well, he had Katherine and her lady-in-waiting being carried around by four porters on a great chaise, which was nice in our theatre, because they kept moving, and so the audience was able to see them at all times.

In the battle scene he had a great cannon designed and a lot of smoke and screaming and yelling. Then I came running in up on to the cannon to do the 'breach' speech. I looked down one day and I saw Pistol picking pockets and I saw people doing this and that and cleaning their guns, and I said, 'Tony, is all this going to go on?' He said, 'Don't worry. There'll be so much smoke, no one will ever see them.' He always *enriched* the scene by having all of that life going on while you're trying to do your big speech.

Before I started working on *Hamlet* I had supper with John Gielgud to talk to him about the play and about the production that I was going to be in. I asked him about certain things in the play. He said, 'Yes, I think I did that.' But he had done it three or four times, so he didn't always do it in the same production, you see. He said, 'You frightened?' I said, 'Yes.' And he said, 'Well, you needn't be. You have Tony directing. He does have a tendency to put all the extras down front and hide the stars, but he won't do that with *Hamlet*.' He had the greatest control of the audience's eye that I ever came across in the theatre. He could make you look at whatever he wanted you to look at, no matter how many people were on the stage or no matter what they were doing.

I remember one time in Minneapolis someone said, 'We can't always understand the actors. They talk so fast.' And Tony said, 'When we want you to hear something, we'll slow down.'

If you had to give a reason why Tony Guthrie was one of the great directors of our century, what would you say it was?

I think his enthusiasm, his almost childlike enthusiasm. His joy, his love of the theatre, and his need to make a lot of those boring plays interesting, which is what his critics accused him of – overproducing plays. His need to entertain an audience was what kept him going. He always used to refer to 'if we are spared' productions, because of his heart attacks. I'm just sorry I never got to do *Peer Gynt* with him, because I found it amazing that the Guthrie Theater did not do a Scandinavian playwright until that third or fourth season with *The Dance of Death*, which was the first. That's the only regret I have about Tony: not getting to work with him in another production like that.

Ellen Geer

ALFRED ROSSI: *You played Ophelia in* Hamlet *the opening season in Minneapolis. As you look back on that experience, was there anything that guided you more than anything else in developing the role with Guthrie?*

ELLEN GEER: Of course; it was in the mad scene, I remember. It was a frightening experience, coming out and doing it for the first time with all those people around. George Grizzard probably felt the same about doing Hamlet. I mean, who can do Hamlet? It's almost impossible to try and do. Everybody has decided views about how they want it to be done. The same with the mad scene. I remember Guthrie did a strange thing at the first rehearsal. He obviously saw that I was nervous, and said, 'Just cough, keep coughing.' I got all upset because I thought, 'I can't play it coughing, what is that?' Very peculiar. So out of nerves and survival I went home and blocked out a whole thing, to get rid of that cough and I went there praying the next time that he wouldn't notice I wasn't coughing, and he didn't. I mean he was so open to what you did.

How did Guthrie react to your getting pregnant, which eventually forced you to leave the company?

Well, I wasn't sure I was pregnant at the time and Tanya had already designed the costume, a jersey dress that fit well. I remember, it was at the first dress-rehearsal, and all of a sudden the jersey fit too well – I noticed the boobs were big, right? Huge. So I tried to fix my hair to match – so I'd balance with the chest and hopefully no one would notice. I remember Guthrie at the note session saying, 'Now, Ophelia looks rather like a whore, doesn't she?' I thought, 'Okay, this is it,' and I went to the doctor and sure enough I was pregnant, and I was worried about finishing the whole season.

I said, 'We've got to be honest about this,' so my husband called him on the phone, and said, 'I'd like to speak to Guthrie.' Guthrie at that time was in the tub and Lady Judith said, 'Oh well, you'll have to tell me, dear, what the problem is.' So my husband said, 'Well, I'd rather talk to Guthrie; it's personal.' Sound of footsteps leaving, then returning. Lady Judith said, 'It's all right, I won't know anything. Tony says for you to tell me, and I'll pretend not to hear.' My husband said, 'Ellen's pregnant.' There was this dead pause on the phone. 'All right, fine, dear, I'll pass the information along.' My husband was sure he heard laughter in the background. She came back. . . . 'All right, dear, you and Ellen come tomorrow for tea. Goodbye.' Nothing was said.

So the next day we went – I felt so embarrassed by doing this on his big opening, you know? I mean I was easy to replace, but I felt bad. So we went to his apartment and Lady Judith was there. He was out of the room. Lady Judith said, 'Let's have some tea.' She did a whole number with the tea – didn't say anything about the baby, nothing. It was frightening; I was shaking. After about ten minutes Guthrie came bounding across the room, *bounding*, and said, 'Oh, congratulations!' And he hugged me and kissed me and said, 'Now, we don't have to say anything more. You work as long as you can. I've always wanted a pregnant Ophelia.' I said, 'Do you mean you want me to start the season?' And he said, 'Of course, and for *Three Sisters* I'd like a chubby Irina.' And then Lady Judith started laughing and said, 'Oh dear, I'm so happy now I can finally say something. I wasn't supposed to know. Congratulations!'

He illustrated a bit for you, as I remember, in the mad scene. He did things like hitting his stomach, and singing those bawdy lyrics. How did you react to that?

I thought it was very exciting, and it came out of Tanya's idea of playing her in black, that it's her father's funeral, and the whole frustrated sex idea that Guthrie brought in was extraordinary. I remember long after we had staged the scene Guthrie called a special rehearsal on learning I was pregnant, and he tried to take it all out because he was worried I was going to hurt myself with so much leaping about and pounding.

Did he ever talk to you about how he thought you did as Ophelia?

Yes. He said, 'You sing beautifully, darling.' He was always very encouraging to me, except for Rosalind in *As You Like It* which he told me 'needed work' and I agreed with him. He used to tell me that I reminded him of Ellen Terry. And so did Lady Judith. The most I talked with the two of them was about the garden, of course, that I built for them – the Shakespeare garden out in front of the theatre. Think they've torn it down by now – interfered with their cement.

How did that come about?

That's just something Pop [Will Geer] and I do. Have a Shakespeare garden at a Shakespeare theatre. Audiences love it. You know, you put in the plant quotes out of the plays as they are put on at the theatre. I wanted it to be in honour of the Guthries so I planted grass in the shape of a clover. I don't know if anybody ever noticed it but the beginning of the walk was the bottom of the stem and then it went into three loops with the Shakespeare plants and quotes nestled in between. That was for them. It was Lady Judith's and our secret, really.

In The Three Sisters *what guidance did he give you as Irina?*

He would talk 'at home' things. He would say, 'You're used to having these material things here.' He always made us feel at home on that set. He didn't do that much direction mentally, it was mainly placement which made you feel the emotional state a scene needed. I remember Guthrie coming on-stage after our first run-through – it was very early on – and he had tears in his eyes, and he said, 'I don't know what else we can do.' That show seemed to just fall in place. I think it was because of the glory of having rep theatre, of people working together. And it's a play that prompts it. But the thing he really stressed was 'I don't want a dirge here.' It's a thing that human beings are funny and sad at the same time. And he really pushed for that beautifully.

Do you remember any of the specific things that he did to illustrate what you just said?

Well, the clearest example was with Zoe Caldwell. Zoe always felt that he went too far with her Natasha – the humour versus reality in a character. They always had a disagreement because he loved the idea of that kind of bossy extreme woman in it, almost to a comment. Zoe instinctively pursued the reality – she was right. Rehearsing Irina one day I hit myself on the rear end in exasperation, and he said, 'My dear, what play are you in? That's terribly vulgar for Irina, don't you think?' And he was right. He helped me get the pacing, the movement, the drive of that speech in the fire scene. He kept telling all of us to think of the fire, because that's usually why the act doesn't work. It's extraordinary what happens with the fear of a fire – that you might be taken – your goods, your material – and they were very into material things. He brought out all those aspects; he never let us forge the fire, *never*.

It's almost as if that type of thing is something geared to a psychological, emotional base, and Guthrie is not usually thought of as a director who was terribly concerned with those things.

It's a fact though; emotional or not, the *fire is a fact*. It *is* really the third act. I think that's why he kept bringing it out. He said, 'Remember when you go to that window there are sirens going on out there. People running and noises outside.' That's what made the third act really work. Because people forget you're trapped in a little, closed room. He used to make sure that we remembered – we were forced to be in that room together. That's why emotions were so split. I remember Tusenbach came in and Guthrie brought out how Irina cannot get away from him, why it bugs her. That was a very important part of it, the crowding.

In the fourth act it was space. People kept missing each other. It was open. Now, that's there for a reason. You never say to yourself, 'Now at this point I want space.' I think it's one of those *inside* things. When people say he didn't talk enough intellectually, I think he was going beyond that, I really do. It was just part of him, and he was able to move people and what-have-you without saying, 'Now the reason we're doing this is because . . . '

Now that you're able to look back what did he think you needed as an actress?

He felt I needed not only age – I mean, you know, just a pure thing of growth – but he got very upset sometimes and he used to call me 'Miss New York' or Zoe 'Miss Australia'. And he used to call me 'awkward goat' sometimes. It's just the thing of learning, you know, learning how to move. I *was* an awkward goat. He helped me in every department. He was extraordinary. He used to say, you know, 'More guts, more guts.' The one time he was really pleased with my work was in *St Joan*, which Douglas [Campbell] directed. At a dress-rehearsal of *St Joan* I remember he was there. Afterwards he came bounding across the stage and said, 'Great guts. Great guts!' And that's all he ever said to me, and it was *everything*. Again, it's one of those things where he didn't have to go into all those talking specifics. He said, 'Hello, how are you?' And he walked on. But he really *meant* 'Hello, how are *you*?' You could tell by his eyes.

How would he go about helping you get more guts?

By putting me in a huge framework, and that's what he did with Lady Anne. I had finally gotten so I could speak to him, right? Two years – it took that long. It was the most exciting scene to work with him, because he was trying something different with the play. He'd done *Richard III* many times. He wanted Lady Anne bored with this whole funeral thing, her 'husband was too old anyway', and so it made it easy for her to go to Richard. In other words, 'Oh God, here we are at another prayer stop, darling.' That's the way he spoke to me. 'Oh, it's hot and my dress is getting so terribly dirty every time I have to kneel down.' I wanted, of course, to play it the usual way, because I'd never been through the experience of doing the play as often as he. He was ready to turn it, and you know how he loved to make fun of religion and royalty. It was *his* religion to give it a little twist. He was way ahead of his time on that score. We're only getting there now. He worked with me on biting ends of words: 'hunch*ed* back*ed* toa*d*'. And he said, 'Now at this point I want you to take your hanky out of the front of your dress, and pull your breasts up a bit. Show Richard the goods.' I, again, was very embarrassed. In those years I didn't know myself or my body freedom. But I was willing to do it, because it was *so* extreme and exciting.

Working on that scene, was part of the interpretation the fact that maybe she was ready for a rather perverse experience with this hunchback?

That was his comment on all royalty, wealth, power. I think it was his comment on the situation and what it was like then, and look at us now, it's the same thing, he's absolutely right. Again, Guthrie was way ahead of his time.

How did that translate itself into the actual work?

He said something like 'Let's have some fun' and 'Let's have her do this'. At first, I couldn't understand because of what was in my head, that this was a lady who was really suffering. He said, 'Now, you stand up here, dear, and oh it's hot, it's terribly hot on this road.' Then slowly we seemed to understand each other, without sitting down and having one of those psychological talks that people love to have. It came out of the work together. He would say a phrase, not 'Set down, set down, your honourable load,' but 'Set . . . down' (old weary voice, drawing slow, deep, bored breath), 'set down your honourable . . . ' He would say what the character was in one phrase and you could understand what he wanted. Then together you could pick out the place for the handkerchief, and the way you fight. You fight with excitement, with sexual excitement. Not just hollering at somebody, but hollering at that man who's interfering with your funeral fun. Fight with that man, so you *can* get sexually excited. It was an innovative scene, and one of the experiences I most enjoyed with Guthrie.

He spoke about the high emotion of grief. When you are at that pitch very strange things can happen. That pitch came out of anger, talking with Richard. The minute he comes, there's this conflict. I don't know if you've ever met a person like that, who thinks that they *should* be unhappy, right? They don't *know* that they should, but they *think* so, and they begin playing the game of unhappiness. 'I'm very unhappy my father died.' You know Guthrie used to say about death that somebody gets run over on a street and everybody goes 'Uh . . . oh!' In other words, we're trained to think and feel a certain way, and yet we might not even know the person. Lady Anne looked *good* doing it. Oh, the grief looked *wonderful* on her. You know the way you bend, and your back is rounded, and you have your hankies, and all in appealing black.

Did he talk much about the scene in sexual terms?

No, no, he didn't. There was a way Richard and Anne kissed, *how* we held, which, of course, came out of Hume [Cronyn], too. But Guthrie almost reversed the roles. At a point, he had Hume crying. Now the Europeans who saw it loved it. Americans weren't sure. It's that thing, again, that we are a new country. Our view of the classics is new. Do you know what I mean? We weren't ready for that concept. Guthrie was always, to me, ahead of his time. I know a lot of people wouldn't agree, but I think so. His knowledge of human nature was superb; now, whether he wanted to *deal* with every aspect of human nature is a different point.

He presented problems to you in directions that you hadn't gone?

Right. Probably never would have had the chance otherwise. But he seemed to do that with everybody, or most Americans. You know what I've found? It's like, again, with *St Joan*. American actors are extremely different. They used to put me down for listening to Douglas when he was directing *St Joan*. We used to have long sessions, and he would give me line readings. This startled all the actors. They thought that was terrible. But I don't, you see. Because Douglas spoke with Sybil Thorndike, who worked with Shaw – he *knows*. What do I know, *me*, young American actor, who's had no exposure to the classics? I think you should be open enough to just suck it all in. How are you gonna learn? Then once it's in, you put your stamp on it, it becomes you. It has to become you, where else can it go? It's gotta come out of you! It's such an ego thing that we Americans go through. I think that's what used to upset Guthrie so, you know, when he would holler and carry on and say, 'This doesn't sound good, that doesn't sound good.' Americans, in general, are afraid of technique, think it stops their truth, whereas technique can only release them to a higher truth that reaches further for their audience.

He didn't like to be a coach, but the only time he would is when it interfered with his production. You remember when he threatened to fire an actress if she cried one more time when he tried to direct her? I mean, it was a disastrous thing. I think if anything interfered, he would get the best thing he could in order to make his production work. That's all. Remember when he couldn't get a sound he needed from an actor? Guthrie would say, 'Trumpets, I want trumpets here.' He would *demand* sound. I mean he would swear at people if they weren't doing it. And *his* production is what he got.

Let's go on to The Cherry Orchard *production which was the second Chekhov he did there. Did you find in working on that his method changed?*

Well, by that time, we were really a company, and he was much easier to talk to, or rather I wasn't such a chicken. I thought it was fantastic that he cast me as Dunyasha, and I asked him if I could have padding. I even asked him if I could have a nose, become more common. And he was excited about all that. He, I remember, helped me with a fat walk. He helped me get a whole fat feeling. He was much more specific in that one actually.

Did he ever indicate to you any of his feelings towards Chekhov?

Chekhov put him in happy tears all the time. He came up one day during *Three Sisters* rehearsal – we had had a good rehearsal, everything was going well – and he taught us this song. I remember him standing there singing, 'Rose, rose, rose, rose, will I ever see thee

red?' He stood there, and his eyes were full. He was a huge humani-
tarian. Although I think his frame and his way, perhaps, made people
not see it as much, they all felt it. You can tell by how they speak of
him after.

With The Cherry Orchard *did you find that he altered anything in
terms of his way of working with you?*

I was able to suggest things. I know lots of people were frustrated
by Guthrie and Campbell. It was just not that way for me at all. I
found it the most glorious experience. And really an honour to be
there – to learn. Where else do we have in this country to learn? I
didn't find them frustrating in any way. I used to get upset when
they didn't like American actors. But instead of getting upset it was
'I'm gonna prove to them that we're just as damn good as the English.
We've got the heart.' And he found that out in Chekhov. He found
that out! We're very close to the Russians, very close; in our basic
gypsy heat, we're very close to that. I think he was just as startled as
all of us were by *Three Sisters*.

*Are there any 'Guthrie stories' that you haven't told me that you'd
like to?*

This was told me, I don't remember by whom, and I was almost
appalled, because I'm an American and my thing about death is a
certain trained response. And what I learned from Guthrie is that it's
calculated, right? When somebody dies you go 'Uh'. You're not even
open enough to feel what you really feel. . . . He had just had a bad
heart attack – this was before Minneapolis – and all his relatives were
around him – he was in an oxygen tent. An aunt opened the tent,
thinking he was gone, but he opened up one eye, when she looked in,
and said, 'Not dead yet, fiddle dee-dee.'

My other favourite story is when he was at a fund-raising event for
Stratford, Ontario. And he had everybody all excited about building
the theatre. Then at the end of the meeting he said, 'The main thing is
to keep your peckers up.' Which in our country means your penis. And
apparently in England it means something else – energy, excitement, I
don't know – it must be something different, but he almost blew the
whole afternoon!

*You've worked with a lot of directors in your career even though you're
a young woman. What made him so special?*

Well, working with him, I don't know if it was my age or what, but I felt that what he was doing was absolutely right. I was sucking in – a sponge – and he made you feel totally secure. I think he was an extraordinary human being, and he knew about human beings more than most. That's why he was such a goddamn good director. He really *knew* human beings. Why else would he start a theatre like that?

Hume Cronyn and
Jessica Tandy

ALFRED ROSSI: *In thinking back on the roles that you were offered at Minneapolis that first season, Jessie – the Queen in* Hamlet, *Olga in* Three Sisters *and Linda in* Salesman *– and Hume – Harpagon, Chebutykin and Willy Loman – were any of those suggested by you initially?*

HUME CRONYN: Well, I certainly didn't suggest *The Miser.*

JESSICA TANDY: I don't think so.

HC: I remember telling Olivier that I was going to act with Tony Guthrie and he said, 'What are you going to do?' And when I got to *L'Avare* he said, 'Molière?' And I said, 'Yes.' And he said, 'Oh my God. Funny as a baby's open grave.' And that's an absolute quote. I thought, 'Oh, oh!' Because Larry's background in classical theatre is, shall we say, somewhat richer than mine.

Do you recall in either of the things you did, Jessica, in Hamlet *or* Three Sisters, *discussions that you had with Guthrie about the work that you were doing?*

JT: The only thing I remember we talked about was that the first scene would be the wedding, which was an innovation. And that took me back for a moment or two, but then I thought, 'Why not?' It wasn't just another day at court; it was a special day. It was very spectacular. I was in a wedding dress and flowers, and it was obvious that that was the occasion.

It was a very interesting set-up in that Hamlet *came on first as if he had come from the back pew of the church. He had come through the double doors up centre and bells started to ring, and he closed the doors and then the trumpeters and drummer came in on the upper level, then the doors swung open and the court swirled around and came in and then Gertrude and Claudius came in there and posed for the photographers.*

JT: You used a word that you can always use about his productions – they 'swirl around', that's exactly what there would be, a great happening on stage. It was exciting. It was a marvellous opening for the season.

Since you both worked in two of the three Chekhov plays that he did, is there anything that you think might account for the opinion of many people that those plays were his best work?

JT: They were new. It was the first time he'd done them. He'd also been involved in translation. All those other plays he'd done before many times. And a lot of the things that he did in those plays – for instance, certainly in *Richard III* – had been done before. He was repeating himself with a different cast and in a different place. But these were absolutely new. It was as though he had never got bored with them yet so he didn't feel he had to gussy them up, but he really got to the nitty-gritty of those plays. He did some naughty things, particularly his Natasha. He was really shocking about her. It's documented that in the original production of *Sisters*, Chekhov was furious with Stanislavski, because in the fire scene when Natasha comes walking through the bedroom, Stanislavski had had her feeling under the bed with a stick and Chekhov was horrified at this. He said, 'She just walks through the room.' That's it. She just opens the door and walks through. And Tony copied exactly what Chekhov *didn't* want. It got a laugh, but it's a cheap act.

HC: I remember this rather vividly. In the script Natasha was an apparently shy, gauche, almost introverted country girl who is in love with Andrey, and little by little in the play's development she grows and develops until she is the power in the household. Well, right from the very beginning, Tony had insisted that Zoe Caldwell create Natasha – against Zoe's will – as a presence, and something of an authority and a threat, right from the beginning, so there wasn't that slow discovery and exciting theatricality of the *development* of Natasha.

The play opened, and, as was so often the case with Tony, he had to go away somewhere. And I remember Tony coming into the green room and Zoe was sitting at the table. There had been some criticism of the interpretation of Natasha, and Zoe had been pretty miserable. He came up, he kissed her and said, 'Good-bye,' and then all I can remember is him saying, 'Got it all wrong, dear. Have a go at it yourself.' Completely reversing. But that was a mistake. And God knows there were other mistakes, but I'd rather put up with a lot of Tony's mistakes than the strokes of genius by some other director.

Tony's failures were sometimes much more interesting than other people's successes.

HC: Going back to those very first few days in Minneapolis, the first rehearsals, I was involved in a really major crisis right from the word go, because I'd been told that I was to do the Malleson adaptation of *The Miser*, and I'd spent quite a lot of time working on it, almost every day. And to suddenly arrive and be told that there'd been a change, and we were doing a whole different approach to the play – I was *very* upset. In fact, I told Tony I wouldn't do it.

So how did he handle it? How did you end up doing it?

HC: Well he asked me to get together with Dougie Campbell and Dougie, who must have been furious that any upstart actor – and that means *any* upstart actor – would challenge the director's authority to do what he liked, was patient and reasonable and explained what he wanted. But I was not persuaded. And then I had a session with Tony, going over this long, point by point letter which I had written to indicate what I felt the strengths and weaknesses were of the two versions. Finally it was resolved on this basis. Tony said, 'Hume, we're not going to let you out. If you insist, we will revert to the Malleson.' Well, I was dead, because can you conceive of what that season would have been like if I had started off my relationship with the director of the first play that I had to do in the Guthrie Theater, by imposing on that director the version of the play that I wanted to do. Now perhaps Henry Irving could have made that stick with some lackey director.

JT: But in those days the director was not the power he is today.

HC: But I was not going to put myself in that position, and I said, 'Well, Tony, if you won't let me go, I will have to do what the director wants to do.' Now, Al, I want to make this very clear – I think Dougie Campbell was right. I think that was the version he should have done. I think it gave him the bones and muscle of the play, but a certain spareness on which he was able to elaborate with the *commedia dell'arte* approach, which would have been much more difficult with the Malleson.

Hume, do you have any special impressions of Tony from that first rehearsal of Three Sisters, *which was the first time you'd worked with him?*

HC: I don't think Tony ever spent much time discussing character with the actors. I do remember one discussion, or argument, with Tony. When I got to know him very well, I'd go over to the house and we'd have long, theoretical discussions which were great fun. And Judy would chime in, and it would just be theatre talk. And I remember Tony making a very strong point once. I think it was apropos to *Richard III*. I thought Tony really buggered that production. I took him to task for his lack of guidance and he, I thought, took defence in saying, 'You know the actor has a very strong creative contribution, and I don't feel justified in saying, "You must do it this way", when his impulse is the other.' I remember that conversation and I felt, 'That is a bit of specious rationalization conveniently produced at this moment.' But I did a play years before with Harold Clurman and, as I remember it, nearly half the rehearsal period was given over to discussions of character – just that. I found that fascinating. With Tony one somehow brushed through that and what was the actor's impulse and then it was just how did one execute it, so that it was theatrically effective. This was Tony's strength and also his great weakness. He had this marvellous theatrical flair.

For example, *Richard III* opened with Gloucester up on the balcony looking down over an almost entirely dark stage and held only in one bright spot. Before the play began, when the house was dark, there was a very ominous musical effect – it was preparatory to the three witches, really – then you discovered Gloucester and he started, 'Now is the winter of our discontent', etc. That's dead wrong. That is not, I'm absolutely positive, what Shakespeare wrote. There should have been the lovely – now we're on a thrust stage with bare boards and you hope for some passion – ambience of spring, sunlight, the sound of music, flutes in the distance, perhaps passers-by below under the balcony, garlands of flowers, and so on. And against this whole Botticelli-like scene a man is saying, 'I cannot live in this atmosphere.' It's ironic. Instead of which he played the ultimate effect. It was dark, moody, perverted, crooked, threatening. One should have discovered that. I mean it was the same damn thing with Natasha. You weren't allowed to come to these moments of discovery. I mean that latent violence, the fury, the perversion, the self-hatred, all should simmer underneath in an atmosphere at the beginning. It's not until much later in the play that they emerge and take over, and that's the tragedy. But if you start with that where do you go? Of course Tony came with such a reputation that it seemed a monumental impertinence to challenge him on a basic concept. But I remember talking to him about that.

Since he had directed the play before, did you ever get the feeling that he was asking you to do things that had worked in another production?

HC: I don't remember at any moment Tony imposing anything on me or the other actors, something that I felt belonged in a previous production. That may have operated very strongly. I saw his production with Guinness – and Guinness is an actor whom I admire extravagantly – and I didn't like it very much, and I think I would never have agreed to play the role, if I didn't think I could do it differently. I had a different concept and some parts of it worked and some parts of it didn't.

But Tony loved visual effects. You remember the appearance of Richard in that coronation cape, a lovely theatrical effect? They practically had to push me on stage to get me started. I only weighed 130 lb wringing wet, and I've got I don't know how many yards of velour trailing behind me with four people holding on to the train, and I've got to get the momentum of getting that started across the stage. And I can't remember whether it was in that scene, but one of those scenes was prefaced by the inevitable Tony Guthrie parade, people pouring out from the vomitories. There were the bishops and priests, and one of the priests stumbled carrying a magnificent jewelled cross and went to his knees, and then got kicked by the bishop behind him to get up to his feet. I mean, that's typical Guthrie.

JT: He always liked to take a swing at the Church. He was a very religious man; it's very strange.

In the same season about which we're speaking, he also directed The Cherry Orchard, *and I suppose Madam Ranevskaya was the most important role you'd ever played for Tony. Is that correct, Jessie?*

JT: Well, one before, which was very innovative, was in *Twelfth Night* to play both Sebastian and Viola. This was at the Old Vic in 1937. It's a marvellous idea. He made it work physically, except that it's really impossible for the actress, because you have to save so much to play Sebastian that you could have used in Viola in order to differentiate them. You also ran a lot backstage, to try and come in the other side. But the confrontation at the end, when they're both on at the same time, he did marvellously.

How did he do it?

JT: Well I spoke all the lines, either one or the other. Earlier in the play Jill Esmond as Olivia had given me a flower, which I had tucked into my hat as Sebastian. So after that, every time I came on as Sebastian, the flower was in the hat. Now when they were both on at the same time – there were a lot of people on stage – I would say one line as Viola, and we would rush together and turn, and the flower would be in the hat, and I'd say the next line, so it was a sort of ballet. It worked, and was very exciting.

I remember that production and also the *Henry V* with Larry, where for the first time the French lesson was done right. He did it *beautifully*. The scene comes after the fall of Harfleur, and there are big battles and speeches and lots of actors. Then suddenly, usually played on the apron there would be Alice and the Princess and the French lesson, and before you'd got attuned to that it was all over, nothing. Not with Guthrie. We finished Harfleur and right at the back of the stage at the Old Vic I was waiting on a little bower on the shoulders of six guardees, and there were court ladies all around. The whole scene was set with flags, tattered or triumphant or whatever. Then two men lifted back two flags in the centre and sang a laughing song, two more came and took the next, and took the next, and took the next – about six of them going back until they were all cleared and then from the very back of the stage down the Princess came on this ridiculous bower, being carried through the streets on the shoulders of these men. Now the audience was ready to listen to the scene, which is very funny, which is very *risqué*, and which had always been passed over before. It was amusing, charming and absolutely wonderful. It was heaven to do.

Having worked with him at times almost thirty years apart, did you find any noticeable difference in the way he directed?

JT: No, not at all. He was as vital and fascinating as ever. I mean you always knew that there were going to be sparks and things happening.

Did he treat you any differently?

JT: No, because you see I don't think Tony prescribed to any adulation for actors or for their achievements at all. He was like Kazan in that respect. When you go to work for Kazan you can put on your jeans and roll up your sleeves and *go to work*. Nobody's trying to impress anybody. Tony was always extremely nice and polite, and I don't think he was very different at all. He was never in awe of anybody, let's face that.

HC: In the book he wrote about the Guthrie Theater he talks about why he engaged us and that is one of the things that I'm proud of. I think he felt we would be a healthy influence in the company.

And it was purely professional. Tony's theories of theatrical democracy are just fine, but you did run into trouble occasionally, because you cannot always expect the same behaviour from someone who's had twenty, thirty, forty years in the theatre on the one hand and someone else who comes in fresh from the university. I think there are certain prerogatives and prerequisites that someone earns over a long period of time that have to be recognized in almost any field.

I remember plumping once for someone with a central and responsible role and carrying a play to get the billing, and that those of us who were doing not much more than carrying spears be listed below in alphabetical order. When somebody came along who did have to play Hamlet it seemed to me that it was not unjustifiable to put their name up on a par with the production designer and the production stage manager and even with the director. I mean, with Tony, and even more so with Dougie Campbell, there was an atmosphere which inclined to prevail in that theatre, which was a bit of a pain in the ass, and that was that all of us were equal but some were more equal than others, and it was a charade really. I mean, there the director was the star and then there was the designer, the composer, the adapter or the author, etc. All those people would be listed and given particular credit. Then there would be an alphabetical listing of the company. Now I personally think that's bull, if it is something like *Hamlet*. Or as a matter of fact almost any of the plays we've talked about, because the responsibilities are not in any way *evenly* divided and some people bring a lifetime of effort to it and others are just starting. It seems to me that if you're going to have a company with, say, George Scott in it, and George plays the little part of the waiter in the third act, let his name appear between R and T down at the bottom. But if, on the other hand, he's playing Lear, it seems to me not unreasonable to let you know that George Scott is playing Lear.

But I know we tried very hard; in fact it was no trial, we wanted to do it. We were damn sure that if anybody was going to be on time for a class, we were going to be on time. And if there was any question of failure to attend, it wasn't going to be us. We were going to be part of that whole thing which had to do with the life and enjoyment and morale of the whole company. It was a marvellous experience for me. I adored him. Those were, in some ways, the best days I've ever had in the theatre, and much of it thanks to Tony Guthrie.

That's one side of it. The positive and the good side. The side that I found hypocritical a bit was that sometimes an atmosphere took over in which the company was assembled and then lectured rather like the third form at school, and you were told that this was what was expected of all ranks, etc. But there weren't all ranks. There were *the ranks*, not all ranks.

Jessica, since you worked with two superb directors on two of the greatest female roles written in this century – Ranevskaya and Blanche – could you compare working with Kazan and Guthrie?

JT: Well, first of all they are each of them absolutely tops. They are the same and different. The sameness is . . . how can I say it? . . . really *honest* work. When you go to rehearsal you don't feel that you're on trial or that you're frightened of making mistakes. You are free to make as many mistakes as you like. It's a working relationship. Kazan doesn't have the flair for the theatrical that Tony had. He could never do all that marvellous, exciting crowd work. He isn't as musical as Tony. Music was very important in Tony's productions. You're liable to get a deeper insight into what you're doing, your character and your relationship with other people, with Kazan. Remember we were doing an entirely different kind of play. Really, I suppose we should compare Guthrie doing *Three Sisters* and Kazan doing *Streetcar* and there isn't an awful lot of difference. It's really bringing out the very best in the play, the very best in the actors.

HC: Gadge would be better at the latter, I think, than Tony.

JT: Well, because Gadge was an actor. So was Tony, but I don't think he really cared about actors very much. I think Tony, in a way, despised actors a little bit. I think he felt that we're kind of children. Kazan doesn't. You're on a level with him.

HC: Kazan is a great friend of mine. I've worked with him twice, but on a much more superficial level than Jessie in *Streetcar*. She really can speak with far greater authority about that relationship. I can speak with almost equal authority about him as a friend and as someone whose work I know quite well.

I think Gadge's work goes deeper than Guthrie's ever did. You see, Tony wouldn't start with the actor and now we've come full circle to something we said earlier on. Tony wouldn't start with building the blocks of character, then having them develop into a behavioural pattern so that finally you came to know how to execute it. It seemed to me that Tony very often started with the execution, and if you happened to be dead wrong in your concept, or if he happened to be dead wrong in what he felt your concept should be, you could be in serious trouble. Because you have all the glorious costumes, you have all the balletic movement, and somehow something was rotten at the core. Now that, I think, can happen to any director but it happened a little too frequently with Tony, because it seemed to me that very often he saw somehow the finished production; it was all in his mind, and he worked towards that. And if you happened to be clued in, as the actor, as to your contribution in one or two important arias or solo passages, and you were running on the same route or, at least, a parallel one, things were liable to happen very well. But if your concept was different and he hadn't checked it, caught it, changed it early on, the marriage was never really satisfactory. That would be far less likely to happen with Kazan, I think.

On the other hand Jessie makes another point. I think that Tony, with his vast musical sense which is not just knowing about music but thinking about so many things musically, balletically, had the most extraordinary grasp, for a director, of all the components of the theatre – music, visual design, choreography, ballet, you know – they all came into being.

JT: The pitch of voices.

HC: Right. There are very, very few directors who manage to combine that.

How did Tony approach that wonderful scene in Cherry Orchard, *which is so well written and was so well played – the party scene in which Lopahin comes in and you were sitting in the one chair on stage and there was a great deal of activity going on around you, with the party upstage. You never moved from the chair, as I recall.*

JT: He was worried about that, because he wanted to get rid of me. He wanted to put me somewhere out of the way in that scene, and I couldn't bear it because I knew that there had to be the two things going on at the same time. So I said, 'I promise you, Tony, I won't do anything to take the attention away from them, but I should be there. The audience should be able to monitor those key things.' It had something to do with his embarrassment, I think, with the emotion. If there was any deep feeling, he would often do something – wave flags or crash tables or something to dull it, to take away from it. But he let me try it, and he realized it was all right.

I think those Chekhov plays were the best work he did in Minneapolis and, of course, the emotion in those plays is very deep. It's curious that he was able to create a milieu which could communicate that to an audience and yet somehow be in keeping with his basic reluctance to deal with emotional scenes.

JT: Well, you must remember that his translator was there all the time, and they must have discussed line by line exactly what was meant and what was going on. When he'd got a finished Shakespeare script he could do what he liked to illuminate that, but there must have been the sort of Kazan-like discussions with his collaborator. Especially when they were trying so hard to find exactly what it meant. In that way I think those Chekhov plays were quite different from anything he'd ever done before. It was a different experience for him.

Did you socialize with the Guthries at all?

HC: I remember some times at the house in Minneapolis when I was alone with him there. We socialized with them a bit. I think we probably saw as much of them as any other actors working with him at that time. I liked Tony enormously. When you started asking that question I suddenly got an image: have you ever seen a field covered with grackles or blackbirds? They come down at certain times of the year and they roost in certain areas. You've got all these busy birds pretty much the same in plumage, and suddenly into them comes this great blue heron. Tony was not only whatever the hell he was – six foot seven or whatever – in height, he was a real giant in every way.

I also remember that he could be unthinkingly quite brutal at times. I saw one incident when I thought he was very unkind to Dougie. Do you remember that bloody photograph taken for *Life* magazine in the first season when we were all in the field opposite the theatre? I was the only person present at the time, and the discussion that took place was really so painful. We were standing there waiting for this to begin and Tony came by, probably without his socks on, and said, 'Are you ready?' And Dougie said, 'What do you mean? Yes, I'm ready', and he said, 'Are you going like that?' 'I thought I would.' 'But you can't. Haven't you got a dark suit?' And Dougie said, 'Well, I'm properly dressed. I've got on a tie and jacket. It's not a funeral.' 'Well, I think you should change.' I mean, it was like father to son in a rather tactless moment. Oh, he could slap you down. I remember one moment in which he turned to me and said rather sharply, 'Hume, you really must remember you are no longer thirty.' This had to do with something that I thought I could play or the way I was approaching something I was playing. Those were the unusual extremes.

JT: Well, there was no malice in any of that. I mean, it was painful for Dougie but there was no malice, I'm sure.

HC: He also had respect for the actor's contribution. I mean, if you said, 'I would like to approach this in this fashion', unless it resulted in an absolute foul-up of his directorial conception, he had great respect for what you wanted to do. When I challenged him, he said, 'Well, I don't think I could impose that on the actor. The actors bring that and then I shape it and give it some direction and fit it into one piece that works together, etc.' Jessie, what's that story about Tony striding over all those prone bodies? Tell it to Al, because that's such a typical one.

JT: He was putting on a pageant for some town in England, and there were hundreds of people all over the place and there was a woman reclining on the grass, you see, and he was all over the place with *all* these people and he finally came back, stepped over her and said, 'Isn't it fun putting on a play?' And that is actually right, isn't it? I mean, that is exactly the epitome of what you feel. 'Isn't it *fun* putting on a play.' You obviously felt he was enjoying it tremendously, and the enthusiasm was terrific.

HC: Tony was the ultimate professional with the very best spirit of the amateur.

Ken Ruta

KEN RUTA: I was attending the Goodman Theater School in Chicago and was going to teach speech. I remember visiting Stratford, Ontario, the first season, and I went to *Richard III*, but could only get a seat in the back row of the old tent. There was a seat next to me that was empty, and about ten minutes into the show this *giant* came in and sat down in it. I never realized until years later that it had been Guthrie sitting next to me. It was that night that I really decided I had to be an actor. I mean, being a Catholic with all that mysticism – it was the first time that the theatre had all that stuff. After that night my ambition in life was to be in a show directed by Guthrie and wear one of Tanya's costumes. And it was ten years later that it all came true.

I remember that party we had before starting first rehearsals for the initial season. The thing that amazed me was there he was at the door greeting everybody. He'd met me once, and there he was introducing me to Judy, and he could remember my first and last name. And of *everybody*. That was one of the fantastic things about him. He also knew how far he could drive you, and he knew how to talk to *you*. He must have found out that I loved the opera because he always spoke to me in musical terms.

ALFRED ROSSI: *Did he use that as a specific way of opening up things for you?*

Maybe. Like that first day of the *Hamlet*, God! I knew some friend of George Grizzard's and George said, 'Would you like to come and have lunch with me?' We had a marvellous lunch and George was nervous, and he was confiding all this stuff to me. We went to that first rehearsal, and Guthrie started saying to me, 'More *legato*, go up another octave,' and all that. Well, George never spoke to me again until about August of that year. He said, 'You know you intimidated me so much. I thought you were some beginning actor and you and Guthrie – I could have murdered you both, the way you two just pounced all over me. You doing all your operatic stuff and me with this little voice.' And he said, 'Those pauses you used to take. I wanted to kill you.' But Tony just loved it. He would say, 'Push Hamlet around some more, he's just a little squirt,' because Tony wanted the Ghost to be so big and wanted Hamlet to be this little runt that got pushed around all the time. He was forever putting me on the top step, and wanted me to wear foot-high boots, which we later cut. I had never worked with anybody like that, we just went wild. He would just see how far he could drive me all the time.

When Tony started rehearsing with you what kind of initial work did he do?

I think this is the sign of a great director. He really said very little. He said he didn't want any 'boogie-boogie' kind of stuff. He wanted someone who was in great pain. That was when he said something about 'pain drives the voice'. He did it with me on the piano once, and I think I almost spoke on three octaves. I remember he said, 'Go as high as you can go and then drop down as low as you can come back.' And it was just sensational. He was a frustrated opera singer, and I guess I am too. He would just say, 'Higher. How high can you go?' And I just kept on going higher. I guess that's why it worked out. He used to tell me he just loved rehearsing that scene, and Jessie Tandy used to say, 'I'm frankly bored with Tony doing those scenes. He's just getting his rocks off. *He* wants to play that part.'

Did he ever demonstrate anything for you?

No, that's one of the great things about him. I can never remember him reading a line for anybody. He'd speak to you some other way. He was always using musical terms like *legato, basso profundo, coloratura,* syncopate that line. I could understand that, but a lot of people didn't.

The first day at rehearsal they had given me the Second Gravedigger too, which wasn't in my contract. So I thought I'd go complain to the management, and I did. And they gave me a raise, after they had talked to Guthrie. I've noticed that I played all the parts that one of Guthrie's favourite actors, Robert Edison, played for him.

Did he see you as a certain type?

Well, obviously not, because the Ghost was sort of your grand old daddy thing and then he cast me as Trofimov in *The Cherry Orchard*, but I think he thought I was a grotesque.

Is that the way he described you?

Yeah, I think that was an English term in the theatre, because Eric Portman used to say that, 'You and Ellis Rabb are both grotesque actors.' I guess the stretch . . . you know . . . that you could go into all sorts of gnarly things, you weren't straight and clean. More or less in the French style of work, i.e. losing yourself in the part rather than losing the part in you.

Let's go to the second season. You were given Pistol in Henry V *and Voltore in* Volpone.

Yes. In the *Henry* he wanted to do something new. He didn't want the clowns to be funny. He wanted to do it sort of Actor's Studio-ish as real people and get away from all that funny business. Well, it was not very good. And at the last run-through we had in the rehearsal room, before we went on stage he said, 'I've made a terrible mistake. It's fucking *awful*. Try and do something with it, make it funny. Just pick up the lines and talk loud. None of that acting.'

Was this a shock to you?

No, because I trusted him. I'd seen awful performances in shows of his, but he could cover it up so brilliantly, put some music over your singing or put a bag on your head or something. But we did it, and I didn't think it was very good, and he knew he'd made a mistake.

I don't think he was well that season. The *Henry* rehearsals weren't going very well. He wasn't happy with a few performances, 'not juicy enough'. He said the same thing about *Richard III* the next season.

They needed more flesh to them, you know, pure vocal pizazz. George Grizzard and Hume Cronyn, you know, do tiny things marvellously with emotional rage, but never had the big voice and presence to fill the theatre, not like Wolfit or somebody like that.

But the *Henry* wasn't a happy production. We were doing the St Crispin's Day scene at dress-rehearsal, and we were all in our positions. We'd run the scene a couple of times, rolling in the cannon and all those things. We were all coming down the aisles and up the vomitories, and he stopped us and delivered a speech that went on for almost two hours. We were all just standing there, and it was completely mesmerizing. It was one of those incredible things. He talked about what the play meant to him. He wanted to compare the Greek ideals of honour with those of the pale Samaritan, meaning Christ – the Christian ideals of honour and death. And it was like music – it spoke to you somewhere inside, and we were just standing there crying. It was very simple – he had one foot on the top of the stage and the other was down, and he just stood there and talked. And he was talking about the Queen, making his jokes, saying that she was this rabbit that had a baby once every two years. He put down everything in the Catholic Church, which he loved to do.

I think the things that he loved he had to put down all the time. Poor Harry Cronin. Harry was a McKnight Fellowship student and also a priest. He played one of the traitors in *Henry V*, and Tony loved torture on the stage. Harry used to come in trussed up like a deer on this pole, and at one point he was cut from the pole and fell to the stage. Well, Tony used to do that *over* and *over*. Poor Harry's knees. He had pads, but *still*. Someone said, 'Tony, that poor man, he could have broken his . . .' And Tony would say, 'Oh no, the Catholics love all that pain.' And, of course, whenever a nun would come to watch rehearsal he would say 'fuck' as much as he could.

At the end of *Henry V* there was supposed to be a great 'Amen' sung. Well, it wasn't loud enough so that they had to hire some professional singers to come in to tape it, and we had to do it in an hour. There were four women and two men. Tony, of course, loved to sing. You could always hear him above everybody else in the tapings: he was a little off pitch. But those women, he just hated them. I remember he said, 'You great fucking cunts! Can't you read music?' Well, they got very upset, and they complained to the composer, Herb Pilhofer; they wanted Tony to apologize.

When he stopped and delivered that long speech, at dress-rehearsal, wasn't that kind of unusual?

Well, the show wasn't working. Like he had cut the wooing scene between Henry and Katherine, because he said he didn't understand it.

But they put it back, didn't they?

Yeah, because George and Kristina Callahan had rehearsed that scene on their own. He didn't understand two-people scenes, especially romantic – he didn't like all that. He really was very sentimental, I know it, deep down inside. But he wouldn't allow himself to show it ever. The kidnapping scene in *Volpone* had a lot of music and Guthrie choreography in it. He would rehearse that over and over again and just sit in the audience with his eyes closed, and I was sitting next to him, and he said, 'That's what it's all about. I don't know what's going on, but I know that's what the theatre is.' Everybody on stage was singing and moving in extraordinary patterns: very operatic. And it was glorious. You knew what the scene was about. You didn't exactly understand what they were saying, but it didn't matter; you could understand it from the way things looked and sounded. He would rehearse that over and over and just sit there with his eyes closed: 'That's what it's all about.' He said – I think it was that opening ceremony of the theatre – what the theatre should be about: the agony and the grandeur of life. That's what he really liked, both ends. The little common things he didn't like.

How did he guide you as an actor?

Very technical things all the time. Musical stuff. And as he got to know me, he knew I was an anglophile, and I knew all these old English actors' names. So he'd say, 'That was awfully Robert Atkins', or 'A bit more Gielgud here', or 'A little Wolfit'. So I could respond to that. Some people he just couldn't get to at all. Since we both wanted to be opera singers it did mean a lot, because we would get together and play records.

What were his favourites?

Oh, it had to be loud and very emotional. I remember I surprised him once. I had heard that he was going to do *Macbeth* with Maria Callas at Covent Garden. He denied it. He said, 'They've never asked me.' I said, 'I've seen it in print.' He said, 'You may have seen it in print, but I was never asked to do it. I would love to do it.' It really would have been wonderful, the two of them. He used to call her 'Cahlosh'. I don't know where he found that pronunciation. The last time I saw him he'd just gotten from Marborough Books the complete Beethoven symphonies, the orchestral score in a $3.98 paperback. And he was going through the book listening to the symphonies with the orchestral score. He had this funky phonograph, 1929 I'm sure, with a straight pin in it. Tanya bought a new phonograph, and she gave him her old one. But he could *survive* on that. That was the *way* he survived.

You know, those old house slippers, walking through the snow, and a sweater that somebody had knit for him that was never cleaned. I remember one time coming to a *Henry* rehearsal he'd walked through a snowstorm, he was soaking wet, and was sick. He borrowed one of the monks' robes, and he was laying down on the floor, and Judith brought that wonderful thermos of hot soup, which we knew was something else. He took the robe off later on, and put on his old red sweater and those wonderful pants with the jockey shorts pulled up over his shirt. And that tuxedo he wore the opening night of the *Hamlet*. He said he bought it from Ralph Richardson. It was the one he borrowed from Ralph when he was knighted. The cuffs were a *little* high. Once I saw him wear a tuxedo and house slippers.

I know you and Tanya Moiseiwitsch are good friends. How would you describe her work with Tony?

The way those two people used to work was so incredible. Tanya, even now, does only one show every six months. The research that she does with the director! I remember it was two years she was designing the *Oresteia* with Tony. Sheaves of sketches were thrown out. So a lot of thought had already gone into it. If you look at the back of her sketches, she has written down everything you ever want to know about your role. She would have things about the vocal quality, even the age and family background, very thorough, particular things. And you knew the first day of rehearsal when you saw the sketch only *you* could wear that costume. That's the great thing about Tanya, I think. However, I don't know who led – her genius or his. The combination was miraculous. He did tell all of us birds in *Volpone* to go to the zoo and really look at their habits.

Sounds Stanislavskian.

Yes. I think that his 'spectacle' days were ending He wasn't happy with the epic any more. Chekhov was his man. He was really going deeper and deeper.

Did you go to the zoo?

Well, I was very lazy and I didn't go; I just used my imagination. One time I remember he said, 'Do something with the shoulders and the neck.' When I sat down and started putting on the make-up and saw these feathers I had around my neck, I remember I painted my neck blood red. I had this beak on, and the hat transformed my head. My hunched shoulders made a hump. That's still Bill Ball's favourite acting bit. I came in with my shoulders hunched and my head way down in and I looked at Volpone's body. And Tony told me, I remember, 'Why don't you lick your lips?' I had used vegetable dye on my tongue too, and so I licked my lips and I thought, 'Oh my God, I should show my neck.' So I dropped the shoulders and stuck this bloody neck from out the feathers. It used to get a gasp from the audience. And Bill just thought that was brilliant. Now that was a combination – Tony and Tanya thought out that whole thing. Everybody was getting an exit hand at one point, the end of Act II; I was jealous and I wanted to do something. He said, 'Just get off the stage. No pause, no turn, no tricks, just keep going, keep going.' But then he'd rehearse that trial scene over and over. It was another one of those scenes he loved, which he'd like to play too, because it was a lot of vocal gymnastics.

The ending of the show wasn't good. I think it was that Dougie and he weren't seeing eye to eye, and he had the brilliant idea that there had to be a fugue finale, sung by the entire cast. So Dominick Argento had to go off that night, and he wrote this fantastic piece of music. Opening night we did it brilliantly (and never did it that well again). It was a fantastic fugue, in about eight parts. It was basically simple, but the difficulty was doing the fugal harmony on that thrust stage, you couldn't hear. So we had to make a recording and sing with it, but it never really made it. Tony left, and it was up to us. And then Tony came back, and the show was not holding at the end. Dougie was playing the house rather than the play. Tony said something, as he did in *The Three Sisters* the season before (which I wasn't in). The *Sisters* opening was beautiful, I remember, then Tony went away. When he came back I met him on the stairs, and we talked about it. He said, 'They've sold out. They're playing for the audience. If the audience laughs, you're doing something wrong. They should smile. The audience is privileged to be at a Chekhov play. They're eavesdropping, but they should never control the actors.' And that was one of the reasons when he did *The Cherry Orchard* the third season we never blocked the fourth act until three days before we opened. He wouldn't rehearse. He said, 'I don't want it to be out of control. The less planned the better. The show is so perfectly cast, you don't need me. I want the show to hold, so I'm not going to do it until the very last minute, because it'll fall apart.'

Do you recall the work on Richard III*?*

The production was based on the one he did at Stratford, with Tanya
and Guinness and Irene Worth. Of course now he had a different
designer, different actors, and that concept didn't work. I don't think
he was very happy in that either. He really didn't want to do it. He
was forced to do it. I think he was getting less and less happy with
Shakespeare, because I think he was forced to repeat successes. Unless
he really loved the play – for example, he'd done *Cherry Orchard*
before, but found more and more in it. But I don't think he found
more and more in *Richard*. He was diddling around with it. I hardly
ever rehearsed Clarence's scene. And when he rehearsed it, he gave me
only one thing. The murderers were supposed to come at me during
the middle of the line. He wanted me to jump one octave, in the middle
of a *word*. I'm sure he just wanted to see if I could do it. It was marvellous, but then it just got to be something technical. But that was
about the only thing he did, and it was very boring because he would
never say a word. Rehearsing it, we got in the theatre and it was just
awful. He said, 'I can't understand a word you're saying, not a word.'
And then we fixed that up, but he was still bored with it. So he wanted
Sandy McCallum to carry me off on his back. And Sandy is all of four
foot I-don't-know-what, and I'm six foot three. He said, 'That'll be
great fun.' It wasn't a happy time, and the show was not that successful.
He was having his fun with the Catholic Church again. He loaded it
with lots of incense, and he got a little bit of *Ivan the Terrible* in there
too, to cover up his boredom with the whole thing. It was one of
those shows that did not improve during the season.

But what I learned from him. I had had a very good speech and voice
teacher at the Goodman, Mary Agnes Doyle, whom Guthrie had heard
about and always wanted to meet. She had been a student of Henry
Sweet, who was Shaw's model for Henry Higgins. Elsie Fogarty, who
was a great voice teacher in England, was her room-mate back in 1905.
So Guthrie had been brought up on the same things I'd been brought
up with in terms of vocal training and speech. It was a matter of using
what I'd been taught. I didn't understand some things when in school,
but now here was someone who knew them and how to use them and
how to help *me* to use and profit from them. And that thing about
saying seven lines on one breath, I mean that was the *minimum*. In
Hamlet I think there was one time when I had to do ten. And I could
do it.

How did he work on The Cherry Orchard?

We read it about a month and a half before we started rehearsal. He just wanted to hear it so we could make little changes. (It was a new translation he and Lola Kipness did.) He didn't want us to sound American or English. That was very technical. But then he did talk about the play, which aroused the ire of certain people in the cast – there was no *lead* in this play. 'This play is about the house, and there are no tears in this play.' That was one thing he always said about Chekhov. 'You ought to always let the audience do the crying. Chekhov wrote happy people. Maybe that's why they're foolish, or they're foolish because they're happy.' And it amazed me.

You know, when you look at a Chekhov script, there are no stage directions, everything's between the lines. But it was so simple the way that thing unfolded. Maybe it was just him being in the room that made it happen. People were working with props right away. It seemed like they were already living in the house. It was very simple, the flow of it; it happened almost by magic. I mentioned that he said it was just because it was perfectly cast, and he didn't have to do anything with it.

Oh, there were little problems here and there. He hated Trofimov's big speech, because he thought it was a lot of claptrap. He said, 'I want you to do something during it', and he had actors on stage swatting flies while I was sketching. (I really did some marvellous sketches. I'm very flattered Tanya has one; I used to sketch the group on the stage.) But he would never work the end scene between Anya and me. That was up to us to do that. He never said 'boo' during rehearsal or opening. Came back to see it and said, 'Oh, it's come a long way. Couldn't have done it myself, I must admit. Not as sentimental as I thought it was going to be.' He would always encourage doing everything you could possibly do (I believe in that technique in acting): just go to the farthest point and then throw out the unnecessary. In this play everybody believed in themselves and their ideals and the harder you believed the more foolish you appeared. Those people don't sit around beating themselves, moaning. They're very wonderful, passionate people, but they're all fools and idiots, and they make mistakes . . . thank God!

Did you ever feel that Guthrie thought the audience was almost unnecessary?

Well, he really talked about that a lot in Chekhov. The audience were *intruders*. One thing he said to me was marvellous. It was during *Volpone*, talking about the greater the play the less the audience understands of it. He said, 'If it's a great play like *Hamlet*, and if they come away with fifty per cent of it, that's really something. You know, as the play gets worse, they understand more.' And he talked about acting too, saying, 'The better you become the more the audience is going to hate you. They may like you at first, but they're jealous of you, if you get to be too good an actor.' They want to come and see you fall down or come on drunk. That's why they keep coming to see you. They want to see you do a bad job at something, equally as much as wanting to be thrilled. There is as much thrill out of seeing you trip, or if you're going to go on at all. Like Judy Garland, 'Is she going to make it tonight?' And then she does make it and it's exciting, but if she stumbles a few times, it makes it all the more exciting.

The actors not quite the gods we thought they were, they're more like us.

I had tickets to see Guthrie's production of *The Makropoulos Secret* at the Phoenix a number of years ago, but couldn't go. And my friends came back and said, 'You should have gone; Guthrie *acted*.' He had gone in as a temporary replacement. I would love to have seen him. Have you seen any of his film performances? I've seen *The Beachcomber* and *St Martin's Lane*. In *St Martin's Lane* he has this scene in bed, practising the harmonica, reading the sheet music; that is the most obscenely funny thing. He was the true grotesque, but marvellous, just marvellous.

Once he started talking about his favourite actors, because he asked me what I'd seen that season in New York. And I said I'd seen Donald Wolfit in *All in Good Time*. He said, 'How did you like him?' I said, 'Well, he was marvellous, but he didn't do any of the things that I thought he was going to do.' He said, 'That's the greatest actor. That man can do anything.' He'd just seen Leo McKern in *Peer Gynt* at the Old Vic that season, and he thought McKern was just stupendous. But his two favourite actors were Donald Wolfit and Flora Robson. He thought Flora Robson was the most beautiful on stage; she just exuded beauty. He said, 'She isn't; God knows she isn't, but she makes you believe.'

Do you have any fond memories of him socially?

The big thrill was being invited to dinner, the first time, at the

Guthries'. I got all dressed up, and I was going to pick up Tanya. Tanya said, 'My, you're awfully overdressed.' Then she said, 'Oh, would you like to have a little martini or something first?' I said, 'Oh, I suppose so.' She said, 'You take ice?' I said, 'Yes.' And the phone rang and it was Lady Judith. She said, 'You can come over now.' We just walked from Tanya's little garage-top apartment to the Guthries' rooftop place and up those many stairs. Tanya had told me to take my drink with me, because it had ice in it. We went up there, I in my tie and vest and all.

There was Tony greeting me with this water glass of warm gin, in his bathrobe and slippers. He invited us in and Judith was in the tub at the time, and she came running back and forth in her little wrapper. Well, nothing ever changed through the evening. Tony sat there in this awful flannel robe, hanging out, plying us with these glasses of gin, which I used my ice cubes in. We had a wonderful meal of a can of Dinty Moore stew, in which was a small box of Sunmaid raisins and what must have been a pint of whiskey. It was brought to you in a plate floating. And we were served the gin out of – they were keeping them for some reason or other – medicine bottles. Tanya had brought over her phonograph (I think Tony's straight pin had since worn out) and we listened to 'Mahria Cahlosh' records. He played Benjamin Britten's *Noye's Fludde*, which includes a lot of hymns. Tony joined in and sang along at the top of his lungs, while the rest of the conversation was going on. And Judith would every once in a while say, 'Please, Tony!' 'Quiet. I'm singing,' he'd say. And she couldn't get a word in edgewise. (Judith told me that he used to have a beautiful soprano voice, because she first fell in love with him when she heard him singing in the choir as a young boy.) Well anyway, we were all just pissed to the gills with the booze pouring in, after that wonderful Dinty Moore stew. But I couldn't believe it – my great night out with the Guthries, and there they were in their bathrobes. Well; the gods are like that when they're up on Olympus.

The last time I saw them was at a dress-rehearsal for *Peter Grimes* at the Met. Judith had been in the hospital quite a lot. She'd given up smoking, she said, but she still had the famous cough. But they were both looking very good. And I think Tony was very proud of that *Peter Grimes*, as well he should have been. It's been revived since. This year the San Francisco Opera did it, but it was Tony's conception and Tanya's costumes. But he talked so much about that *first* production of it in London right after the war when the gods were with them, because there was a heavy fog that night, and it actually filled the theatre. He said it was just magic: you couldn't see where the theatre left off and the set began. But the gods were always with him.

You know, he reminded me of loads of childhood things. He was a great-grandfather I can barely remember who used to beat you at Christmas time. He was a great father image. I think he was everybody's daddy.

Barrie Stavis

ALFRED ROSSI: Harper's Ferry *was the first original script produced at the Tyrone Guthrie Theater. How did the play come to Tony's attention?*

BARRIE STAVIS: I had known Tony since 1955. It was he who had recommended *Lamp at Midnight*, my play about Galileo, to the Bristol Old Vic, which resulted in a production in 1956 with a cast which included Peter O'Toole, Rachel Roberts, Robert Lang and several other splendid actors. So in 1960 I wrote to Tony asking him permission to send *Harper's Ferry* – it was then titled *Banners of Steel*.

He asked to see the play, and on August 13th he wrote from Stratford, Canada: 'I've read the play and offer you respectful congratulations on what I really do think a noble and moving piece of work. Of course, it is, as you yourself agree, *far* too long. I think there are many small cuts which could be stylistically to its advantage. I would like, however, to make a more dramatic suggestion.

'The second act – the battle of Harper's Ferry – is far more suited to film than to the stage. You have been ingenious but, even so, lots of these short scenes of chasing, shooting, wrestling, etc., would be *very* hard to stage and could *very* easily be ridiculous. None of this is the *sort* of thing for which the theatre is suited.

'If Shakespeare could leave the battle of Agincourt out of *Henry V*, I don't see why you can't leave the battle out of your play.

'We don't *need* to see what has been clearly foreshadowed, in fact, occurring.

'Act III could begin with some narration of the few necessary facts. I don't know *precisely* how, but I'm sure it could be done. And then, *muy pronto*, you're down to manageable length and have avoided most of the stickiest passages.

'Again and again I found the grandeur and simplicity of Brown *most* moving. He's grandest when simplest, and when least preachy and most practical.

'Washington's a good part. It's a great merit of the play that the "good" people aren't white, nor the "bad" ones jet-black; also that the coloured people aren't sentimentalized.

'The suggested staging is bold and, in my view (except for Act II), perfectly practical.

'I think Hunter is done less than justice. He would be more moving, and I believe truer to nature, were he to be shown not solely as intelligent and just, but also humane. There was, after all, an important matter of principle at stake in John Brown's trial as well as the slavery matter. Brown *had* committed treason. People simply cannot be permitted to take the law into their own hands, however convinced they and their friends may be of the rightness of their cause.

'All in all *splendid* work – not yet quite ready to be offered to read.

'Best wishes and warm congratulations and I'm flattered to have been allowed to read it.'

What did you do about his suggestions?

Tony gave me exactly the insight I needed about the cutting, and, in fact, when the play was published I quoted from his letter in my introduction and acknowledged my profound debt to him.

Then what happened to the play and Tony's relationship with it?

When the Tyrone Guthrie Theater opened in 1963, I went to Minneapolis and saw the season, visited with my friends in the company, and, of course, visited with Tony and Judy. During one of these visits I had a substantial talk with him, raising the question of doing the play at the Guthrie.

He was blunt and to the point – as he usually was when necessary. He said, 'I couldn't under any circumstances consider the play at this time because we must first form a professional theatre based on the classics and the semi-classics. If we were to do a new play during our early years, these crucial formative years, and it were to be a failure, it would injure the theatre. It would take us several years to recover from such a blow.' I understood his position and agreed with him, painful as it might be to me.

Well, I saw the plays at the Guthrie in 1963 and 64, and, naturally, visited with him and Judy, and we would see each other in New York when he'd be there working or passing through. During our talks those early days of the Guthrie Theater, Tony frequently uttered the thought that it takes ten years for a newly formed repertory company to really function as a *company*, and that during that period of time the theatre should do classics or semi-classics only.

That first season of the Guthrie was an astounding success – a powerful community response in the shape of an enormous number of subscriptions. The second year, the same thing. Evidently Tony felt that it might be safe to shove his timetable of ten years up a bit because along towards the end of the second year he said, 'We may begin to be in a position to discuss your John Brown play a year or two from now.' I was dazed, I tell you. I said, 'Tony, I'll wait.'

Then during the third year of the Guthrie in 1965 Tony said, 'We can start talking about this for 1967.' By that time, that is for the year 1967, Douglas Campbell and Peter Zeisler would be the Artistic Director and Managing Director respectively, which meant, you understand, that the decisions would have to come from Dougie and Pete, not Tony, but, naturally, his recommendations would carry enormous weight.

Doug and Pete felt that because it was a new play and an important step for the theatre, we must be assured that Tony would direct the play. You see, they not only wanted to assure that this departure from previous Guthrie Theater policy would be approved by the Board of Directors, but they also wanted to assure a good audience response. From my end, Tony's directing the play was a culmination of one of my great hopes and he was the *only* person I would have allowed to direct the play at the Guthrie.

Since Doug and Peter wanted a formal statement from Tony that he *would* direct the play, by agreement with Dougie I sent a copy of the script to Tony. This is his response to me which is dated September 27, 1965:

'My Dear Barrie, *Banners of Steel*: I've read it again carefully and I like it and admire it *very much*. It's a piece of work of which you can be proud.

'The battle scenes are immeasurably better now than in the version which I read before. I think they are now exciting and stageable and tell the story.

'If I say candidly what I now feel not to be quite right, it's the very end. All moves with splendid inevitability and with exactly the right degree of moralization up to the point where John Brown speaks to the journalists.

'Then follows a rather interesting scene (3–1–1); but I wonder if it should not *precede* the more important scene where Brown realizes that by talking to the journalists he can do as much for The Cause as if the Harper's Ferry affair had succeeded. *That* is a crucial point and very rightly you place it at the most emphatic possible juncture – viz. second act curtain. But it leaves you with rather too little material for a third act.

'I wonder whether the play shouldn't be in two, not three, parts; and whether after the present second act curtain, you shouldn't get far more quickly to the end.

'I don't think the point about his getting the trial delayed and the plea of insanity are important. From the time of his capture, it is perfectly clear that the authorities are going to find him guilty and hang him – and anyway everybody *knows* that he was hanged, there is therefore no "suspense" in the audience; scenes are not of interest simply if they suggest that just possibly he *may* escape the hangman.

'Therefore I find a great deal of the material in 3–2 uninteresting. It seems to be trying for a suspense which doesn't exist. I do see that possibly a big noble speech for Brown is required; but even of that I'm not sure. He wasn't the sort of character who, like Sydney Carton, goes to the scaffold with a memorable line.

'Likewise, I think 3–3 tries too hard for pathos. The situation is bigger than pathos. By all means have a *very brief* farewell between Brown and his wife – and the more restrained and dignified the better. We are after tragedy here, not pathos, 3–4 has this dignity; but could be better still.

'All this I'm expressing so poorly – just putting down the thoughts in any sort of order, not pausing to tidy them up, or to express them "tactfully". But you'll understand.

'To sum up: I think the material in 3–1 – the point of view of the slave-owners and the perception by Hunter (and a bit by Washington) of the immense gravity of the issues – all that is good and should be in the play; but I believe it ought to, and could, precede the scene in the hospital where Brown speaks to the reporters.

'Thereafter the play should move to the end without a single unnecessary word. The tempo of the acting here will have to be slow and pausy; and I don't think there ought to be any rhetoric. We *know* what the end has to be, we must therefore get there as quickly as the dignity of *tragedy* will permit.

'Incidentally, I don't think in the scene between the husband and

wife that there should be a *return* to the topic of the outrages on the
dead bodies. That has been powerfully dealt with in Kagi's description
of Newby's end. That's enough.

'I've been interrupted twice since starting this letter, so the "continuity" gets wilder and wilder.

'Title: I think *Banners of Steel* is too romantic – sounds like an
adventure "yarn" for boys. Would you consider *Harper's Ferry?*

'Plans? In my opinion – and I'll write this also to Douglas – I think
it would be a V.G. play for us to do in M'polis – perfect for the stage,
and utterly apropos (so far as a foreigner may judge) for the times. I
feel that Douglas ought to play Brown, and that may present a problem
in his first season as director; but that's for him to say.

'If dates can be arranged to everyone's convenience, I would be
happy to direct it.

'To conclude; I really do congratulate you most sincerely and
humbly. It's a very impressive achievement.'

What was your reaction to this letter?

I was shocked and stunned when I first read it. I had thought there'd
be no more, or relatively little, work on the script – and here's this
letter of Tony's staring me in the face. I read his letter about five times
that day, every few hours. Read it really slowly and let it sink in. I
also remember that I deliberately didn't look at the script that day. I
think I would have been overwhelmed by the problems and would
have frozen. I fell asleep with the problem on my mind and woke up
with it. I was in anguish, physical anguish. Each night I deliberately
thought about the problems just as I was falling asleep, and I think it
was the third night, maybe the fourth, that my subconscious must have
been heavily at work because I awoke refreshed and with a profound
feeling that I would crack the nut within the next few days.

That morning I began studying the script with Tony's letter before
me. By the end of the day I saw not only how it could be done as Tony
suggested, but, more important, that Tony's thought of making it
into a two-act play was better than my initial decision to make it into
three acts. It would take maybe a week to do, but I knew that I'd
encounter no difficulties.

We were in correspondence during the intervening year. Then he
came to the States on a number of projects, one of them being *Harper's
Ferry.* And so one morning he came to my apartment and spent the
entire day working on the play with me. He entered with a marvellous

curtsy at the door and a little bouquet of flowers 'for the lady of the house'. Then within five minutes, like a whirlwind, we were plunged into the work. He began by saying, 'The procedure will be that I'll read, and anything you want to stop me on, you stop me. And any time I want to stop and talk, I will.' And he started reading the play, and read it through to the end. Very expressive, often very moving. I remember one point in the play he saw a connection, or perhaps the way to do a scene that he'd not thought of before and he stopped dead, and his voice was low with emotion and he said, 'That's splendid, Barrie.'

As he read along he'd stop and say, 'I'd like this sharpened', or 'I'd like this cut'. We would discuss it and I'd do the writing right then and there and we'd set it. A few times he'd ask me, 'What are you trying to achieve at this particular moment with these four speeches?' (Or five, or six, as the case might be.) I'd tell him and he'd say, 'Well, write it down exactly the way you just said it to me. Write it down.' So I wrote it. We continued in this way, setting the play, speech by speech.

Working this way with Tony was exhilarating and I'm sure his presence sparked me because I was rather eloquent and yet sharply to the point, and so the work flowed smoothly and rapidly through the day. You understand what we were doing. It was an examination of exactly what happens on the stage, minute by minute.

But though the work went smoothly it was a long, hard day. Very tight work. What floored me was that during this entire time from early morning until he left at about six, he didn't have to go to the john once. He was in my house for some nine hours, had lunch and consumed (not liquor because he wanted to be very sharp) but water, tea and coffee. And I thought, 'Jesus, what powers!'

The other thing was that at about four in the afternoon I began to fail. I have great physical energy, stamina and concentration, but towards the end of the day I began to get groggy. And Tony kept pushing me, 'Come on, dear boy, we mustn't . . . ' I said, 'Tony, I'm tired', and he replied, 'I have another appointment after this and I do want to complete the script today.' I was exhausted and he was fresh. And he was humming! I'm failing and he seemed to get more and more charged as he went along, more and more joyous, as it were.

Towards the end of that glorious but physically exhausting day for me, we had a rather interesting discussion about a scene at the end of the play between John and Mary Brown which I loved very, very much. It's the scene in the prison when Mary comes to visit John the night before he's to be hanged. Tony said to me, 'Oh no, Barrie, it's just too sentimental', and he made quite a number of square brackets to show me his proposed cuts. I said, 'Tony, you can't want to cut this out', pointing to one of his proposed cuts. 'And this!' I said in horror, as he square-bracketed one of my most favourite speeches. He answered matter-of-factly, 'Yes, I do.' I said, 'You're cutting off my arm.' He said, 'I want you to see what I propose doing. I want this to become a more spare scene.'

I think I can illuminate *why* Tony was proposing those cuts. When Doug Campbell was discussing the play with me a couple of years earlier, he said that he very much liked to have a painting as a metaphor for a play and he wondered if I could name a single painting which would give him insight as to the quality that I'd like to see emerge on the stage. I gave him a reproduction of El Greco's 'View of Toledo' which is housed in Room 21 of the Metropolitan Museum of Art in New York City. It's a canvas I stand before almost every time I go to the museum. There are unusual green tones in the lower half of the canvas and the blue and grey clouds in the upper half of the canvas are not at ease – they have a twisted, whirled-around and almost tortured look. The middle section, which is the town itself, sprawls over the hills and has a mysterious quality, as if strange and terrifying things happen there frequently and could happen on the very day you, the viewer, are looking at the canvas. In addition, it is a remarkable coincidence that El Greco's 'View of Toledo' looks so much like Harper's Ferry during John Brown's day. There is the river, the bridge, the church spire, the craggy hills. For me El Greco's canvas has always been a perfect metaphor for Harper's Ferry.

Well, I mentioned Doug's request to Tony and gave him my copy of the reproduction to refresh his memory. Tony studied 'View of Toledo' and then talked with me about Grant Wood's *American Gothic*! No matter how much Tony knew of America, he really didn't have it in his bones. He was still an Englishman, a limey, as he often with amusement called himself. You see, in part his image of John Brown and Mary Brown was *American Gothic* – not mine in a thousand years. And so, as you can see, with the image of *American Gothic* in his mind, he could never allow on the stage any kind of sentiment between John and Mary Brown.

Then when the work on the script was completed and all I wanted to do was flop on the floor and pant and let the sweat of fatigue roll down, he said, after humming a few bars, that we must set up the doubling and tripling scheme. I recall the speed with which he laid out the scheme, saying 'So-and-so can play this part. . . . How many pages between this scene and that scene?' and when I told him he said, 'Yes, that'll be enough time for a costume change.' He did it so fast I almost couldn't follow it, and it's *my* play.

I walked out of the house with Tony to accompany him to the subway station. My apartment is just at Park and Ninety-sixth Street in Manhattan and the trains which are above ground up to this point go underground the length of Park Avenue until they reach Grand Central. Of a sudden Tony walked across the street and looked down at the tracks. There were the signal lights, the semaphores, and the tracks stretching into the distance. I suddenly sensed that I had lost Tony. I looked at his face and there was a small smile; he seemed far away. Ever since childhood Tony loved trains. I knew I mustn't intrude. So I stood stock-still, somewhat away from him. With equal suddenness he returned to the present moment and said quite briskly, 'Musn't be late for my dinner appointment', and he started loping off for the subway entrance – with me walking hard to keep pace with him.

Do you recall the first rehearsal?

I remember that the first cast meeting was in the evening. Now you must understand I'd seen perhaps thirty productions of Tony's and seen him in rehearsal fifteen or twenty times. However, this was the first time I'd seen him start with a play from the beginning and work through to the end. Usually, as you know, a director has actors sit around a table and read for two or three days until they're familiar with the play. Then the director puts the actors on their feet. This has been my long training. What happened at this first rehearsal was that he had the actors read for about twelve minutes, perhaps ten pages of manuscript, and that was it. They then went into specific rehearsal that same night. I was astonished.

Later on that night as I walked him home after the rehearsal I said, 'Tony, don't you have the cast read the play *fully*?' He said, 'What for?' And I said, 'What for!' I had no words, you see. 'What's your theory?' I asked. He said, 'The actors who have small parts get impatient while the bigger actors are reading. When their time comes they generally overact and throw the whole thing out of kilter. They're preening. This is their big chance. The lead actors are pretty well primed. They

I

know what they have do to. So why not get on? Why waste these two or three hours?' The point is, that night he demanded of the actors that they reach a certain height almost instantly. Later on Ed Binns, who I'm pretty sure is a Method actor, said to me: 'This is like being plunged into water sixty degrees below zero. I don't know where I am. I'm numb.' And then he said, 'This has never happened to me in my life. I need more time to get into the role. A part like this, John Brown, is a monumental central character. I need *more* time than that. To be forced to act, to make relationships!'

Tony demanded not only articulation, but sense in the lines. By that I mean he *demanded* readings. He demanded not finished readings, but readings which conveyed the power of the speeches. This is twenty minutes into your first rehearsal! He was demanding responses, and at the same time he was staging the play. He would say, 'Why are you doing this?' and the actors would be floored. I wasn't prepared for this at all. I'd never seen this in my entire life. And I've been around. I'm no kid.

But after reflecting upon what happened that night, I came to certain conclusions. One, he had many of the actors do the initial reading of ten to fifteen minutes because he wanted to get a feeling about them. A fair number were new that season and they were unknown to him and he wanted to find out what their qualities were. And he found out what he wanted to know in those first ten to fifteen minutes. The second thing is that Tony attacked people at the opening rehearsal. He let people know who was the boss; he really numbed them in that first rehearsal. I saw him do this with *The House of Atreus* that same season of 1967 and also with my play *Lamp at Midnight* which he directed about two years later.

On reflection, I think Tony was too harsh with some of the actors during the first few rehearsals, and demanded too much, especially the very first one. But what was remarkable was that by the third or fourth rehearsal things smoothed out; Tony was absolutely marvellous with the actors, and they adored him – and usually acted at the top level of their capacities. A very heady experience.

Once Tony was into rehearsals, when did he start, if at all, suggesting changes to you?

All the work we had done earlier paid off. There was relatively little to be done. I had to make some adjustments, but all minor. For example, one day he phoned me at eight in the morning about a scene and he said. 'Barrie, we need some preliminary lines to establish the fact that this is the apple orchard. Just about four or five, no more.' I said, 'I'll meet you a half-hour before rehearsal time.' We met at ten-thirty that morning and I showed him what I had written. He read and said, 'Let's put something in about the apple pie.' I did, and thus we established the apple orchard in the action of the play.

Now he did something else which amazed me. And I have to refer to the first season's *The Three Sisters*, that's 1963. If you remember, George Grizzard, who played Solyony, looks out in the direction of the audience and blows, and makes a few passes with his hand as though he were wiping a window, and you were to imagine that windows were above the settee and that George was melting the frost from them in order to look out into the garden. And I thought, 'What's Tony doing?' It seemed to me that Tony had used a realistic concept on a stage where you'd want to stay away from this kind of physical illusion. I couldn't understand. Well, in rehearsals of *Harper's Ferry* he did the same kind of thing about the apple orchard and we played the scene that way in performance. The two characters involved in the scene stooped as though they were climbing under low branches to get into this enclosed bower of the apple orchard. At first I was offended by it. I said, 'This is exactly what I don't want to do.' But I accepted it, though I never quite liked it. Tony needed it for *his* purposes and that was all right with me, but I never quite liked the fact that they stooped under the low branches. The lines he suggested were great, but I thought the action belonged in a typical proscenium arch production.

Let me tell you something else in similar vein. In the opening of the play, after the prayer, there is the preparation for breakfast. Tony in the first rehearsals said, 'Make the clatter, make the clatter', for the dishes and the food and the eating and things like that. I felt that this advice was wrong, because I'm not concerned with the physical reality of their eating and its so-called realistic representation on the stage. I'm concerned with something way beyond that. I thought that the stage should be used in a different way – actually the way Tony taught me and hundreds of other theatre practitioners.

I said, 'Tony, you're drowning the lines with realistic business.' And he said, 'They're not that important. The essence of it will come through, and it's nice that you see the waking up in the morning and the preparations for breakfast.' But what interested me was that as the rehearsals went along, bit by bit, the noises and physical action abated, and ultimately it became almost a miming of the food preparation and the eating. It was just the spoon up and the spoon down and they were sitting quietly while other action was going on. Within ten days that realistic stage business was eliminated and the emphasis was on the dialogue and a more overt objective movement – and I had not had a single talk with Tony on this matter except for that one conversation I just referred to.

Some people have detected in Tony Guthrie a conscious rebellion against anything that was too sentimental, anything that was overtly emotional. Did you notice that?

That's quite right. First of all, Tony had an abhorrence of any kind of physical demonstration on the stage. Now we know of his enormous devotion to Judith, and Judith's enormous devotion to him. I saw it in a hundred ways, the tenderness they had for each other. But Tony was unable to tolerate any sign of physical affection on the stage. When Martha and Oliver came into the orchard in that same scene that we were talking about, it was a scene of love. My lines state explicitly that they make love. This is the only place they have, this bower of the apple orchard, because the farmhouse is crowded, and they have no privacy there. The men sleep in a kind of dormitory in the attic, and the women sleep in another little place.

The two actors who were playing the parts went off and worked on their scene and then came back and played it for Tony and myself. We were the only people in the theatre at that time, just the four of us. It is a tender love scene. Michael Moriarty played Oliver and I still have vivid memories of his stunning performance for Tony and me. I remember it affected me emotionally. It did take too long in terms of the design of the act and of the total play. When I say 'too long' I mean they were going through lots of motion, too many responses, which would have to be pared down. That would have been Tony's job, to give it balance within the total act. But Tony cut it very drastically, and I thought almost castrated the scene. And it didn't have the physical passion and the tenderness which the writing called for, and which the actors in that demonstration gave it. This, you must understand, despite the fact that Tony was equally as impressed with Michael Moriarty's performance as I was. We talked back and forth about Michael's performance and I remember commenting to Tony that I thought in about five years Michael would be ready to play a marvellous Hamlet. Tony looked at me in a sort of doubletake;

the next day he said something like, 'I daresay you're right about Michael playing Hamlet.' But still he cut the scene. He said, 'I want to get on to John Brown and his needs as soon as possible.' And yet I would point out to you that with Chekhov Tony's tenderness and compassion were just incredible.

I'll tell you something else, too. Tony used to be very acerbic in many human relations in his earlier years. He used not to suffer fools. Yet towards the end, in the last five years or so, he became more and more gentle. His thoughtfulness and his goodness towards actors and playwrights and directors and scenic artists we all know. But he became very tender in human relationships. He became more patient with people. Again and again when we would be together and something would happen which shouldn't have happened, he'd give a little shrug and say, 'Well, we have to bear with this.'

Lamp at Midnight opened in New Jersey and played there for two weeks prior to its national tour. We played evenings, but had extra rehearsals in the afternoons. After rehearsals Tony and I had dinner, then we had about an hour before curtain. There was a nice quiet street in this Jersey town and we would walk together very quietly, and sometimes he'd take my arm. He used to like to walk in step, and sometimes I'd deliberately break step, and he'd make a little skip and come back again in step. It was just very gentle talk all the time, very quiet and very mellow and very dear. Those were my dearest times with him.

Do you think Tony's decision about the scene had anything to do with his affinity for the bigger action of the play, the greater theme?

Tony was ill-at-ease, downright uncomfortable with any kind of physical demonstration on the stage. Presumably it was because he was always concerned with the larger action, the larger dimension. For example, I want to tell you how he did one mass scene which I thought would take several hours to work out; he did it in about ten minutes. This is the scene in which John Brown takes refuge with his men in the Fire Engine House and there's going to be an attack to dislodge them.

There are about ten actors on the stage, the US Marines, who are led by Lieutenant J. E. B. Stuart (the General Jeb Stuart of the Confederate Army during the Civil War), who are going to charge the Fire Engine House. Tony claps his hands and says, 'All right, come on, come on, men.' So they all charge in, the most lively, most ridiculous, and poorly designed composition on the stage you could ever see. And he called out to one man, 'Would you mind moving up about two feet and as you come in hold it until so-and-so comes in, and directly after he comes in you fall right behind him, and would *you* do the following . . . ' Now you must understand, he saw it *once*. He said, 'You have it?' They said, 'Yes.' Then he said, 'Would you come in again?' And of course they didn't have it. So very patiently he began choreographing it, and asked so-and-so to come back six inches and so-and-so to move forward several inches and all of a sudden a spatial pattern began to emerge. Now all of this that I'm describing to you took no more than five minutes. By the end of ten minutes this was the most beautifully designed pattern of people rushing in, attacking, and overpowering the fort. Ten minutes, the whole thing.

Do you think he had a preconception of how he wanted to stage that? Or was he just simply reacting to whatever was being given him?

My thought, based on my experience with him as I watched him work on other scenes of *Harper's Ferry* and also on *Lamp at Midnight*, is that he would have modelled anything that was shown to him. In other words, he would take whatever was presented to him as raw clay. Had the actors come on the stage in another grouping, he would have taken that grouping and modelled it, and it *too* would have been a wonderfully staged and choreographed attack on the Fire Engine House. What I'm saying is that any grouping that had been presented to him would have been used as a point of departure. The attack could have been done in any of a dozen different ways: equally effective, but different. He was perfectly ready to let what finally was seen by the audience be based on the chance of how the actors came in at that instant.

On the other hand, there was another piece of staging that was vastly different. I'm talking now about a scene in the first act. In view of the fact that neighbours are passing by on the road which is not far away, the people in the house have to be quiet. There was always the tension of some neighbour coming in to snoop and then men having to rush up into the attic to hide. Then there is a storm, and the men who have been cooped up for weeks on end and under great strain are told they can make all the noise they want, because the storm will drown out the clamour. So there are pig squeals, shrieks, wild marching and there is screaming, singing and all that. A wild outbreak after the pent-up

strain and enforced quiet of many weeks. Then somebody starts singing a song. Because they are homesick one joins, then another, and
with the passage of the storm you have the soft singing of 'Lorena'.
It is extremely effective indeed. From that you go into the scene of
going to bed, all carrying lighted candles. Now in that scene of noise
which is covered by the storm he asked, 'Who knows how to stand
and walk on his hands?' One actor said he did. Tony said, 'You may
do that, and I want you and you and you to do the marching, and you
men do this over here.' He designed that scene, and then he didn't like
that design. Two days later he reworked the design and I believe three
days later he reworked it again. He fiddled with that scene maybe four
or five times before he got what he wanted. There was an image in
his mind which he wanted to see created on the stage. He changed the
scene over and over until he got what he wanted. The attack scene,
on the other hand, was a modelling scene, where he took the
rawish half-formed clay they gave him and used it for his directorial
needs.

How did you work on Lamp at Midnight *with him?*

I think it's best summed up in my remarks and acknowledgements in
the latest edition of *Lamp at Midnight*: 'In preparation for the nation-
wide tour of *Lamp at Midnight* Tyrone Guthrie worked with me line
by line, scene by scene. Though the play was then twenty-two years
old and had a long list of successful productions, he examined it as
though it were a new, untried script. His probing and questioning
provided the impetus to rework many lines. Several times I changed
the tonal qualities of an entire scene. My debt to him remains constant.'

I'm talking about a play which was twenty-two years old and which
had had over one hundred productions at that time. We sat and again
he made me justify every line. And many of the line changes to be found
in this latest edition stem from his pushing me, his probing. 'I think
this can be said in a sharper way, Barrie.'

I had done the preliminary casting, and he spent two or three days
with me and saw the people I had screened. Then he did the final
casting. And again what amazed me was how he was able to judge an
actor's capacity by just talking with him for two or three minutes. It
floored me to see how he interviewed actors. He had them in for all of
three minutes each. He rose very graciously every time an actor came
in and he just talked with them. He didn't read them at all. Then he

got up and graciously ushered them to the door and out. It was like a treadmill, the speed with which he did this. He must have interviewed twenty or twenty-five actors an hour. I said, 'Tony, not even to have them read a line!' He said, 'That's not necessary, dear boy.'

His judgement was absolutely splendid. What's more, he was able to keep all the actors in mind, and he never took any notes. I had to write notes like mad and have pictures of the actors in front of me. He was able to work out a first-rate doubling and tripling scheme for *Lamp at Midnight* using only sixteen actors. And he did it without ever having an actor read a line.

I can tell you from personal experience that Tony was able to judge the capacity of an actor for a role by just sitting and talking with him across the table for two minutes. And they were so flattered that the great Guthrie had ushered them in and taken them to the door as they left and each interview was two minutes! I had this long list of actors to be interviewed and I thought it would be a long day, but he knocked it off before lunch. Then I had another long list. Knocked it off before five o'clock. He said, 'Let's call so-and-so back and so-and-so back.' Oh, he did have one person read. That was for the part of Galileo's daughter Polissena, because he was very desirous of a certain quality. At the call backs, he just talked more. A little longer time. Five minutes, eight minutes. He was able to discern what actors could do by talking with them.

Where did you start the rehearsals of Lamp at Midnight?

In New York. We were to have two weeks of rehearsal, but it was going to play two weeks in Jersey which would give Tony time to do polishing then as well. A week before rehearsals were to begin I got a call from Tony, who was in Ireland, to tell me that he had pneumonia, and the doctor had forbidden him to leave. Pandemonium! He thought he would be able to leave a week late which would give him one week of rehearsal time. So it was agreed that I would direct the play for a week. Now I want to tell you, Al, it's a terrible position for an author to be directing his own play when the actors had signed up because they wanted to work with Guthrie. It was horrendous for me. What I had to do at that first rehearsal was to be very brusque and very sure of myself though I was quaking inside all the time, and I knew they were saying, 'Ha, ha, ha, where's Dr Guthrie?' So I carried on, having no other choice.

Meanwhile I was in transatlantic phone communication with Tony.

He agreed to leave and did – arriving one week late. He left Ireland against his doctor's strong protestations. He came because he felt an obligation to me and the play. He came and was a tired person that entire week. I took care of him. I called for him in the mornings and drove him to the rehearsal hall. I drove him back. I fed him coffee and hot chocolate and biscuits during the day. I made him sit down. You know he liked to stand and move around during rehearsals. I made him sit as much as possible. But he was awfully tired. We would be driving in the car and he would doze for a few minutes between places. He needed sleep and rest, and I was very worried, indeed. After the play opened he stayed with the company out in Jersey and worked with them. I came out there every day to be with him and to make sure he was all right. And we had these lovely walks after dinner for an hour or so. By then he was pretty well rested, but it disturbed me tremendously that he would doze off at any given moment. His energies were not at their best.

After he arrived, did he immediately go into the script with Lamp at Midnight?

Well, remember the company had had six or seven days of rehearsal under my direction. Now my programme for that week had been that we worked on each act for two days. And the morning after he arrived I told him what I had done and he said, 'I may do the same', because he had only six and a half days to mount this play. He came in, and he was introduced and there was the usual applause. I was saying, 'Thank the Lord, this ordeal is over for me.' What a position to have been thrust into! What he did was have the actors run through the entire play once to see what I had done and what they were doing. The minute the play started – you remember I remarked to you about attacking – he attacked again. The play starts with Galileo's daughter Polissena singing. The song was adapted by me from an early seventeenth-century piece of music which I had heard in Italy. The minute it started Tony got nasal, satirically imitating the tune. He said, 'I don't know whose toes I'm stepping on, but this is terrible. I must have better music.' I said, 'Tony, it's my toes and it's perfectly all right. If you want another piece of music, we'll have another piece of music.' I got a friend who in two days wrote the music which was used.

Tony had immediately attacked to let everyone know who was the boss. He was in the saddle instantly. As for the directorial work I had done, well, he ripped it to shreds, which was no surprise. He had a different image of how the play was to be directed.

Actually, he shouldn't have come, he was a sick man. He came out of friendship, loyalty, devotion, honour, everything you could want. And he made the play and saved the production. I couldn't have brought it to fruition.

Len Cariou

ALFRED ROSSI: *What roles did you play under Tyrone Guthrie's direction?*

LEN CARIOU: I played Orestes in the two Minneapolis productions of *The House of Atreus* that we did. We did the original production in 1967, and revived it again in 1968, and took it on tour to New York and Los Angeles. I also did a Barrie Stavis play, *Harper's Ferry*, in which I played one of Brown's right-hand men.

At the very outset of the work on The House of Atreus, *how did Guthrie present what he wanted to do with the production?*

He approached it as being a symphony and we did it, of course, in Greek *cothurni* and with masks in the way the Greeks did it originally. I was referred to as the *trumpet* of the piece. Indeed, that's really what I was according to the orchestration.

It was part of the general work, but the one trumpet sound that he really desperately wanted was my entrance to the palace gates where I knocked on the door to get my mother to come to the door. I would then gain entrance and kill Aegisthus. So the moment was orchestrally developed. I made my first entrance over my father's grave, then there's the scene with the Chorus and my telling them of my visit with Apollo, and what Apollo has told me. Then they say, 'Well, we think it's time to act.' So then I made an exit and returned in a huge entrance, in which I came from the right vomitory of the Guthrie stage, leaped my father's grave, and came up to two incredibly high doors, which were over twenty feet. My line was 'You there within the palace', which I played almost like a trumpet. It was very high and sustained on one note. Orchestrally, Dr Guthrie was building for that entrance and my voice was meant to top what had gone on with the Chorus and the orchestra from backstage.

Did he do anything to illustrate specifically what that sound was to be?

No, he didn't. He just went with my intuition. He built the scene up gradually as we went along. Of course, as we were rehearsing we didn't have an orchestra, so the demand on me was not great vocally, until we got into the last week. The first time that I made the sound that I wanted to make, and hoped was what he wanted to hear, he paid me an incredible compliment. He stopped the rehearsal and he said, 'That is wonderful. That is an incredible sound you've made. That is exactly what I mean.' He congratulated Fran Bennett, who is our vocal coach, and then went on and on and on.

There was another moment that I recall vividly: it's when you and Electra swear vengeance for Agamemnon's murder. How did he work on that?

He hadn't been specific until one day we were doing it. We had, as I recall, done most of our own physical choreography. All he really said was 'I want you on top of the grave, and I want the Chorus to move in around.' We were doing, rather arbitrarily, whatever we wished until finally he wanted it to be more specific. He showed me a position that he wanted to see – the sword above my head, and he said, 'It's really like a Samurai warrior, taking a position before the kill, going into the frog-like crouch that they go into before they make their sound and then their move to strike.' That's really all he ever said about it.

Was his way of working on that scene typical of the work of the production generally?

I would say that it was typical. He had an outside shape, and he took what you contributed and what he then contributed on top of that, then he edited what was extraneous, and you came out with this scene, and from an audience's standpoint there is not one iota of this blocking or shape or colour or visual image that's been left to chance. But it wasn't cut and dried from the beginning. He let us have our head and then he would say, 'Well, I'll take that and I'll take that, but there's something missing.' He would introduce that into our heads, and we would add that to it, and maybe we would keep what he introduced and get rid of one of the things that he had already taken *from us*. It was that kind of a process.

Let me throw something at you. One time I talked to Bill Hutt in Stratford, and he said the wonderful thing about Tony Guthrie is that he gave you so much freedom as an actor. A little bit later I talked to Michael Langham and I told him what Bill Hutt had said and Langham said,

LEN CARIOU

*'I think what Guthrie gives is the illusion of freedom.' And later still
I talked to Tony himself. I said, 'Bill Hutt said this and Michael Langham said that and what's your reaction to their comments?' He looked at
me, paused, and said, 'Well, dear boy, freedom is an illusion.' So having
that preface, how would you compare the amount of freedom that you had
in that particular production?*

Well, I think I agree with both the people, strangely enough. That
sounds like a cop-out, but it's not. I think that very definitely there
is an illusion of freedom, because as I pointed out already there's a
definite structure to the piece as he sees it. But then I think that's what
directing a play is about. I think you have to have some form and
structure, so that you can put your actors into it and then be able to
look at it, and say, 'Well, do I change it, or not change it? Does it
work, or doesn't it work within the structure as I see it?' I think it's
his prerogative, quite frankly.

Not that I think we're puppets, because I never felt like one. I
couldn't elicit enough response from him as far as I was concerned. I
felt a little frustrated in the sense that he didn't say enough to me. He
wasn't discouraging at all, but I naturally had my worries about the
thing. I would elicit some kind of comment from him if I said, 'Is that
what you mean?' And he said, 'Oh yes, that's what I mean.' But that's
all he would say and he would never elaborate. He would never say,
'Yes, but . . . ' or 'No, but . . . ' and enlarge on the point, which is
obviously what I was begging him to do. He was just being kind of
naughty with me and letting me go my own way. I think he was trying
to tell me to figure it out for myself.

*You said you were looking for something from Guthrie, and it came at
a time when you were feeling frustrated. Can you explain that further?*

I think I was probably frustrated with my own inadequacy. He, I
think, was allowing me to grow up as an actor. He knew that it was not
easy, but neither was he going to nurse me through. He was going to
make me go through the hell that one has to go through during that
kind of a play. It demands something of a person that very few modern
classics or even the Shakespearian classics do. You start at C above
middle C instead of starting at middle C, where you do with most
plays. You really have to sustain it and it's very difficult. You have to
be in tremendous physical condition. You have to be mentally positive.
You have to be very sure of yourself technically as an actor. And then

you have to find the core of the human being that is there, knowing that you're going to be behind the mask and so on.

It's one thing to do in rehearsals when you're working without all the trappings; it's another thing to do it in full clothing with masks and *cothurni*. I rehearsed quite a bit with them, so I got to the point where I used to do camp things 'on point' with the *cothurni*. They were especially made by people in Minneapolis, and were quite extraordinary, because I'd been in a pair in the *Oedipus* production that Guthrie had done in Stratford, and they were incredible – they weighed a ton. These were made of a special kind of compressed styrofoam or something. It was done in layers and just kept being built up and built up and built up.

Talking of the accoutrements of the production, namely the cothurni, *the padded costumes, the masks, etc., did Guthrie give you any suggestions dealing with those so they became more organic for you as an actor and as a character?*

We, of course, rehearsed most of the time with the *cothurni*, and that gave you some kind of idea of how tall you were. I think I was six foot four. What he really gave us were hints of style more than anything, because we were working with a full mask, so that one led with the head even in rehearsal without the masks on. There came a point after we'd been rehearsing for about two and a half weeks that they gave us plastic mock-up masks that we could use for rehearsal purposes. They were just like putting on a batter's or football helmet. But you sensed it being there and having it covering your nose and the fact that your mouth and your chin were the only things that were exposed.

Did he ever illustrate the way he wanted people to move their heads, necks, bodies?

Absolutely. He would get up and do what he thought it should be. On several different occasions he put on a mask. Most of us had never done this kind of play before and so why not? Show them what he means. It's a lot easier sometimes to show. And in one gesture you go, 'Oh, I know what you mean.' Then you could put it to sleep, and never worry about it again.

You said Guthrie seemed to know what he wanted to see, and it was up to you to do whatever you needed to get what he wanted. Was this more by implication than explication?

By implication chiefly. For instance, he would work with the Chorus as I described earlier in the first entrance that I made, and he had built it in such a way that you had to top it. We worked that way through the entire play. In other words, he would build a shape outside with the Chorus, which meant that you had to ride the crest of that wave that they were building. He never said, 'You get in there and do it. They're here, now you've got to come up to that.' He let you go and go until you realized, 'Well, wait a minute here. I'm being left behind.' There were occasions when one would stop and say, 'Look, I'm lost here and I'm the central character in the piece and I don't think this should be done. I don't think I should say the speech this way. I would like to say it another way.' And he said, 'Well, then say it another way. You go ahead.' I said, 'Well, could you at least start at a lower pitch, so that I can feel my way along without having to feel I'm fighting the sound of these other ten people?' And he said, 'Absolutely.' So we did it and eventually we ended doing exactly what we were doing in the first place, but I was comfortable with it and I had indeed initiated from within my own self the same result he wanted.

As you got closer to the actual production (I think there were a couple of previews) were a lot of the actors, as I sensed when I saw them in Minneapolis that summer, extremely fatigued to the point of exhaustion?

It's an abnormal thing, doing a Greek tragedy. The company had been in a constant state of rehearsals for five months of a seven- or eight-month season. So it wasn't that they weren't used to that kind of work. Some of them, the new ones who had never done rep before, yes, naturally. By the time we did *Atreus* that year, we were already playing three plays.

The way Guthrie choreographed them physically – people in somewhat grotesque positions for long periods of time – caused a physical tension. If you didn't find a way to relax within the context of that position which was held for sometimes five to ten minutes at a time, you'd be exhausted. I think once they got the costumes on they were able to relax more than they were when they didn't have them on. The costumes were shapeless, so you could get inside of them, and *physically* cheat, but not cheat the audience. You would not have the tension that you would have if you were just wearing street clothes in a rehearsal situation.

Was there any particular comment by Guthrie that now seems to stand out as a rather significant statement that opened up things for you?

There were several times he embarrassed the hell out of me, because I had long passages to say and I was trying to get a flow to them and I would take my time and take an enormous breath and then try and phrase it in a certain way. There were several times when he would stop the rehearsal right there. I took the breath to begin and he said, 'Stop. That is the most exciting thing in the theatre. When he took that breath, that's what the theatre is all about. That expectation. I heard him. You heard him. That is magnificent.' Well, I went beet-red. You know how he used to go around and take a huge breath and pull his entire upper body up and then be able to go and go and go. It's like you do when you sing. What it did was give me a concrete base to work on.

Did you think that he was pleased with the production of Atreus *the first year?*

Oh yes, I think he was terribly pleased. He came backstage after the opening, I remember, to the dressing-room, gave me a great big bear-hug and crushed me to his navel. He said, 'Bravo, dear boy, bravo. Wonderful performance.' Then, of course, I think he was about to cry, so he left the room.

There's one great funny story on opening night. Robin Gammell was playing Cassandra in the first play and had an entrance from Agamemnon's carriage, if you remember, down the ramp after Agamemnon and Clytemnestra had gone in, and the Chorus chanted, 'God, god, god, Apollo, Apollo, Apollo, Apollo, Apollo, Apollo.' Cassandra was meant to come down the ramp, make a complete circle on the stage, stop and then go on with the speech. Well, on opening night Robin came running down the ramp, tripped and fell flat on his face. The Chorus never stopped talking, so nobody in the audience knew what was going on. At the end of the first play, Guthrie came back and Robin was in the dressing-room next to me, madly tearing off his Cassandra costume to put on his Electra costume, with the make-up change and the entire thing. The door to his dressing-room was open, and meanwhile I'd been standing around for an hour and fifteen minutes going crazy getting ready to do my number in the second play. Dr Guthrie came walking back, which surprised me. I hadn't expected to see him back there before the thing was over. So I said,

'Dr Guthrie, how's it going?' He said, 'Well, it's going very well. Except Cassandra, the silly cunt, tripped on her frock.' And then he turned on his heel. Robin, who was absolutely demoralized by the fact that he had tripped at all and was in the middle of putting on his tights for Electra, said, 'You son of a bitch.' He came right out into the hallway chasing Dr Guthrie who was seen going across the back-stage area having a great giggle.

You've brought out here Guthrie's rather unique way of commenting on what actors did or didn't do. It was always with humour.

Let me tell you this. I mean, he really got me good. One day we worked in the morning and broke for lunch, and we were pretty tired. When we came back he said, 'I want to pick it up where we left off.' So I started begrudgingly into a line which was something like 'I have motives enough to drive me on, the will of the gods, the grief of my father', and so on. And he said, 'Stop, stop, stop. "Grief of my father" sounds like a Hero Sandwich.' What do you say after that? Everybody on the stage just fell apart, and I was just standing there like some idiot. He turned his back to me and went up the stairs and had a bit of a giggle to himself. But the real key to the story is that Tanya Moiseiwitsch then told me why he had said it. He had gone to the green room in the Guthrie Theater and went to the sandwich machine and saw 'Hero Sandwich'. He had never heard of or seen a Hero Sandwich. He had it for lunch, and thought it was the funniest thing in the world. The first chance he had to use it, he used it.

The production of The House of Atreus *was revived in Minneapolis and then done in New York and Los Angeles. How do you feel he coped with the problem of bringing a production that was designed for a specific space in Minneapolis, a thrust stage, to New York, in which it played a proscenium house?*

I think he resented the fact that he had to do it for a proscenium stage because finally in Minneapolis he was able to do a Greek tragedy in the same kind of arena that the Greeks had done it in. So what he did was build a three-platform stage that he put on top of the Billy Rose Theater's normal stage, so that we had the levels. They were not nearly as long nor as wide as the Guthrie's levels, but we didn't feel like we were in a terribly foreign place. We had just rehearsed in a room somewhere at the University of Minnesota. We didn't have any idea of what we were going to end up with, but once we got it on the stage, I think it amazed almost everybody how well it worked.

Do you have any memories of his reaction to the reception in New York?

I think he had a pretty good idea that that's how they'd react to it, which was noncommittal. I think Guthrie expected it to be lukewarm, which it was. But I don't think he was ready for the diatribe that Barnes threw at him. None of us were. That came really out of left field. I recall Judith Crist, who had given us huzzahs for the perform-ance, the next day – when Barnes came out – she went on the air and said, 'You're crazy, Clive Barnes.' And she said to the public, 'Go and see it. He didn't see the same thing I saw.' That kind of production – you either love or you hate.

How about when Atreus *went to Los Angeles and played the Mark Taper Forum? It is a thrust theatre, but is certainly smaller than the Guthrie stage. Did you get any indication of how Guthrie felt the response was in Los Angeles?*

The response was very good in Los Angeles, and he recognized it as such. I personally felt the theatre was too small for the scale of the production. It's a very intimate theatre, as you know. Vocally, I think we were too much for them. We had a lot of music, and we had a lot of high-pitched Chorus work. It just seemed to be too much for that hall. I think really deep down in his heart Dr Guthrie felt it was too, but I don't think he wanted to meddle with it. The only adapting was going to be entirely up to us as a company. He knew when he saw the Taper. He said, 'We're going to blow them right out of the theatre. But we have done this production, we are very proud of it, and this is why we're bringing it to you.' However, it did modify itself as we went through the run while we were there.

Is there any other experience that you had with Guthrie relating to The House of Atreus *that you might want to tell me about?*

I recall that after we had opened the play and were in running it, a lot of us felt that it was probably the last major thing that he would ever do. I think he felt that it was, too. It was like his last statement, in a sense, having gone through all the Shakespearean things and having ended a career on the stage, certainly in this country, doing a Greek tragedy. There was nothing said about it, but thinking in our romantic way, with him going away. . . . He wasn't at all well at that time. He had the blood-clot in his leg, and when we were doing *Harper's Ferry*, for instance, he did an awful lot of direction from a stretcher on the steps because he was supposed to keep that leg straight. It was really a stretcher that they'd piled up at one end so that he could be in kind of a hospital bed, and he could see what was going on. He really should not have been working at all. Of course, he lived for four years after that. It seemed to be a culmination of a career. It was not only me that thought that. I think Dougie Campbell felt that it was the last major work that he would do, and that anybody in North America would ever see. If my history serves me correctly, it was.

What do you think is the primary reason Dr Guthrie was one of the outstanding directors in modern theatre?

I would say, primarily, that he served the playwright first. Then he imposed things on what the playwright had done to see if it would, in fact, sustain that imposition. For instance, all the Shakespearean plays he did on such a grand scale that everyone came to know as *his* style. He knew that Shakespeare could sustain anything, and as we know now Shakespeare can sustain any abuse and still come out on top. He knew that. I don't believe that he ever abused it to the point that it's been abused by other people on this continent. He had a tremendous sense of the theatrical and knew that when you came to the theatre, the theatre was an event. It was something that was larger than life. It was not ever to be a soap opera, no matter what kind of play you were doing, and you could never reduce it to that level. It was always one step above normalcy. The normal way you talk, for instance – you don't talk that way on the stage. You have to project, so that it immediately lifts it out of the realm of being a normal situation, no matter whether you're doing *Uncle Vanya* or *The House of Atreus*. He approached it as an event, and it was meant to entertain. It was meant to hopefully enlighten people about certain aspects of certain societies, and in so doing to try to link societies together through the times. I think nobody ever did it any better. The only other guy is Michael Langham.

Who was the protégé of one William Tyrone Guthrie.

Absolutely.

L to R. Tyrone Guthrie, Alfred Rossi, and Stella Adler at the Jack I. and Lillian L. Poses Brandeis University Creative Arts Awards ceremonies, New York City, 1965.

Scene from *The Three Sisters*, directed by Tyrone Guthrie, Minneapolis, 1963.

Tyrone Guthrie rehearses *Peter Grimes* at the Metropolitan Opera House, New York City, 1967.

Tyrone Guthrie welcomes the acting company of the Tyrone Guthrie Theater, Minneapolis, 1963.

L to R: Peter Zeisler, Tyrone Guthrie, and Donald Schoenbaum outside the Billy Rose Theatre, New York City, 1968.

Michael Langham

ALFRED ROSSI: *When did you meet Tony Guthrie?*

MICHAEL LANGHAM: In 1947.

I was the Director of the Arts Council Midland Theatre Company in Coventry and Tony and Judy came down to see my production of *The Doctor's Dilemma.* I was extremely nervous, but with characteristic dispatch they put me almost instantly at ease.

He saw the show. The only thing in it of which I was proud was the sequence when Mrs Dubedat goes to change her clothes after her husband has died. In the text this offstage event is covered by some Shavian 'fill', where the doctors rhapsodize on the manner of his death, thus giving Mrs Dubedat, on the one hand, time to change into the colours she believes her husband would have appreciated, and Shaw, on the other, the opportunity, with her startling re-entry, to shock not only the doctors but the audience too. To fill the resulting theatrical slack, I devised some funereal choreography. This was unquestionably due to Guthrie's influence: if you can articulate with movement or grouping what is already being said with words, you will reinforce the impact of the work. Audiences don't need to listen *all* the time; they can get the point by *watching* for a while and then be fresher to *listen* later on. I don't think that now, but I believed it then. Anyway, I devised a figure-of-eight procession of pontificating doctors around the dais in Dubedat's studio. I thought it splendidly, theatrically showy. But the night Tony saw it the stage had been wrongly set and there was no room to move behind the dais, so the smooth, rhythmic funeral was transformed into an ugly, spastic hopscotch.

After the performance I introduced Tony and Judy to the company. Both of them were supremely positive, and Tony made some hilarious, mischievous comments about his compatriot Shaw. Seeing the company's glowing reaction to this, I was induced momentarily to wonder which of these two Irishmen was the most effective exponent of the 'life force'.

276

Next day the Guthries had to travel to Bristol, so I offered to drive them to catch a train in nearby Birmingham. This was in the days of gas rationing, 1947. En route we had a pleasant talk and I began to warm my hands at this man. His background was similar to mine except that his family was now resigned to his being in the theatre; mine, as yet, was not. 'Why don't I drive you further towards Bristol?' With a sense of responsibility typical of postwar Britain Tony asked, 'Is this government gas?' Of course it was. But I said, 'I like talking to you. Is that irresponsible?' Well, I drove them to Bristol and got to know them. From then on we were firm friends.

I find it very hard to talk about him as a director. Our relationship became progressively that of son and father, and in later years, of brother and brother. My own father had died when I was a month old and although I enjoyed a delightful stepfather, I never knew a real dad until I met Tony, apart from the harbourmaster of Haifa whom I met as a prisoner of war and who became a kind of *paterfamilias* to many of us who were young and had no experience of life at that time. But Tony fulfilled this personal need.

Anything I say about him as an artist must be judged in this context.

Do you remember what he said about the first time he'd seen you direct?

He was most encouraging, but as disinterested as I was in directing Shaw. 'All you can do with Shaw,' said Guthrie, 'is to fan the actors out in a semi-circle, put the speaker at the top, and hope for the best.'

I'm wondering if at that early point in your career you could tell that he influenced your approach to directing, or is that realization retrospective?

I believed then that his was the only kind of theatre that mattered, the only one I could believe in. He was the master of it. Blindly, perhaps, I was aware of his influence to lead me to the only theatrical expression that seemed worthwhile.

It's hard to analyse genius, but I think in this respect Tony was a genius. He had enormous influence on people's lives, and when a friend thought he was making up his own mind about how he should live, the truth often was that Tony had told him not only what to think, but what to do. He was not, however, a Machiavellian manipulator; he loved and rejoiced in people – many of whom I personally found boring. This was a special part of his genius.

What happened after that? Did he see other productions of yours, or did you have other social engagements with him?

I went from Coventry to Birmingham, and Tony was directing *Henry VIII* at Stratford-on-Avon while I was Artistic Director of the Birmingham Rep a few miles away. He came to see a play I'd directed. He loathed it but thought my work provocative. It was *The Marvellous History of St Bernard* by Henri Gheon in a series of illuminated-manuscript settings. It was designed quite beautifully by Paul Shelving. Tony brought Anthony Quayle, Artistic Director of the Stratford Memorial Theatre, with him. As a result I was asked to co-direct *Julius Caesar* in the next Stratford-on-Avon season with Gielgud as Cassius and Quayle as Antony. Subsequently Guthrie asked me to direct *Othello* at the Vic.

Well, by the time I'd been engaged by Guthrie at the Vic we'd talked about families. You always did with Tony. I mean he was very curious to know exactly who was who and how they got there and everything else. And he'd been to my home in Scotland, and he'd met my mother and my brothers and sisters and they'd liked him. He'd been there in the middle of a terrifying gale, one of the worst hurricanes, certainly in this century, to hit the British Isles. He stood at the window with my mother, who was tiny, just over five feet, and watched massive, wonderful trees going down like matchsticks. Seeing this spirited woman taking it all so coolly moved him enough to speak about the incident most eloquently thereafter. He was acutely responsive to other people's qualities.

Did he invite you to his home?

Oh, yes, to his homes and lodgings all over the world. Especially his home in Ireland and his tiny London apartment in Lincoln's Inn Fields.

What was your impression of that?

First of cats and fish. I remember once when my wife was about to sit in a chair Judy Guthrie screaming, 'Mind the cod!' Myrtle, their cat, was studiously trained in cat-box terms, however. Myrtle would be out playing and hunting in the gardens of Lincoln's Inn Fields, four storeys below, and whenever she felt the urge, she'd bound up the four flights and dutifully bless the cat-box.

I couldn't believe two such tall people could live – with obvious contentment – in such cramped quarters. Lovely worn oak stairs and floors, but no room to breathe. They had one or two rather valuable pieces of old furniture. A 'character' brass double bed – more princess than queen. And I remember Tony, with almost parental proprietary satisfaction, polishing an ink-stained circular walnut table (which he'd bought as an amazing bargain) and reflecting in the glory of its shine.

Did Tony help with cooking or did Judy do all of that?

Judy did all the cooking, and the disposal of garbage, sometimes forgetting there were screens on the windows. In Stratford, Ontario, the screens were often clogged with tea-leaves. Judy kept forgetting. But she made super tea. Tony played housemaid.

Stratford, Canada? How did that come about?

I remember when Tom Patterson's famous phone call came through: 'Will you come and advise?' 'I'll go anywhere if you'll pay the fare.'

At this time I was directing another play at the Old Vic and the rumour had just spread that Tony had fallen out with the Vic Board. Whether he had been sacked due to policy disagreement or chosen to go voluntarily, no one quite knew. I was very shocked, and the company also, so I rang up, and Judy answered the phone. 'The company is so outraged about what's happening,' I told her, 'that they are prepared to go on strike tomorrow night.' Judy said, 'How very febrile of them.' (At the time I didn't know what febrile meant; could it have something to do with Myrtle?) 'It's their business to keep working.' And she lectured me most wisely about emotional overreaction. Eventually Tony came to the phone and was sufficiently moved by the company's gesture to sob.

The truth was that he'd been displaced by the superior political footwork of a colleague who wanted to 'rescue the Vic'.

So Stratford, Ontario, came at a propitious moment in his life. His resentment of the picture-frame stage had been fermenting. Here was a possible chance to build the theatre he had, for so long, wanted.

I think Stratford became his favourite child. Certainly, at this moment, it filled a void in his life.

Do you think it could have had something to do with the fact that it was in another country? After all, he'd been rejected after having done what he did for the Old Vic in the thirties and forties and even the fifties and then, as you say, having been dropped; was it possibly the attraction of going as far away as he could?

No, Tony was too resilient to run away from anything. But oddly enough he never liked the big metropolis. He didn't understand it enough to satisfy his temperament. He spent a lot of his life in London, and I imagine he found aspects exciting – especially the village-like atmosphere of the South Bank, where the Old Vic was – but he could never get his long arms around the place. He could do that with almost any other city in Britain, like Glasgow, for example, or Edinburgh or Bristol. I don't mean to imply that he wanted to avoid the challenge of a big metropolis, only that he felt able to offer more in smaller places because he understood them better.

Did he talk to you at all about your possible involvement at Stratford?

Not before the first season in 1953. I stayed at the Old Vic after he left, because I'd been asked to direct *Romeo and Juliet* there. I didn't, because I got extremely ill. Tony came to see me in hospital. 'What you need is a good holiday.' I said, 'I can't afford it.' 'What's your bank?' I said, 'No, I don't want anything like that.' He rang my wife and said, 'Michael's being very bourgeois and suburban, refusing a loan from a friend.' And he put money in our account and we had a holiday somewhere on the English south coast, which affronted Tony; despite his suspicion of 'abroad' he had expected us to go to the south of France at least.

Later he said, 'I think you should go to Canada.' Well, I had just been to Australia, and I didn't really want to go to Canada. Besides, I had a career going for me in Britain. But he made Canada sound like the only place worth working in. He had great persuasive powers. However, it wasn't till the following year that I bought the idea – that if I didn't fall flat on my face with my first offering at Stratford, I'd agree to take that Festival over.

The strange thing is that, before Stratford, I had never seen Tony work. We had talked much about work, but we hadn't been available to attend each other's rehearsals. My first year in Stratford changed this. He was directing *The Merchant of Venice*. I was directing *Julius Caesar*. I still revered him enough to be scared. I'd go to his rehearsals and watch spellbound. He'd come to mine and help. He'd see me trying to cope with a crowd scene, and he'd say, 'Do you mind if I jump in here?' What could I answer? And he'd work with a group on one side of the stage, improvising reactions to what was happening, and then turn, waiting for direction from me. I perspired much during this ordeal in the Stratford tent – but never because of a lack of encouragement from Tony.

How would you characterize a Guthrie rehearsal, as one director looking at another director?

The main thing was that he somehow kept a rehearsal rhythmic. All the cast were assigned to pumping life into a dead body. This had to be rhythmic. The pulse had to pulse; the alternative was death preserved. This made for a rhythm that everybody understood – survival – and they were functioning at the same pace as the director, instead of the director being way ahead.

He always said that he believed in what dry-as-dust pedagogues contemptuously call 'the play way'. He believed in no human activity unless it could be fun. He was embarrassed at being thought solemn. He was nauseated at being thought earnest. Consequently, in rehearsals, in public speeches and in everything he wrote, he never really said what he meant by his work.

Of course he thought deeply – but he seemed frightened of thinking too deeply. He saw himself, paradoxically, as a round person, a cherubic personality. And he used to say, 'When I die I think I'll get out of my coffin on the other side and someone will say to me, "I'm Tony Guthrie, who are you?" And there won't be the smallest resemblance between the two of us. Life will have put its imprint on one of us and not on the other.' He believed this happened to everyone: that there could be no reconciliation between how we start out and how we end up.

Do you think that might account for what seems to be an apparent dichotomy in this man: great fun and yet on the other hand strangely disciplined, conservative, autocratic in some of the philosophy he espoused?

I think he was always, subconsciously, the Laird – a Scots expression meaning the Boss, the Gentleman Farmer, the Benevolent Landlord. It was as if Guthrie were always in charge of an estate, and everyone else was presumed to be working for it. But he *was* a benevolent laird. He really cared for the lives of the workers.

This attitude was similar to what had been imbued in me during my formative years. I didn't sustain it as long as Tony. He carried it through his life, largely because he always had the Annagh-ma-Kerrig estate in Ireland to go back to. When his mother died he instantly took on full responsibility for the estate; and not only for the people who worked on it, but for the whole village.

I think this trained sense of duty applied anywhere that he worked,

K

provided the place resembled a manageable estate. Maybe he didn't thrive personally – no matter what the success – when working in New York or London, just because these two cities *weren't* manageable estates.

Talking of New York . . . the first time I went to New York was soon after I arrived at Stratford in 1955. He said, 'If you're going to New York, let me organize it.' And so he arranged for us to live near Brooklyn Heights (where he was staying) and put up at the St George Hotel. 'You have to understand that New York is a *port*. That's the first thing you have to know about it. And you have to be able to see the Statue of Liberty and know what the country is meant to be about.' (If we took turns holding each other by the heels out of the window we could just manage to glimpse the Statue of Liberty round the corner.) He was going to take us on our first New York night out. We were ordered not to take a cab – he was always thrifty – but the subway. We were scared to take the subway because we thought we'd get lost, if not murdered. So we took a cab and didn't tell him.

He had invited us to a luxurious French restaurant on Third Avenue (since, alas, defunct). It seemed an extravagant choice for Tony whose favourite dish was bacon and eggs, but he was clearly bent on making this an evening to remember. After dinner he was going to take us to *Inherit the Wind* with Paul Muni. The meal was delectable; Tony was in great form; wine flowed. So did the conversation. So did the liqueurs. At last I ventured, 'It's getting on, Tony, we really ought to . . . ' '*Trois cognacs*,' he barked in a Churchillian French understandable only to the English.

We arrived about three-quarters of an hour late at the theatre. 'You have seats in the name of Guthrie.' 'Yes,' said the box office bloke, 'that'll be . . . ' Tony was outraged. 'That's for *three* acts; what's the price for *two*?' The box office man dropped his head on the counter in total confusion. 'Forget it,' said Tony. And we went over the road to a bar and gossiped through the night.

Did you notice any major changes in Guthrie's work as you observed him over the years?

I must say that having *seen* the last half of the first part of his career and been a devoted fan, and then having *worked* with him through the last part of his career, I couldn't but notice an enormous difference in the quality of his work when his mother died, which was in 1957. She had been blind for some years. Whenever he had been home,

Tony had spent much time reading aloud to her and generally caring for her needs, such as purchasing special playing-cards for the blind – she was always a demon for solitaire.

On her deathbed Mrs Guthrie went into a coma, during which she insisted (with Tony by her side) on mumbling through an inventory of the garden shed: fifty-six flower-pots, three trowels, six lengths of twine, four rakes, one grass-mower, three besoms, forty-six lengths of wire-netting, etc., etc. Suddenly she rose from her pillow and in the clearest, youthful voice, said, 'Tony, I can *see!*'

Immediately afterwards she died.

Tony pondered on the possible meaning of her last remark for the rest of his life.

Just before her death, I had invited him to direct *Twelfth Night* at Stratford, Ontario. It was the first production I'd seen him do that was wholly relaxed. There was no passion to prove a point, to be clever, to be brilliant – in short, to show off. It involved far less effort than had been apparent in his previous productions, for it came from within him. It was the first really mature work I'd seen him do.

I think when his mother died, some kind of pressure went out of his life – he was no longer trying to prove to her that being in the theatre wasn't a bad thing after all. When she went, that pressure vanished. It was an important moment in his career and it affected all that followed, whether what he did was, by critical standards, good or bad.

You have had the distinction of taking over positions that Tony held in two of the most influential theatres in North America, if not in the world. What kind of pressures did that place on you?

Well, in the case of Stratford, which I knew was very special to him, I first felt, 'I can't do it.' But when someone of his stature demonstrates such confidence you feel impelled somehow to try to justify it. The first years were a great strain, both personally and professionally. I think I was a tyrant to work with. I didn't care if anyone liked me or not; I was just determined, as anyone could see by the grittedness o my teeth, to make the thing work somehow just because of the faith he had in me. That pressure passed with the years.

The case of the Guthrie Theater in Minneapolis was quite different. The Guthrie was suddenly in trouble; there was even a question of whether it could survive. Tony was very influential in my agreeing to go there. But before taking the job, I had to ask myself, 'Is this the pattern of my life now? Am I to go wherever Tony's been? Am I always going to be following in his footsteps?' That seemed a dull prospect, though I wouldn't have known whose else to follow in. He'd just been to Australia, and I wondered if that meant that I was shortly going there to take over his job in some Kangaroo Pleasure Dome. But such apprehension didn't last. And when I took on the Guthrie Theater, I felt none of the pressure I'd felt at Stratford. Not simply because I was older and more confident, with more under my belt, but because Tony had made far less impact in Minneapolis than he had in Stratford. I was quite shocked to find how mildly he was revered locally. It wasn't as if a great man had come to Minneapolis and made something fantastic happen, which is what I'd felt at Stratford. I had been replacing God at Stratford. There was none of that in Minneapolis.

What was your opinion of him as a Shakespeare director?

I didn't think much of any of the Shakespeare productions he did during the Guthrie Theater years. But in his early productions, he always made me aware of an enormous canvas, fascinatingly peopled. A case in point was his *Henry VIII* at Stratford-on-Avon. It was a teeming, sweaty vision of a period of history, of its characters and personalities, of its political intrigues, of its seaminess and its smell.

An incident, typical of Guthrie direction, occurred in the scene where Katherine of Aragon, in response to the threatened divorce, pleads her wounded case to the King. By Henry's choice this was made into a public, not a private scene, although she strove to keep it private between husband and wife. In the middle of her long speech, Henry started tapping a ruler on a table . . . rap . . . rap . . . rap. Quietly and slowly at first, while he beamed with an ever-so-winning expression of long-suffering boredom to his sycophantic court; then louder and more insistent, as she continued (in the face of ribald laughter) with a parallel growth of desperation. This 'rap-rap' not only served to make her speak louder and therefore unwittingly publicly; it also served to show the world that he, Henry, regarded her remarks as unworthy even of attention and that the world, including the Pope, had better take note. A seductive, private plea was ruthlessly made public, laughable and, in the end, painfully touching. The production was full of such inspirations.

I know that you were with him on the opening night of The Tenth Man *in New York. I wonder if he was attracted to the play because he was influenced by the Habimah production of* The Dybbuk?

284

Probably. I know he regarded his time in Israel as a rich learning experience. It was a world he'd never known before. And he felt a deep sense of debt. Directing *The Tenth Man* was part of his paying it. And it was by no means a 'goy' attempt at a Jewish play. He had dug right underneath it all and there was a warm, loving sense of unified purpose between him and the company, which in itself was remarkable – I'm sure he could not have pulled this off without the earlier experience of directing *Oedipus* and *The Merchant* for the Habimah. Incidentally, it was typically Guthrie-esque that in the latter production the whole company was Jewish, excepting two Christians whom he chose to cast as Shylock and Jessica.

I'm surprised he saw the opening. He has been known to avoid the first nights of his plays.

Not in my experience. Although he once persuaded me not to attend one of my own first nights. It was my début at the Vic and I was just entering the auditorium when I heard a pistol shot behind me. It was due to Tony's large hands coming together and producing a sound greater and more arresting than any hand-clap I've ever heard. (Guthrie's rehearsals were sporadically peppered with such gun-fire.) He was standing in the lobby. 'Where are you going?' 'To watch the play,' I answered defensively, feeling I'd been caught red-eyed in an act of voyeurism. '*Not* very intelligent. Your own rhythm is beating faster at the moment than anyone else's in London; you'll find the whole thing unbearably slow. Come up to the office and distract yourself with some designs that just arrived.' My face must have betrayed a degree of frustration, for he added, 'We can always slip in at the back every now and then to watch the showy bits.'

I had a pleasant evening. Had I followed my instincts, it would have been miserable. It was, as Tony knew, my first show in London.

As a director where was he strong and where was he weak?

He had the initial advantage of being well-read and well-educated. Considering the classic status of most of the works he directed, this was a great advantage. Most directors, including myself, are insufficiently equipped in this respect, and we have to do (often hurriedly) huge amounts of homework just to get us to first base. Tony, in my experience, never seemed to do any homework at all; so I once asked Judy when he found time to prepare his productions. 'Goodness knows,' she said. 'While he's walking about, I expect.'

I've known of no one with a better capacity to orchestrate a text. This was at once an enormous strength and a potential weakness, because his orchestration would sometimes be so authoritarian as to smother some subtleties of human content. But it was a wonderfully crafted musical gift. I suspect, however, that he might have achieved greater qualities in his work if he'd let the structure of orchestration occasionally lapse in order to explore something that happened to be coming out of an actor.

I have known no one more capable of inspiring a company, especially a large company, to ensemble playing. Nor of anyone better equipped to make the smallest player feel like a star, or to make a star feel like a small player. His prodigious powers of invention together with his infectious sense of life being a game were vastly instrumental in his success with actors.

All of us in the theatre tend to be introspective and self-important about what we're doing. Tony gave us the face-slap we needed. He forced us to be extrovert; to reject indulgences. 'You're *feeling* it, you silly girl,' he said to the actress playing Jessica in *The Merchant* at Stratford in 1956. 'Your job is to make *us* feel it.'

Guthrie's successes were mainly with extrovert playwrights – Marlowe, Shakespeare, Jonson, Wycherley, Schiller, Capek, Brecht, Wilder. I don't think he was at ease with introverted plays containing much sub-text. They were temperamentally unsuited to him. It was therefore all the more surprising when, towards the end of his career, he returned triumphantly to an author with whom he'd had little success earlier on. His Chekhov productions in Minneapolis were richly and beautifully realized. It was as if those tumble-down Russian estates had suddenly fused with Tony's own not-unChekhovian, upper-middle-class, tumble-down estate in Ireland, with its many relatives, guests, retainers and servants. And, as opposed to speaking through his professional craft, he was at last speaking unguardedly through his domestic heart. This was possibly the last creative flame of his theatrical career.

During the final years Annagh-ma-Kerrig and all it stood for seemed to become the most important thing in his life. That was maybe one reason why the Chekhovs worked; they related closely to his concern for the estate in Ireland. Making a go of the jam factory that he proposed to set up there was now a priority; it was to be a last gesture, and it's a terrible tragedy it didn't happen. Many of his final productions and lectures (which were often admittedly boring) were undertaken solely to underwrite that jam factory.

Tell me your version of what the jam factory was, and why it didn't work.

I don't know enough to answer that properly. I only know that he wanted desperately to make a world in that Irish bog of his, from which the inhabitants – especially the young ones – wouldn't keep feeling impelled to go away. So he instituted the jam factory. He had a grave sense of responsibility to his miserable country and its terrible divisions. He broadcast patient, finely reasoned talks on the BBC (printed in *The Listener*) in an attempt to halt that age-old war of religious bigotry. I think he was feeling, as he got older, that his job was to look after his roots, and that he should use his career in other parts of the world solely to support his responsibilities at home.

With the exception of the Chekhov, you seem to speak in relatively negative terms about his work at the Guthrie Theater.

I didn't see it all. Indeed the only play I saw which I've not yet referred to was *Volpone*. It was very compelling and entertaining, though I thought he'd let himself get locked into a brilliant idea – the bird-vulture idea – and that he'd allowed it to become so powerful that it pushed everything else out. But then Tony himself *was* a bird, in a way, a very tough bird. He'd say that himself, laughingly, 'I'm a tough bird; but I'm a cherub inside.'

I must admit the word cherub never occurred to me.

Well, he was the most rounded of personalities.

Yes. He was one of the most rounded personalities I've ever known, in terms of being able to relate to people on the simplest of levels and yet feel at home with the more educated aristocrats of the world, too. It's like water seeking its own level. Wherever he was he seemed to be at home.

Because he belonged to himself. He really knew himself. And he wasn't going to be thrown off balance by giving a speech to the Royal Academy.

He told me one time that all he really ever did was change the title of his speeches.

That may have been true by the time he got to Minneapolis. But by then his career was in a decline – the sort that is made inevitable by the advance of years.

When I first went to Canada, I attended a big speech he gave – Chamber of Commerce – lots of Toronto businessmen, about three hundred. Tony stood up with no notes and spoke about the future of the Stratford Festival for an hour and a quarter.

His capacity to think and talk on his feet, using lengthy, always arresting, sometimes brilliant phraseology, was remarkable. He'd subtly indicate, for example, at the start of a phrase, that he was leading you on a precarious journey into the unknown. He'd already persuaded you to believe in him as your guide; he'd seemed to have you firmly by the hand. But he invariably chose the most perilous possible routes. Your gratitude, therefore, when you finally arrived breathlessly richer for the experience, at the magic haven of the phrase's end, was unbounded.

On this occasion in Toronto, Tony was about to make the final 'kill' to the demanding challenge of his Stratford speech. The businessmen felt it coming and didn't seem to appreciate its potential burden. Sensing this, Tony digressed from the subject of Stratford and for twenty hilarious minutes talked about everything else. We rolled in the aisles. Then, with no warning, he returned to his original challenge and rammed it home. All the businessmen rose as one in response. And Stratford gained some considerable economic underpinning.

Do you have any other thoughts about him that you'd like to share with me?

Tony had so many people to stay with him at Annagh-ma-Kerrig – it was open house to anybody, almost. One such visitor came to see me last year and give me a snapshot of Tony taken on the front steps of Annagh-ma-Kerrig. It is slightly out of focus, giving the appropriate impression that a mist has risen from the surrounding bog; Tony is wearing a tweed jacket, flannel pants and carpet slippers, and standing with his arms outstretched in welcome. This is the last image I'd like to leave in your mind about my impression of the man – of the laird.

An Impression of the Memorial Service held on Wednesday, 16 June 1971 at St Paul's, Covent Garden, for Sir Tyrone Guthrie

CONSTANCE TOMKINSON: It was a lovely June morning, warm and sunny, and I arrived at St Paul's early as I knew the church would be packed. The service was at 12 noon and at 11.30 a.m. the church was half full. By the time the service started the church was packed to the gunwales with people standing outside under the portico.

The congregation was the same mixture of old and young, rich and poor that we had had in our house when we celebrated his knighthood several years ago and had told him to make up his own guest list. So these were the people Guthrie would have been pleased to see there. This was the same mixture expanded, made up of famous actors and actresses and those who had been 'resting' for some time, singers, producers, conductors, writers, stage technicians, designers and critics. There were people with household names and television people with household faces, mixed with the unknowns.

It was the right setting for the service – the 'actors' church' for centuries and a stone's throw from theatres in which Guthrie had worked – not too large, not too grand, beautiful and full of atmosphere – the perfect set for the occasion. The whole thing was so well stage-managed it could have been rehearsed for weeks. The performers, if you could call them that, picked up their cues and were in position exactly when needed.

Lady Guthrie had chosen the hymns that she knew her husband would like and in the choir were the best voices in the country. I don't suppose they had sung anything but solos for years. On the opening hymn 'The Lord is my shepherd' the professionals sang out loud and clear but the rest of us had such a lump in the throat that we could hardly be heard.

Dame Sybil Thorndike was assisted into position by her son and she looked so frail that one felt that at her great age it was going to be too much for her but when she started to speak the Shakespeare sonnet her voice rang out just as strong as if she were playing St Joan as a girl for the first time. Lady Guthrie said to me the following day, 'Wasn't Sybil electrifying?' and indeed she was. Geraint Evans followed her with the song 'I will lift mine eyes up unto the hills', sung like some Welsh angel. When the last note had died out Laurence Olivier was in the pulpit and started reading from John Bunyan's *The Pilgrim's Progress*. It was an intimate reading, geared to the size of the audience and perfectly in tune with their feelings. It was simply and gently read with great depth of feeling. This was so affecting that we all had to muster up courage to rise and sing 'He who would valiant be'. You could feel the emotion in the church and hear it in the quavering of people's voices as they sang. When we sat down there cannot have been a dry eye in the church.

Alec Guinness was already in the pulpit and for a second you were reminded of his vicar in *Kind Hearts and Coronets* but the moment he spoke that fey vicar vanished. He was now playing himself. The written address cannot capture the flavour it had on delivery, which was masterful. The humour of the address saved us all. The terrible gloom passed, people's faces started to brighten. When he got to the point of Guthrie's command we all knew so well, 'Rise above!' there was a great burst of laughter – it was extraordinary – partly relief and partly because Guinness had brought Guthrie back. I suddenly felt, 'He isn't gone. He's still with us – now.' Many others must have felt the same. I could see him striding down the aisle, towering over us and saying 'We'll take that again – faster!' He had taken over the production and it was all as it used to be. Guinness had rallied us all.

When we rose to sing 'Praise my soul, the King of Heaven' we sang out loud and clear – nearly raising the roof. As Lady Guthrie, who had been so brave, walked down the aisle with her usual unstiff, unstuffy dignity we were able to face her with steady, comforting smiles – not the tearstained faces she would have seen a short time back.

I do not believe that St Paul's, Covent Garden, in all its long history can have ever had a better memorial service – not since it opened in 1633. It was a perfect production with an unbeatable cast and, most important for all concerned, it was a labour of love. It was a fitting final curtain for one of the truly great men of the theatre.

Address Delivered by Alec Guinness at Sir Tyrone Guthrie's Memorial Service

William Tyrone Guthrie

'A great tree has fallen'.

Those were the words used by an old family friend on the rather Chekhovian Guthrie estate, when it became apparent that death had claimed Tony Guthrie. Tony was found sitting in a wooden chair in his study, his hands folded on his lap.

There are some names – not many – which when they crop up over a dinner table, on a walk, or round a fire, immediately seem to take charge of the conversation. Guthrie has been pre-eminently such a name over thirty-five or forty years; giving rise to a wealth of anecdote, laughter, admiration, love and speculation. The strength of his personality has been a vitalizing influence on all who knew him. And will continue to be so.

That he was a very great man of the theatre, whose ideas and energies have spread across the English-speaking world – and not only the English-speaking – we all know. He was, I suppose, our own, original, home-grown *enfant terrible* of the theatre – galvanizing, delighting and shocking a whole generation of performers and spectators, long before more recent 'terrible children' were born or thought of. And he showed no signs, even at the age of seventy, of relinquishing his provocative activities.

The range of his achievements in opera and drama is formidable. *Who's Who in the Theatre* lists ninety-six productions, not including those he did for the Scottish National Players between 1926 and 1928, or at the Cambridge Festival Theatre from 1929 to 1930. Add to that several works for radio, and a handful of books and plays. Everyone will have their own favourite productions; my list would certainly include *The Anatomist, Love's Labour's Lost,* the revelation of *Measure for Measure* and *The Cherry Orchard* with Laughton, Flora Robson and the Liveseys, *Henry V* with Olivier, *Peer Gynt* with Richardson and *All's Well* at Stratford, Ontario. He enjoyed huge success at the New York Metropolitan Opera, apart from his achievements at Covent

Garden and the Wells, at the Old Vic and in Australia. He has left behind two splendid theatre buildings – in Ontario and in Minneapolis – and greatly influenced the new Playhouse at Sheffield and the Octagon at Perth, Australia.

He was marvellous with the young, giving them much needed confidence. Sometimes he saw – or thought he saw – talent in unlikely places, but whoever came under the spell of his charm and energy emerged the richer.

But he was not only a great man of the theatre, he was great in himself. Extremely witty – sometimes devastatingly so; generous with money and time to a fault; interested in all men and loving most; of wide-ranging imagination and sympathy. I think the clue to his greatness lies in the fact that he was never 'all things to all men' but, on the contrary, always totally himself to all men. He never cut his cloth, or trimmed his sails, to suit other personalities, but gave wholly himself. A man of the greatest integrity. I am sure he was the same to all of us who knew and loved him. We may have slightly different memories of events, or stories, or witticisms, or kindnesses – but basically they are all the same. He had great personal humility – and rather hoped for it in others. And riding above all else was his laughter – rich, ironic, kind and memorable. I have always associated both the Guthries with laughter.

Some eighteen years ago, when the building of the Stratford, Ontario, theatre was supposed to be under way, Tony and I visited the site. The eventual theatre was impressive, but what greeted us that morning, a matter of weeks before the first night, was a hole in the ground about six foot deep and ten foot across. I was horrified and expressed my feelings. Tony fixed me with his bright hawk eye, and with the merest inclination of the head, said, 'Rise above it!' It was a phrase he constantly used and it was applied to almost anything irritating; from a cup of tepid and revolting canteen coffee, to a failed spotlight, or the total disappearance of all costumes and scenery on tour. He was even known to tell an audience to 'rise above it' when an evening's entertainment looked like proving unsatisfactory. A clutch of Scandinavian crowned heads, before the war, were similarly advised when hustled, on a night of terrible storm, from Elsinore Castle to the ballroom of the Marienlys Hotel for the opening of the Olivier *Hamlet*. Incidentally I think it was the excitement, improvisation and experience of that particular night which sparked off his passion for the open stage, and his dismissal of the proscenium arch. 'Rise above it' must have been heard all over the United States and Canada, by the Finns in Helsinki (where he rather surprisingly coupled productions of *Oedipus* and *The Merry Widow*), in Tel Aviv and Australia, as well as in St Martin's Lane and the Waterloo Road.

Wherever he and Judy found themselves they made a very recognizable home, and dispensed the warmest and most beautifully casual hospitality. It could be a covered punt on the Avon (in which they lived for weeks on end) – where a meal would be washed down with brandy swigged from a Heinz tomato soup tin – or at Annagh-ma-Kerrig, with its fine lake and relaxed air – or the sooty draughty house in Burnley during the latter years of the war – or – and above all – and blessed is its memory – the small ramshackle flat in Old Buildings, Lincoln's Inn. It was an oasis for many of us – for advice, to discuss plans, or just for sheer pleasure and laughter. And there were not only Tony and Judy, welcoming, but also their beloved and much discussed Myrtle. I fear it was too much, even for the most enchanted guest, to keep pace with Myrtle's vast number of kittens.

His interests were wide – and very human. He loved and had a knowledge of wild flowers and of trees, and retained a boyhood passion for steam railway engines. He was fond of music and enjoyed singing. He sang charmingly; rather loudly, very clearly, and sonorously. He was very caught up with Freudian and Jungian psychology, and greatly influenced by Dr Ernest Jones, on whose theories he based at least two or three productions. He admired Victoriana, loved cats and travel and talk, and gave his full attention to people – and particularly humble people. It was typical of him, on a very cold night, surreptitiously to push a hot-water bottle across the stage to a shivering Titania.

Rehearsals were always immensely lively, never a slack or unconcentrated moment. I can hear his fingers snapping up and down the stalls – a sure sign that he was going to call out 'Faster, faster!' He was a demon for speed in speech. And there were the inspirational moments of genius. Andrew Cruickshank reminded me the other day of how – in *Henry VIII* at Stratford, with Anthony Quayle – Guthrie told the whole tale of the Reformation, and the break with Rome, in a piece of silent business which took only seconds to act. Of course, rehearsals weren't all fun all the time and there were sometimes moments of friction. He could be very schoolmasterly. Personally I don't think I got through any production with him without a bicker somewhere along the line. But he was always the one who made the gesture of reconciliation – usually by some extravagantly absurd and funny statement. But once we had a row which, through my fault, reached proportions whereby we were non-speakers for two days. It all had to do with the severed head of Hastings in *Richard III*. Tony's gesture of reconciliation was to give me, very solemnly, a small brown paper bag of rather squashed cherries.

He was a firm advocate of decentralization – in almost everything. The present crop of civic theatres, springing up throughout the country, are a direct result, I feel, of his spadework, and the voicing of his ideas over the past twenty years. His concern for the high unemployment figures around his home in County Monaghan led to his organizing, a few years ago, a jam factory which employed nearly forty people and relieved much hardship in the district. Unfortunately outside misfortunes forced this into liquidation earlier this year. Tony lost a considerable amount of his own money in the venture, but that didn't disturb him at all – only the distress of the surrounding unemployment again. You can imagine how his memory is revered round and about Annagh-ma-Kerrig where he was very much a father figure. And yet, for all his star quality, and the profound influence he has had on so many diverse characters, I doubt if he thought anything of himself. He gave of his energy and, rather exasperatingly, took too little care of his health. His wife said that if the Ladies Guild of Timbuctoo wrote, suggesting he might give a talk over tea, he would consult his diary and then write back, 'Delighted! Can fit you in nicely on Thursday, on my way from Minneapolis to Belfast.'

He was an Honorary Doctor of Literature of St Andrews and Chancellor of Queen's University, Belfast. He was extremely pleased, I think, with his title of doctor and was known on the other side of the Atlantic as Dr Guthrie. On one occasion this led to a minor embarrassment. Some years ago, staying in a vast hotel in Brooklyn, the telephone went in the middle of the night and the operator said, 'Dr Guthrie, there's a gentleman in Room 204 having a heart attack. Would you go along please?' So, like a flash, Tony went along. When I asked him, some days later, what he had done, he said, 'Made him a strong cup of tea and held his hand. *Much* better in the morning! Advised him to call in his own doctor.' Tony informed the hotel staff that he was *not* a medical man. But sure enough at 3 a.m. the following morning the telephone went – 'Dr Guthrie! The lady in Room 903 has got Spanish flu!' The conversation from then on is possibly not suitable for St Paul's, Covent Garden.

Those of us who were associated with the first season in Ontario witnessed a heart-warming phenomenon – largely due to Tony Guthrie's personality – and that was the welding together of a rather sharply divided community. These were Episcopalians, Presbyterians, Methodists, Catholics and Baptists and so on – including also that sect which feels it vanity to wear buttons – and none of them had much to do with each other. With the building of the theatre, and Tony's six feet four inches striding about and smiling on all, strict teetotallers began to keep whisky and gin in their houses for visiting Anglicans, Baptists – not greatly given to colour – bought and planted geraniums round the theatre, and at the dedication Catholics deigned to join in the Lord's Prayer with everyone else. A Guthrie triumph.

A great and giving man. Our hearts go out to Judy. She has given me permission to recount the following piece of dialogue, which is totally Guthriesque. When the doctor arrived, just after his death, he looked at Tony and said, 'Surprising humility.' Judy replied, 'Yes, surprising humility; but quite tiresome!' The doctor thought for a moment and then said, 'Surprising humility, and – yes – quite tiresome!'

William Tyrone Guthrie. May his noble soul rest in happy peace, in the God he trusted.

Appendix

A Representative Listing of Stage Productions Directed by Tyrone Guthrie

1926–28	Scottish National Theatre Society, Glasgow	
1929–30	Festival Theatre, Cambridge	*Naked*
		All for Love
		Six Characters in Search of an Author
		Gentleman Dancing Master
		The Rivals
		The Machine Wreckers
		Marriage
		Warren Hastings
		Volpone
		The Cherry Orchard
		A Doll's House
		Rosmersholm
		Measure for Measure
		The Merry Wives of Windsor
		Lady Audley's Secret
		Tobias and the Angel
		Iphigeneia in Tauris
1931	Westminster Theatre, London	*The Anatomist*
1932	Lyric Theatre, London	*Dangerous Corner*
1932	Westminster Theatre, London	*Love's Labour's Lost*
		Follow Me (Author Also)
1933	Arts Theatre, London	*The Lake*

1933	Memorial Theatre, Stratford (England)	*Richard II*
1933–34	The Old Vic, London	*Twelfth Night* *The Cherry Orchard* *Henry VIII* *Measure for Measure* *The Tempest* *The Importance of Being Earnest* *Macbeth*
1934	Wyndham's Theatre, London	*Sweet Aloes*
1934	His Majesty's Theatre, London	*Mary Read*
1935	Whitehall Theatre, London	*Viceroy Sarah*
1935	Queen's Theatre, London	*Short Story*
1936	New York	*Call It a Day*
1936	New York	*Sweet Aloes*
1936–37	The Old Vic, London	*Love's Labour's Lost* *The Country Wife* *Hamlet* *Twelfth Night* *Henry V*
1937	Elsinore, Denmark	*Hamlet*
1937	Lyceum Theatre, London	*Paganini*
1937	Queen's Theatre, London	*The School for Scandal*
1937–38	The Old Vic, London	*Pygmalion* *Measure for Measure* *Richard III* *A Midsummer Night's Dream* *Othello*
1938	Vaudeville Theatre, London	*Goodness, How Sad!*
1938–39	The Old Vic, London	*Trelawney of the Wells* *Hamlet* *A Midsummer Night's Dream*

1938–39	The Old Vic, London	*She Stoops to Conquer* (with Frank Napier) *An Enemy of the People* *The Taming of the Shrew*
1941	The Old Vic, London	*King John* (with Lewis Casson) *The Cherry Orchard*
1943	The Old Vic, London	*Abraham Lincoln* *The Russians*
1944	The Old Vic, London	*Guilty* *Hamlet* (with Michael Benthall)
1944	Liverpool Playhouse Repertory	*Uneasy Laughter (He Who Gets Slapped)*
1944	Savoy Theatre, London	*The Last of Mrs Cheyney*
1945	Liverpool Playhouse Repertory	*The Alchemist*
1945	The Old Vic, London	*Peer Gynt*
1946	The Old Vic, London	*Cyrano de Bergerac*
1946	Booth Theater, New York	*He Who Gets Slapped*
1946	Covent Garden, London	*Peter Grimes*
1947	Covent Garden, London	*La Traviata*
1947	Duchess Theatre, London	*He Who Gets Slapped*
1947	The Habimah Theatre, Tel Aviv	*Oedipus Rex*
1948	Broadway Theater, New York	*Oedipus Rex* (Habimah production)
1948	Helsingfors Theatre, Helsinki	*Oedipus Rex*
1948	Assembly Hall, Edinburgh	*The Three Estates*
1948	Sadler's Wells, London	*The Beggar's Opera*
1949	Assembly Hall, Edinburgh	*The Gentle Shepherd*
1949	Helsingfors Theatre, Helsinki	*The Taming of the Shrew*
1949	Sadler's Wells, London	*Carmen*

1949	Memorial Theatre, Stratford (England)	*Henry VIII*
1950	Memorial Theatre, Stratford (England)	*Henry VIII*
1950	Sadler's Wells, London	*The Barber of Seville*
1950	Sadler's Wells, London	*Falstaff*
1950	Gate Theatre, Dublin	*Hamlet*
1950	Assembly Hall, Edinburgh	*The Atom Doctor* *Queen's Comedy*
1950	The Old Vic, London	*The Miser*
1950	London	*Top of the Ladder* (author also)
1951	Lyric, Hammersmith, London	*The Passing Day* *Danger, Men Working* *The Sham Prince*
1951–52	The Old Vic, London	*Tamburlaine the Great* *A Midsummer Night's Dream* *Timon of Athens*
1952	Assembly Hall, Edinburgh	*The Highland Fair*
1952	Metropolitan Opera, New York	*Carmen*
1953	The Old Vic, London	*Henry VIII*
1953	Festival Theater, Stratford (Canada)	*Richard III* *All's Well That Ends Well*
1954	Assembly Hall, Edinburgh	*The Matchmaker*
1954	Festival Theater, Stratford (Canada)	*The Taming of the Shrew* *Oedipus Rex*
1954	Haymarket Theatre, London	*The Matchmaker*
1955	Festival Theater, Stratford (Canada)	*The Merchant of Venice* *Oedipus Rex*
1955	Gaiety Theatre, Dublin	*The Bishop's Bonfire*
1955	Assembly Hall, Edinburgh	*A Life in the Sun*
1955	Royale Theater, New York	*The Matchmaker*

1955	Phoenix Theater, New York	*Six Characters in Search of an Author*
1956	The Old Vic, London	*Troilus and Cressida*
1956	Martin Beck Theater, New York	*Candide*
1956	Winter Garden Theater, New York	*Troilus and Cressida*
1956	Winter Garden Theater, New York	*Tamburlaine the Great*
1957	Belasco Theater, New York	*The First Gentleman*
1957	Festival Theater, Stratford (Canada)	*Twelfth Night*
1957	Phoenix Theater, New York	*Mary Stuart*
1957	Phoenix Theater, New York	*The Makropolous Secret*
1958	Belfast, Ireland	*The Bishop's Bonfire*
1958	Metropolitan Opera, New York	*La Traviata*
1959	Memorial Theatre, Stratford (England)	*All's Well That Ends Well*
1959	Booth Theater, New York	*The Tenth Man*
1960	Phoenix Theater, New York	*HMS Pinafore*
1960	Martin Beck Theater, New York	*Love and Libel*
1961	London	*A Time to Laugh*
1961	Phoenix Theater, New York	*The Pirates of Penzance*
1961	Plymouth Theater, New York	*Gideon*
1962	The Old Vic, London	*The Alchemist*
1963	The Tyrone Guthrie Theater, Minneapolis	*Hamlet* *The Three Sisters*
1964	The Tyrone Guthrie Theater, Minneapolis	*Henry V* *Volpone*
1964	Scott Hall, University of Minnesota, Minneapolis	*Six Characters in Search of an Author*

1965	The Tyrone Guthrie Theater, Minneapolis	*Richard III* *The Cherry Orchard*
1966	Bristol Old Vic (American tour also)	*Measure for Measure*
1966	Alvin, Theater, New York	*Dinner at Eight*
1967	Metropolitan Opera, New York	*Peter Grimes*
1967	The Tyrone Guthrie Theater, Minneapolis	*The House of Atreus* *Harper's Ferry*
1967	The National Theatre, London	*Tartuffe*
1968	The National Theatre, London	*Volpone*
1968	The Tyrone Guthrie Theater, Minneapolis The Billy Rose Theater, New York The Mark Taper Forum, Los Angeles	*The House of Atreus*
1969	Dublin Festival	*Swift*
1969	Belfast, Ireland	*Macook's Corner*
1969	The Tyrone Guthrie Theater, Minneapolis	*Uncle Vanya*
1969	USA National Tour	*Lamp at Midnight*
1970	Old Tote Theatre Company, Sydney, Australia	*Oedipus Rex*
1970	Melbourne Theatre Company, Melbourne, Australia	*All's Well That Ends Well*
1971	The Phoenix Opera Group, Brighton Festival	*The Barber of Seville*

Index

Entries in **bold type** indicate a conversation

Adler, Stella, **111–13**
Albery, Bronson, 41, 157
Albery Theatre, *see* New Theatre
Alchemist, The, 51, 109, 179
Alexander the Great, 132
All in Good Time, 247
All's Well That Ends Well, 22, 36,
  61–2, 181, 291
Amarcord, 14
Ambassadors Theatre, London, 145
America, 13, 43, 70, 79, 133, 140,
  145, 150, 177, 187–9, 196, 275,
  283, 293
American Gothic, 256
Anatomist, The, 121, 291
Anderson, Robert, 215
Andrews, Harry, 35, **114–17**
Annagh-ma-Kerrig, 13, 15, 43,
  45–6, 48, 56, 60, 147, 149, 281,
  286, 288, 293–4
Arms and the Man, 90, 100
Arts Council of Great Britain, 89,
  144, 177–8
Arts (Festival) Theatre, Cambridge
  19, 35, 170
Arts Theatre Club, 202
Assembly Hall, Edinburgh, 124
As You Like It, 71, 219
Athenaeum Club, London, 71
Atkins, Robert, 37, 242
Australia, 57, 174, 177, 280, 284,
  292–3
Avon, river, 117, 122, 293

Ball, William, 201, 244
Banners of Steel, see *Harper's Ferry*
Barefoot in the Park, 201

Barnes, Clive, 274
Baxter, Stanley, 15–16, **122–33**
Baylis, Lilian, 32, 33, 39, 156
BBC, 85, 140, 148, 190, 289
Beachcomber, The, 72, 187, 247
Beaumont, Binky, 78, 112–13,
  192, 195
Becket, Thomas à, 26
Belfast, 13, 47, 140, 147, 294
Bennett, Frances, 268
Benthall, Michael, 175
Bernstein, Leonard, 200
Billy Rose Theater, New York,
  273
Bing, Rudolph, 207
Binns, Ed, 258
Birmingham Repertory Theatre,
  278
Bishop, George, 34
Bochner, Lloyd, 106
Boston, Massachusetts, 196, 203
Brando, Marlon, 82
Brecht, Bertholt, 286
Bretherton, Judith *see* Guthrie,
  Judith
Bridges-Adams, W., 37, 38
Bridie, James, 121
Brighton, 46–7, 57, 144, 208
Bristol, 277, 280
Bristol Old Vic Theatre, 250
British Broadcasting Corporation,
  see BBC
Britten, Benjamin, 248
Broadway, New York, 15, 113,
  203, 210
Brook, Peter, 37, 67–8, 75–6, 83,
  123
Brooklyn, New York, 282, 294

Brown, John, 250–6, 258, 261–2, 267
Brown, Mary, 253–4, 255, 256
Browne, Coral, **104–10**
Buchanan, Jack, 104, 105
Bunyan, John, 290
Burnley, 15, 40, 78, 167, 293
Burns, Helen, 211
Burrell, John, 41, 100
Burton, Richard, 94, 131

Caesar and Cleopatra, 73
Caldwell, Zoe, 220, 221, 228
Callahan, Kristina, 241
Callas, Maria, 242, 248
Cambridge Festival Theatre, 19, 35, 170, 291
Campbell, Douglas, 46, 183, 215, 221, 224–5, 229, 233, 236–7, 244, 252, 254, 256, 275
Canada, 14–15, 26, 53, 68, 75, 106, 133, 140, 151, 157, 163, 172, 177, 184, 190, 199, 280, 288, 293
Čapek, K. M., 286
Cariou, Len, **267–75**
Carmen, 156
Cass, Henry, 32
Cassidy, Claudia, 100
Casson, Ann, 46
Casson, Lewis, 31, 71, 88–92
Chamberlain, George, 15, 39–40, 44, 49
Chapman, Edward, 134
Chekhov, Anton, 15, 55–6, 67, 74, 224–5, 228, 236, 243–4, 246–7, 261, 286–7, 291
Cherry Orchard, The, 67, 224–5, 231, 235, 240, 244–6, 291
Chicago Tribune, 100
Chilcott, Barbara, 106
Citizens' Theatre, Glasgow, 124, 129, 135, 144, 153
Clarke, Cecil, 61, 155
Clegg, Mrs, 190–1
Clift, Montgomery, 142
Clurman, Harold, 230
Cohen, Alexander, 205–6, 210

Cooper, Gladys, 78
Coriolanus, 94, 178
County Monaghan, Northern Ireland, 13, 294
Covent Garden, London, 55, 242, 291–2
Coventry, 276, 278
Coward, Noël, 153
Crime and Punishment, 74
Crist, Judith, 274
Critic, The, 96
Cronin, Harry, 241
Cronyn, Hume, 223, **227–37**, 240
Cruickshank, Andrew, 99, **118–21**, 293
Cyrano de Bergerac, 15, 35, 53, 59, 65, 114

Daily Telegraph, 34
Dana, Leora, 199
Dance of Death, The, 217
Davis, Donald, 106
Davis, Murray, 106
Dean, James, 129
Death of a Salesman, 227
De Mille, Cecil B., 123
Derwent, Clarence, 208
Detroit, University of, 213
Dietrich, Marlene, 208
Dix, Dorothy, 33
Doctor's Dilemma, The, 276
Donat, Peter, **210–13**
Donat, Robert, 210, 213
Douglas-Home, William, 135
Downie, Andrew, 46
Doyle, Mary Agnes, 245
Dybbuk, The, 284
Dyck, Sir Anthony van, 53

Eaves Brothers, 209
Edinburgh, 55, 121, 124, 126, 142, 148, 189, 196, 280
Edinburgh Festival, 15, 55, 121, 126, 142, 148
Edison, Robert, 239
El Greco, 256
Elizabeth, the Queen Mother, 154

Elizabeth II, HM Queen, 13, 141, 148, 166
Elizabethan Theatre Trust (Australia), 174
Elsinore (Helsingör), Denmark, 33, 96, 292
Elsom, Isabel, 208
Empire Theatre, London, 31
Enemy of the People, 203
England, 23, 34–5, 64, 68, 70, 74, 76, 79, 112, 115, 119, 140–42, 164, 175, 188–9, 237
Escapade, 192
Esmond, Jill, 158, 232
Evans, Edith, 36
Evans, Geraint, 290
Evans, Maurice, 32

Fanny, 202
Fellini, Federico, 14
ffrangcon-Davies, Gwen, 27
Fein, Maria, 208
First Gentleman, The, 15, 202–5, 210, 212
Flowers Are Not For You to Pick, The, 147
Fogarty, Elsie, 225
Forsyth, James, 47
Forsyth, Louise, 47
Forty Years On, 75
Fox, Mrs Robin, 47
Freud, Sigmund, 42, 59, 136, 204, 293
Frost, Robert, 215
Furse, Roger, 99

Gable, Clark, 98
Galileo Galilei, 250, 264–5
Gammell, Robin, 272–3
Garland, Judy, 247
Geer, Ellen, **218–26**
Gheon, Henri, 278
Gibson, John, 42, **144–52**
Gielgud, John, 15, 36, 58, 62, **69–76**, 89, 120, 216, 242, 278
Ginsbury, Norman, **202–4**, 205

Girls, Les, 159
Giselle, 42
Glasgow, 124, 135, 144, 153, 280
Glasgow Citizens' Theatre, 124, 129, 135, 144, 153
Globe Theatre, London, 192
Goodman Theater School, Chicago, 238, 245
Goodness, How Sad, 78
Gordon, Ruth, 60, 80, 186–7, 192, 194
Granville-Barker, Harley, 70–1, 72, 118, 120–21
Gray, Charles, 109
Greco, El, 256
Greet, P. Ben, 88
Griffith, Kenneth, **161–8**
Grizzard, George, **214–17**, 218, 238, 240, 241, 259
Group Theater, New York, 111
Guinness, Alec, 14–15, 23, 35, 46–7, **58–64**, 65, 67–8, 71–2, 92–3, 100, 118, 231, 245, 290–5
Guthrie, Dr Thomas, 29, 114
Guthrie, Mrs, 282–3
Guthrie (née Bretherton), Judith, 14, 28–9, 39–41, 43–5, 47–8, 57, 64, 78, 80–81, 85–6, 90–92, 104, 108, 117, 122, 136–7, 142, 149, 153, 159–60, 167, 197, 199–201, 206, 212, 218–20, 230, 238, 243, 248, 251, 260, 276–7, 278, 279, 285, 289–90, 293, 295

Habimah Theatre, Tel Aviv, 284–5
Hall, Peter, 123, 170, 175–6
Hals, Franz, 53
Hamlet, 15, 21, 33–5, 58–9, 65, 67, 71, 74, 93–6, 100, 118–19, 214–16, 218, 227, 233, 238, 243, 245, 247, 292
Hardy, Robert, **137–43**
Harmonia Gardens, The, 189
Harper's Ferry, 250, 252–7, 259, 262, 267
Harrison, Rex, 78, 87, 91

Harvey, Martin, 81
Hayes, George, 32
Haymarket Theatre, London, 72,
  106, 165, 167
Helpmann, Robert, 134
Helsingör (Elsinore), Denmark,
  33, 96, 292
Henry II, king of England, 26
Henry V, 33, 94, 96–7, 214, 216,
  232, 240, 241, 243, 250, 291
Henry VIII, 15, 22, 25–7, 31, 50,
  53, 73, 115, 119, 137–8, 139,
  140–42, 162, 173–4, 278, 284, 293
Herlie, Eileen, 187, 189, 193–4
He Who Gets Slapped, 111
Hill, Arthur, 186–91
Hiller, Wendy, 202
Hitler, Adolf, 88, 119
Holbein, Hans, 53
Holder, Geoffrey, 200
Hollywood, 202, 209
Homecoming, The, 176
House, Eric, 185
House in Malone Road, The, 49
House of Atreus, The, 15, 54, 258,
  267, 271–4, 275
HMS Pinafore, 102
Hunt, Hugh, 104–5, 174–5
Hunt, Martita, 99
Hutt, William, 181–5, 268, 269
Hyson, Dorothy, 26, 27–8, 134

Ibsen, Henrik, 74
Importance of Being Earnest, The, 66
Inherit the Wind, 282
Iona Community theatre company,
  144
Ireland, 13, 23, 43, 44–7, 56, 64,
  73–4, 113, 136, 140, 145, 148,
  151, 177, 187, 199, 204, 264,
  278, 281, 286
Irish Festival Theatre, 145, 148
Irving, Henry, 229
Israel, 43, 113, 140, 151, 212, 285
Italy, 119, 265
Ivanov, 74

Jackson, Barry, 67, 118

Jane Eyre, 72
Jeans, Isobel, 78
Jeans, Ursula, 134
Jones, Dr Ernest, 59, 293
Jones, Inigo, 125
Jonson, Ben, 286
Julius Caesar, 278, 280
Jung, Carl G., 293

Kanin, Garson, 189
Kasznar, Kurt, 198–201
Kazan, Elia (Gadge), 232–6
Kean, Edmund, 94, 164
Kind Hearts and Coronets, 290
King, Dennis, 111
King John, 89
King Lear, 32, 70, 118, 121
Kipnis, Lola (Leonid Kipins),
  55, 113, 145
Knox, John, 132
Komisarjevsky, Theodore, 32, 37,
  17, 74, 120
Kronborg Castle, Helsingör, 15,
  33, 34

Lamp at Midnight, 250, 258, 261,
  262, 263–6
Lanchester, Elsa, 72
Lang, Robert, 250
Langham, Michael, 104, 268–9,
  275, 276–8
Langner, Lawrence, 188
L'Avare, 227
Last of Mrs Cheyney, The, 104–5
Laughton, Charles, 15, 31–3, 50,
  66, 72, 98, 187, 202, 291
Lawrence of Arabia, 167
Learned, Michael, 210, 212
Leigh, Vivien, 34, 167–8
Leighton, Margaret, 35
Levene, Sam, 192
Life in the Sun, 142
Life in the Theatre, A, 204
Life magazine, 236
Liff, Biff, 188
Lincoln's Inn Fields, 15, 28,
  43–4, 62, 66, 85, 108, 137,
  154, 158, 278, 293

Listener, The, 287
Liverpool, 40, 41, 51, 52, 64
Liverpool Playhouse Theatre, 40, 41, 51-2
Livesey, Roger, 291
London, 29, 34, 40-41, 42, 46, 51, 56, 58, 66, 69, 74, 76, 87, 101, 105-6, 109, 126, 144, 149, 194, 196, 204-5, 211, 248, 280, 282, 285
London, University of, 90
Los Angeles, 267, 273-4
Love's Labour's Lost, 19, 58, 66, 74, 291
Lunt, Alfred, 108

Macbeth, 31-2, 88-9, 95, 174, 242
McCabe, Mrs, 47
McCallum, Sandy, 245
McCarey, Leo, 209
McCowen, Alec, **192-7**
McKern, Leo, **177-80**, 247
MacLeod, George, 144, 148
McMaster, Anew, 32
Macready, W. C., 164
Macropoulos Secret, The, 247
Malade Imaginaire, Le, 70
Malleson, Miles, 36, 178, 229
Manchester, 40, 48, 101, 202
Man Who Came to Dinner, The, 104
Marienlys Hotel, Helsingör, 33, 292
Mark Taper Forum, Los Angeles, 274
Marlowe, Christopher, 35, 161-4, 166, 286
Marshall, Armina, 188
Marshall, Norman, 202
Marvellous History of St Bernard, The, 278
Mason, James, 183
Matchmaker, The, 15, 55, 186-7, 190, 192, 196
Matthews, A. E., 78
Measure for Measure, 15, 31, 291
Medea, 90
Memorial (later, Royal Shakespeare) Theatre, Stratford-on-Avon, 32, 278

Merchant of Venice, The, 181-2, 184-5, 280, 285-6
Merrick, David, 187-9
Merry Widow, The, 293
Metropolitan Museum of Art, New York, 256
Metropolitan Opera Company, New York, 55, 156, 207, 291
Midland Theatre Company, Coventry, 276
Midsummer Night's Dream, A, 15, 104, 134, 169, 176
Milanov, Zinka, 207
Mills, John, 84, **134-6**
Mills (née Bell), Mary Hayley 135-6
Milton, Ernest, 89-90
Minneapolis, 13, 15, 23, 25-6, 54, 69, 73, 76, 100, 103, 151, 214, 217-18, 225, 227, 229, 236, 251, 254, 267, 270-71, 273, 283-4, 286-7, 292, 294
Minnesota, University of, 15, 273
Misanthrope, Le, 70
Miser, The, 36, 178, 214, 227, 229
Moiseiwitsch, Tanya, 14, 25, **50-7**, 61, 66-7, 70, 173, 218-19, 238, 242-6, 248, 273
Molière, 70, 227
Moriarty, Michael, 260-61
Morley College, Brighton, 46
Morley, Robert, 67, **77-86**, 87, 142, 202, 211
Morse, Robert, 196
Muni, Paul, 282
Murray, Gilbert, 90
Mussolini, Benito, 119
My Sister Eileen, 104

National Theatre, London, 15, 35-6, 70, 96, 102, 167
New Jersey, 261, 264-5
New (later, Albery) Theatre, London, 35, 40-42
New York, 15, 20, 22, 25, 29, 74, 79, 102, 109, 136, 167, 196, 202-5

Nichols, Mike, 201
Nottingham Playhouse Theatre, 178
Noye's Fludde, 248

O'Casey, Sean, 86
Octagon Theatre, Perth (Australia), 57, 292
Oedipus Rex, 14–15, 53–4, 95–6, 112, 177, 181–3, 270, 285, 293
Old Vic Theatre, London, 15, 28, 31–3, 35–7, 39, 49–51, 58, 60, 66–7, 69–71, 75, 79, 93, 97, 100, 104, 106, 132–4, 141, 153–7, 161, 164, 166, 169, 178, 203, 231–2, 247, 278–80, 285, 292
Olivier, Laurence, 15, 21, 33–6, 41, 58–9, 89, 93–103, 134–5, 158, 167–8, 227, 232, 290–2
One Pair of Eyes, 140
Ontario, 15, 53, 60–61, 76, 292, 295
Opera House, Manchester, 101
Oresteia, 22, 54, 243
Othello, 15, 97, 99, 104, 278
O'Toole, Peter, 96, 167, 250

Parker, Carolyn, 54
Passing Day, The, 146
Patterson, Tom, 60, 279
Peer Gynt, 15, 35, 74, 100–1, 203, 217, 247, 291
Pericles, 38
Peter Grimes, 55, 248
Philadelphia, 187, 206, 212
Philip, HRH Prince, 141, 180
Phoenix Theater, New York, 198, 247
Picasso, Pablo, 54
Pilgrim's Progress, The 290,
Pilhofer, Herb, 241
Pinter, Harold, 176
Pirates of Penzance, The, 167
Planchon, Roger, 75
Playhouse Theatre, Liverpool 40–1, 51–2

Playhouse Theatre, Nottingham, 178
Playhouse Theatre, Sheffield, 204
Plowright, Joan, 36
Poel, William, 34
Portman, Eric, 240
Power, Tyrone, 199
Prevost, Annette, 15, **39-49**
Prince's (later, Shaftesbury) Theatre, London, 40, 41

Quartermaine, Leon, 72
Quayle, Anthony, 15–16, **19-30**, 50, 74, 99, 102, 119, 137, 278, 293
Queen's Comedy, The, 132
Queen's University, Belfast, 13, 140, 294
Quiet Place, The, 199

Rabb, Ellis, 215, 240
RADA (Royal Academy of Dramatic Art), 19, 287
Redgrave, Michael, 97
Reed, Carol, 77–8
Reinhardt, Max, 113
Rembrandt, 23, 53
Requiem (Verdi), 56, 149
Richard II, 32
Richard III, 61–2, 97, 181, 222, 228, 230, 238, 240, 245, 294
Richardson, Ralph, 15, 35, 41, 59, 65, 74, 82, 89, 97–102, 115, 243, 291
Roberts, Rachel, 250
Robson, Flora, 15, 31, 66, 247, 291
Rogers, Paul, **169-76**
Rogers (née Boxall), Rosalind, 172–3, 175
Romeo and Juliet, 27, 280
Ross, 136
Royal Academy of Dramatic Art (RADA) 19, 287
Royal Court Theatre, London, 149
Royal Shakespeare Theatre, Stratford-on-Avon, 32, 278

Ruta, Ken, **238–49**
Rutherford, Margaret, 78, 87
Ryan's Daughter, 177

Sadler's Wells, London, 31–2, 39, 44, 48, 292
St Andrews, University of, 13, 294
Saint-Denis, Michel, 71, 95, 120
St James's Theatre, London, 135
St Joan, 19, 221, 223–4
St Martin's Lane, 247
St Paul's, Covent Garden, 82, 151, 289–90, 294
San Francisco Opera Company, 248
Schafer, Natalie, 199, 200
Schiller, J. C. F. von, 286
Schneider, Alan, 200
School for Scandal, The, 69, 72
School for Wives, The, 70
Scotland, 13, 124, 144, 148, 278
Scott, George, 233 C.
Scott, Robert, 137
Scottish National Players, 291
Seneca, 75
Seyler, Athene, 66
Shaftesbury Theatre, London, 40, 41
Shakespeare, William, 25, 31–3, 35–7, 62, 71, 73–4, 81, 88–9, 94, 97–8, 100, 116, 119, 139, 162, 173, 176, 212, 215, 220, 230, 236, 245, 250, 269, 274, 275, 284, 286, 289
Shakespeare Folio, 36
Shatner, William, 106
Shaw, George Bernard, 68, 73, 120, 224, 245, 276, 277
Shaw, Glen Byam, 37
Sheffield Playhouse Theatre, 292
Shelving, Paul, **278**
She Stoops to Conquer, 134
She Wore a Yellow Ribbon, 209
Shiels, George, 145
Short Story, 77, 87
Six Characters in Search of an Author, 66, 112, 198, 200–201
Slezak, Walter, 202–3, **205–9**, 211–12
Spaull, Guy, 211

Squirrel's Cage, The, 147
Stanislavsky, Konstantin, 83, 111–13, 228, 243
Stavis, Barrie, **250–66**, 267
Stephens, Robert, 36
Stewart, John, 147
Stratford-on-Avon, 15, 22–3, 25–6, 32, 35–8, 50, 66, 81, 115, 119, 122, 125, 137–8, 141, 166, 170, 206, 278, 284, 293
Stratford, Ontario, 14–15, 53, 60–61, 125, 156–7, 181–2, 184, 190, 225, 238, 245, 250, 268, 270, 279–80, 282–4, 286, 288, 291–3
Streetcar Named Desire, A, 234, 235
Stuart, General Jeb, 261
Sweet, Henry, 245
Swenson, Inga, 212

Tamburlaine the Great, 15–16, 20, 22, 25, 35, 65, 106, 108–9, 112, 155, 161–2, 164, 199
Taming of the Shrew, The, 181, 183–5
Tandy, Jessica, 100, **227–37**, 239
Tartuffe, 15, 35–7, 68–70, 72, 74–5
Tebaldi, Renata, 207
Tel Aviv, 107, 156, 293
Tempest, Marie, 65, 67, 77–8, 87–8, 91
Tempest, The, 31
Tenth Man, The, 102, 284–5
Terry, Ellen, 219
Thatcher, Torin, 96
Theater Guild, USA, 112, 188
Thorndike, Sybil, 31, 35, 78, 87-**92**, 224, 289–90
Thorpe Davie, Cedric, 120
Three Estates, The, 15, 121, 123–4, 126, 128, 148
Three Sisters, The, 219–20, 224–5, 227–8, 230, 234, 244, 259
Time for Laughter, A, 79
Tomelty, Joe, 146–7
Tomkinson, Constance, **153–60**, 172, 289
Top of the Ladder, 84, 128–9, 135, 144

Traviata, La, 40, 207
Trelawney of the Wells, 78
Trewin, J. C., **31-8**
Troilus and Cressida, 15, 35, 38,
  67, 71, 110, 170-72
Twelfth Night, 31, 53, 74, 94, 100,
  181, 231, 283
Tyrone Guthrie Theater,
  Minneapolis, 13, 15, 54, 177,
  217, 229, 233, 250-52, 273,
  283-4, 287

Uncle Vanya, 54-5, 113, 275

Valk, Frederick, 182
Valois, Ninette de, 39
Verdi, Giuseppe, 56, 149
Viceroy Sarah, 202
Victoria Regina, 206-7
Victoria Theatre, Burnley, 40
'View of Toledo' (El Greco), 256
Volpone, 36-7. 69, 214, 240-43,
  247, 287

Wager, Michael (Mendy), 199
Wales, 40, 88-9, 91, 177
Waterloo Road, London, 33, 35,
  166, 293

Wellington public school, England,
  142, 148
West, Mae, 110
West End, London, 15, 72, 76,
  105, 113, 121, 143
Westminster Theatre, London, 19,
  35, 58, 66, 74
White, Colin, 124
Wilbur, Richard, 70
Wilder, Thornton, 55, 142, 195,
  286
Wiley, John, 206
Williams, Harcourt, 32
Williamson, Nicol, 175
Wilson, Mitchell, 113
Winter Garden Theater, New York,
  20, 23, 25
Winter's Tale, The, 14
Wolfit, Donald, 15, 22-3, 35, 66,
  106, 154-5, 161-7, 240, 242, 247
Wood, Grant, 256
Worth, Irene, 142, 245
Wycherley, William, 286
Wyndham's Theatre, London, 42
Wynyard, Diana, 79, 139

Zeffirelli, G. Franco, 72
Zeisler, Peter, 215, 252